HAMLET,
Prince of Denmark

William Shakespeare

THE EMC MASTERPIECE SERIES

Access Editions

EMC/Paradigm Publishing
St. Paul, Minnesota

Staff Credits:
For **EMC/Paradigm Publishing**, St. Paul, Minnesota

Laurie Skiba
Editor

Eileen Slater
Editorial Consultant

Shannon O'Donnell Taylor
Associate Editor

Jennifer J. Anderson
Assistant Editor

For **Penobscot School Publishing, Inc.**, Danvers, Massachusetts

Editorial

Robert D. Shepherd
President, Executive Editor

Christina E. Kolb
Managing Editor

Sara Hyry
Editor

Allyson Stanford
Editor

Laurie Faria
Associate Editor

Sharon Salinger
Copyeditor

Marilyn Murphy Shepherd
Editorial Advisor

Design and Production

Charles Q. Bent
Production Manager

Sara Day
Art Director

Diane Castro
Compositor

Janet Stebbings
Compositor

ISBN 0-8219-1633-5

Published by EMC/Paradigm Publishing
875 Montreal Way
St. Paul, Minnesota 55102

Printed in the United States of America.
10 9 8 7 6   **xxx** 12 11 10 09

Table of Contents

The Life and Works of William Shakespeare iv

Time Line of Shakespeare's Life viii

The Historical Context of *Hamlet, Prince of Denmark*. x

Echoes xiv

Illustration. xvi

Dramatis Personae 1

ACT I. 3

ACT II 53

ACT III. 95

ACT IV. 149

ACT V 187

Plot Analysis of *Hamlet, Prince of Denmark* 226

Creative Writing Activities 240

Critical Writing Activities 242

Projects 248

Glossary 250

Handbook of Literary Terms 257

William Shakespeare

William Shakespeare

William Shakespeare (1564–1616). William Shakespeare may well be the greatest dramatist the world has ever known. His mother, Mary Arden Shakespeare, was from a well-to-do, well-connected family. His father, John Shakespeare, was a prosperous glove maker and local politician. William's exact birthdate is unknown, but he was baptized in his hometown of Stratford-upon-Avon on April 26, 1564, and tradition has assigned him a birthdate of April 23, which was also the day of his death and the feast day of Saint George, England's patron saint.

Shakespeare attended the Stratford grammar school, where he studied Latin and perhaps some Greek. At the age of eighteen, Shakespeare married Anne Hathaway, eight years his senior, who was with child. Altogether, William and Anne had three children, a daughter Susanna and twins Hamnet and Judith. He may have worked for a while as a schoolteacher, for there are many references to teaching in his plays. By 1592, however, he was living in London and pursuing a life in the theater. Shakespeare continued to provide for his family and to expand his holdings in Stratford while living in London. He retired to Stratford-upon-Avon at the end of his life.

Shakespeare's Professional Career

By 1593, Shakespeare was a successful actor and playwright. His history plays *Henry the Sixth,* Parts 1, 2, and 3, and *The Tragedy of Richard the Third* had established him as a significant force in London theater. In 1593, when an outbreak of the plague forced the closing of the theaters, Shakespeare turned to narrative poetry, producing *Venus and Adonis* and *The Rape of Lucrece,* both dedicated to a patron, the Earl of Southampton. When the theaters reopened, Shakespeare plunged back into his primary vocation, and wrote thirty-seven plays in less than twenty years, including *The Taming of the Shrew; A Midsummer Night's Dream; The Merchant of Venice; Twelfth Night, or What You Will; All's Well That Ends Well; The Tragedy of King Richard the Second; The Tragedy of Romeo and Juliet; The Tragedy of Julius Cæsar; The Tragedy of Hamlet, Prince* of Denmark; *The Tragedy of Othello, the Moor of Venice; The Tragedy of King Lear; The Tragedy of Macbeth; The Winter's Tale;* and *The Tempest.*

Around 1594, Shakespeare became a shareholder in a theater company known as The Lord Chamberlain's Men. The troupe quickly became the most popular in London and performed regularly at the court of Queen Elizabeth I. By 1599, they were wealthy enough to build their own theater, a large open-air playhouse they called the Globe, and in 1603 they bought the Blackfriars, a small, artificially lighted indoor theater for winter performances. After the death of Elizabeth in 1603, Shakespeare's company was renamed The King's Men, in honor of their new royal patron, King James I. Shakespeare's final non-collaborative play, *The Famous History of the Life of Henry the Eighth,* was performed in London in 1613. Later that same year, he collaborated with John Fletcher to write a play called *The Two Noble Kinsmen.* At that time he was probably living again in Stratford, in a large house called New Place that he had bought in 1597. When he died in 1616, survived by his wife and his two daughters, Shakespeare was a wealthy man. He was buried in the Holy Trinity Church in Stratford-upon-Avon, where his bones rest to this day. The stone over his grave reads,

> Good frend for Jesus sake forbeare,
> To digg the dust encloased heare:
> Blest be the man that spares thes stones,
> And curst be he that moves my bones.

The Publication of Shakespeare's Plays

Shakespeare did not personally prepare his plays for publication, and no official collection of them appeared until after his death. A collection of his sonnets, considered by critics to be among the best poetry ever written in English, appeared in 1609. Many individual plays were published during his lifetime in unauthorized editions known as quartos. Many of these quartos are quite unreliable. Some were probably based on actors' memories of the plays. Some were reprintings of so-called prompter's copies used in production of the plays. Some may have been based on final manuscript versions produced by the author. In 1623, seven years after Shakespeare's death, his friends and fellow actors John Heminge and Henry Condell published a collected edition of thirty-five of Shakespeare's plays. This collection is known to literary historians as the First Folio. In the centuries since 1623, and especially during the last century and a half, editors have worked diligently to compare the various early printed versions of Shakespeare's works to determine which version or versions of each play best represent Shakespeare's intent.

Shakespeare's Finest Achievement

Fragments can be tantalizing. They tempt people, awakening a desire to reconstruct the missing pieces. Since very little is known of Shakespeare's life beyond a few official records and mentions by others in diaries or letters, many people have been driven to speculate about the private life of England's greatest author. Such speculation is made all the more difficult by the fact that Shakespeare did not write in a personal vein, about himself, but rather concentrated his vision on the lives of others. Reading his plays, or seeing them performed, we come to know many of his characters better than we know most people in our lives. A characteristic of Shakespeare's greatness is that his work takes us on journeys into parallel universes, into other minds, so that his characters' innermost feelings, dreams, wishes, values, motivations, and even contradictions become accessible. This is, perhaps, Shakespeare's finest achievement.

The Authorship of Shakespeare's Plays

The fact that Shakespeare was a commoner and led, according to the few facts we have, a rather ordinary life, has led many people to speculate that his plays were written by someone else—by the Earl of Oxford, perhaps, or by Ben Jonson, but there are good reasons to believe that Shakespeare was, indeed, the author of the plays attributed to him. One reason to accept the traditional attribution is that the plays show an understanding of the lives of people in all stations of life, from the lowliest peasants to men and women of the court. We know that Shakespeare came from a middle-class background and later moved in court circles, and this fact is consistent with his understanding of people from all walks of life. At the very least, a careful reader must conclude that the plays attributed to Shakespeare are the work of a single author, for they have a distinct voice not to be found in the work of any other dramatist of his day—a voice that has enriched our language as none other has ever done.

The Uniqueness of Shakespeare's Work

No brief summary can begin to catalog the many virtues of Shakespeare's work. He was a gifted observer of people, capable of creating unforgettable characters from all stations and walks of life. He used one of the largest vocabularies ever employed by an author, filling his plays with concrete details and with speech that, while not always realistic, is always engaging and believable. His plays probe the range of human experience. They are romantic in the sense that they are full of intensely conveyed passion. However, the plays rarely strain credibility or sink into sensationalism or sentimentality. Shakespeare's language tends to be dense, metaphorical, full of puns and word play, and yet natural, so that it comes "trippingly off the tongue" of an actor. A scene of Shakespeare tears across the stage, riveting and dramatic, and yet it bears close rereading, revealing in that rereading astonishing depth and complexity. Shakespeare wrote his dramas in a combination of prose, rhymed poetry, and blank verse always appropriate to the character or scene at hand. His plays have contributed many now well-known phrases to the English language. They have inspired audiences to laughter, joy, pity, fear, sadness, despair, and suspense for over four hundred years. In fact, his works have been performed more often and in more countries around the world than those of any other dramatist. To begin to read Shakespeare is to enter a world, one might say the world, for his art is, as Hamlet says it should be, "a mirror held up to nature"—to human nature. To read him well is to begin to understand others and ourselves. As Ben Jonson wrote, Shakespeare's art is "not of an age, but for all time."

Time Line of Shakespeare's Life

April 23, 1564	William Shakespeare is born in Stratford-upon-Avon, to parents Mary Arden Shakespeare and John Shakespeare.
April 26, 1564	William Shakespeare is baptized.
1582	William Shakespeare marries Anne Hathaway.
1583	Shakespeare's first daughter, Susanna, is born and christened.
1585	Anne Hathaway Shakespeare gives birth to twins: a boy, Hamnet, and a girl, Judith.
1589–1591	Shakespeare's first histories, *Henry the Sixth,* Parts 1 and 2, are produced.
1592–1593	*The Tragedy of Richard the Third* is produced. Not long afterward, the plague afflicts London and the theaters close. Shakespeare writes *Venus and Adonis* and *The Rape of Lucrece.*
1592–1594	Shakespeare's first comedy, *The Comedy of Errors,* is produced.
c. 1593	Shakespeare begins his sonnet cycle.
1593–1594	*The Taming of the Shrew* is produced.
1594–1595	*Love's Labor's Lost* is produced.
1595	*The Tragedy of King Richard the Second* is produced.
1595–1596	*The Tragedy of Romeo and Juliet* and *A Midsummer Night's Dream* are produced.
1596–1597	*The Merchant of Venice* and *Henry the Fourth, Part 1,* are produced.
1596	Shakespeare's son, Hamnet, dies at age eleven.
1597	Shakespeare acquires a fine home called New Place in Stratford-upon-Avon.
1597	Shakespeare produces *The Merry Wives of Windsor,* possibly at the request of Queen Elizabeth I.
1598	Shakespeare produces *Henry the Fourth, Part 2.*
1598–1599	*Much Ado about Nothing* is produced.
1599	*The Life of Henry the Fifth, The Tragedy of Julius Cæsar,* and *As You Like It* are produced.

Shakespeare's Globe Theater opens.	1599
The Tragedy of Hamlet, Prince of Denmark is produced.	1600–1601
Twelfth Night, or What You Will and *The History of Troilus and Cressida* are produced.	1601–1602
All's Well That Ends Well is produced.	1602–1603
Queen Elizabeth I dies. Shakespeare's troupe serves James I and becomes known as the King's Men.	1603
Measure for Measure and *The Tragedy of Othello, the Moor of Venice* are produced.	1604
The Tragedy of King Lear is produced.	1605
The Tragedy of Macbeth is produced.	1606
The Tragedy of Antony and Cleopatra is produced.	1607
The Tragedy of Coriolanus and *Pericles, Prince of Tyre* are produced.	1607–1608
Cymbeline is produced.	1609–1610
The Winter's Tale is produced.	1610–1611
The Tempest is produced.	1611
The Famous History of the Life of Henry the Eighth is produced.	1612–1613
Shakespeare collaborates with John Fletcher to write *The Two Noble Kinsmen*.	1613
Shakespeare dies and is buried in Holy Trinity Church in Stratford-upon-Avon.	April 23, 1616

Hamlet, Prince of Denmark

In English-speaking countries, *Hamlet, Prince of Denmark* is the most widely produced of all plays. Since it was written almost four hundred years ago, the play has been seen by millions of people and has been translated into hundreds of languages. In the past few years, two motion picture versions of the play, one starring Mel Gibson and the other starring Kenneth Branagh, have packed theaters throughout the world. No work in English has received more critical attention or has given rise to more diverse critical interpretations. As a glance at the Echoes feature on pages xiv and xv will show, *Hamlet* has given several well known stock phrases to the English language, and even those who neither read plays nor go to the theater recognize at least some of its lines and can conjure up a mental image of its central character, dressed in black and meditating over the skull of Yorick.

What are the secrets of this play's unparalleled success? A simple answer is that it appeals to different people for different reasons. Those who want an action-packed tale full of ghosts, murder, sword fights, and intrigue will find it here. Those who want powerful emotion powerfully portrayed will find it here as well—love, loss, lust, revenge, treachery, and madness. The play also pleases the intellect, for it contains profound examinations of ultimate questions of life and death.

The Sources of the Play

Shakespeare, like Chaucer before him, often reworked familiar stories. The story of Hamlet is no exception. Shakespeare drew his plot from two sources, a now lost Elizabethan tragedy, most likely written by Thomas Kyd and commonly referred to as the *Ur-Hamlet*, and a French version of the story appearing in François de Belleforest's *Histoires Tragiques*, published in 1570. Belleforest's tale was in turn based upon the story of a Danish prince named Amleth appearing in the *Historiae Danicae*, or *History of the Danes*, by Saxo Grammaticus. Most of the major events of Shakespeare's version appear in Saxo's history: Horwendil, king of

Denmark, is killed by his brother, Feng. Feng then marries Horwendil's widow, Gerutha, and rules in his stead. The son of the murdered king, Amleth, vows to take revenge and feigns madness to avoid becoming himself one of Feng's victims. A young woman is called upon to seduce Amleth to test whether he is truly mad, but Amleth learns of the scheme and avoids revealing himself. As a further test, Amleth is brought for a conversation with his mother in his mother's bedchamber, and one of Feng's counselors is placed in hiding to eavesdrop on the conversation. Amleth discovers the eavesdropper and kills him. Feng sends Amleth and two members of his court to England, along with a letter demanding that the king of England put Amleth to death. Amleth substitutes for the king's letter one requesting that the king's henchmen, accompanying Amleth, be killed. Amleth returns on the day of his own funeral, kills the king, and later explains his actions in a speech. He then is elected to fill the seat once held by his father.

From Saxo Shakespeare took the main elements of his plot. From Belleforest he took the suggestion that Hamlet suffered from melancholy. From Kyd and other contemporary Elizabethan tragedians, he took the figure of the ghost and the tradition of the revenge drama. Shakespeare's genius lay in grafting onto the barbarous tale of revenge a profound meditation on the value of human action and the role in human life of divine providence.

The Intellectual Climate of the Play

Although the events of this play are set in medieval Denmark, the characters and situations resemble more closely a Renaissance court of Shakespeare's time, complete with romantic intrigues, foppish courtiers characterized by their affected speech, and young men who go off to study in the capitals of Europe. One such young man is Prince Hamlet himself, who has been, we are told, a student at the University of Wittenberg. This often overlooked fact provides a key to understanding the deeper meaning of the play.

Wittenberg was the university of Martin Luther, who initiated the Protestant Reformation. Among the other challenges that Luther made to the traditional authority of the Catholic church was his radical theory concerning the relative value of human action and divinely extended grace. Catholic dogma and practice held that, by receiving the sacraments, such as Holy Communion and Extreme Unction, one could obtain absolution from sin and thus achieve salvation. Luther argued that every person is born into the world inheriting the sin of our first parents, Adam and Eve, and that because of our basically sinful nature, we cannot through our own actions make ourselves perfect enough to stand before God. According to Luther, we must depend, instead, on the grace God extends to us despite our essential unworthiness. The more extreme proponents of the Lutheran view went so far as to claim that all events were predetermined and preordained by God and that human actions were irrelevant to the unfolding of His plan, evidenced by providential occurrences in human lives. Such was the avant garde of thought in Shakespeare's day, and it is not surprising that Shakespeare, a man of wide-ranging intellectual interests, should treat these radical ideas in his work.

At the beginning of this play, Hamlet is presented with a challenge: His father has been murdered by his uncle. The murderer sits on his father's throne and sleeps with Hamlet's mother in his father's bed. Hamlet is asked by his father's ghost to take revenge on the uncle, and Hamlet vows to do so. Critics have debated for centuries why Hamlet does not immediately leap to his revenge and kill his murderous, adulterous uncle. In fact, this has been called the central "problem" of the play. By nature, however, Hamlet is melancholic and scholarly. He is given to religious and philosophical speculation and wonders often about whether acting on the ghost's command might damn him, about the value of any human action, and about the ultimate value of human life.

The ghost's challenge tests the very issues that Luther raised: the value of action, the question of whether by one's actions one can achieve salvation, and the relative role in human affairs of human action versus divine providence. Hamlet himself is torn. He longs to live up to the model of his heroic father, who slew the king of Norway in single combat, but his inclination is to escape this world altogether. Hamlet's distaste for worldly things is increased by his horror and disgust at his mother's involvement with his uncle, and so Hamlet's resolution is "sicklied o'er with the pale cast of thought." Even though he has great cause to do so, Hamlet proves unable to act. His paralysis, the cause of so much concern to critics, is the heart of the play and its central subject. That Hamlet behaves badly, especially in his interactions with Ophelia, that his plans go astray, that even he, despite his superior mind, cannot figure out on his own what to do is precisely the point, and this point is missed by those directors and actors who choose to portray Hamlet as a swashbuckling hero. It is because Hamlet is not a conventional hero that he is of such abiding interest.

The Texts of *Hamlet*

Shakespeare probably composed *Hamlet* in the interval between 1598 and February of 1601. The play contains several references to the story of Julius Caesar, told by Shakespeare in a play that was performed in 1599. The text of *Hamlet* survives in three versions, those of the First Quarto, the Second Quarto, and the First Folio. Of these, the First Quarto is an extremely abbreviated and mutilated text, believed to have been an unauthorized, reconstructed version based on the memory of an actor who had performed in the play. The longest existing version, nearly twice as long as Shakespeare's *Tragedy of Macbeth,* is the Second Quarto, which scholars believe to have been typeset, with numerous errors, from Shakespeare's own manuscript. The version that appeared in the First Folio of 1623 is believed in some ways to be superior in that it contains some deletions that Shakespeare later made in his text. Most *Hamlet* texts are of the First Folio. This text is unique in that it presents both the First Folio and Second Quarto versions. However, the Folio version also contains what are obviously typesetting errors. In the version of the play presented in this book, lines that appear only in the Second Quarto but not in the Folio are set off by boxes.

One unresolved problem of this play is that both the Second Quarto and Folio versions are too long to have been presented in Shakespeare's theater. We can assume that in performance many lines and perhaps whole scenes were cut or considerably abbreviated. Unfortunately, no acting version except the corrupt First Quarto has survived, and for this reason we may never know how the play actually appeared on Shakespeare's stage. That the play is so long has led some scholars to speculate that Shakespeare poured much of himself into it, writing for his own benefit what he knew would have to be curtailed in performance. If this is so, then the text of *Hamlet* provides us with a tantalizing look into the mind of the greatest of all dramatists at the crucial midpoint of his career.

Echoes: Famous Lines from Hamlet

Act I

"A mote it is to trouble the mind's eye."

"But look, the morn in russet mantle clad
Walks o'er the dew of yon high eastward hill."

"Seems, madam? nay, it is, I know not 'seems.'"

"But I have that within which passes show,
These but the trappings and the suits of woe."

"O that this too too solid flesh would melt."

"Frailty, thy name is woman!"

"Foul deeds will rise,
Though all the earth o'erwhelm them, to men's eyes."

"Occasion smiles on a second leave."

"Neither a borrower nor a lender be."

"to thine own self be true."

"I am native here
And to the manner born"

"it is a custom
More honor'd in the breach than the observance."

"Something is rotten in the state of Denmark."

"Adieu, adieu, adieu! remember me."

"one may smile, and smile, and be a villain!"

"There are more things in heaven and earth, Horatio,
Than are dreamt of in your philosophy."

Act II

"Thou still hast been the father of good news."

"brevity is the soul of wit"

"Though this be madness, yet there is method in't."

"As the indifferent children of the earth."

"I could be bounded in a nutshell, and count myself a king of infinite space"

"What a piece of work is a man"

"as much modesty as cunning"

"they are the abstract and brief chronicles of the time."

"use every man after his desert, and who shall scape whipping?"

"O, what a rogue and peasant slave am I!"

"the play's the thing
Wherein I'll catch the conscience of the king."

Act III

"To be, or not to be, that is the question"

"To die, to sleep—to sleep, perchance to dream"

"there's the rub"

"death,
The undiscover'd country, from whose bourn
No traveler returns"

"Thus conscience does make cowards of us all"

"Nymph, in thy orisons
Be all my sins rememb'red."

"Get thee to a nunn'ry."

"O, what a noble mind is here o'erthrown!"

"Speak the speech, I pray you, as I pronounc'd it to you,
trippingly on the tongue"

"o'erstep not the modesty of nature"

"whose end, both at the first and now, was and is, to
hold as 'twere the mirror up to nature"

"The lady doth protest too much, methinks."

"a cry of players"

"though you fret me, yet you cannot play upon me."

"I will speak daggers to her, but use none."

"This is the very coinage of your brain."

"I must be cruel only to be kind."

Act IV

"The King is a thing"

"Nothing but to show you how a king may go
a progress through the guts of a beggar"

"How all occasions do inform against me"

"Of thinking too precisely on th' event"

"But greatly to find quarrel in a straw
When honor's at the stake."

"This nothing's more than matter."

"For bonny sweet Robin is all my joy."

"And where th' offense is, let the great axe fall."

"There is a willow grows askaunt the brook"

Act V

"Alas, poor Yorick! I knew him, Horatio, a fellow
of infinite jest"

"Imperious Cæsar, dead and turn'd to clay,
Might stop a hole to keep the wind away."

"Sweets to the sweet"

"The cat will mew, and dog will have his day."

"There's a divinity that shapes our ends,
Rough-hew them how we will."

"the interim's mine"

"There is special providence in the fall of a sparrow."

"the readiness is all"

"I have shot my arrow o'er the house
And hurt my brother."

"A hit, a very palpable hit."

"A touch, a touch, I do confess't."

"Absent thee from felicity a while"

"the rest is silence"

"Good night, sweet prince
And flights of angels sing thee to thy rest!"

"Rosencrantz and Guildenstern are dead."

"purposes mistook
Fall'n on th' inventors' heads"

The Globe Theater

Shakespeare's Birthplace

Dramatis Personae

CLAUDIUS, *King of Denmark*

HAMLET, *son to the late, and nephew to the present, king*

POLONIUS, *Lord Chamberlain*

HORATIO, *friend to Hamlet*

LAERTES, *son to Polonius*

VOLTEMAND
CORNELIUS
ROSENCRANTZ } *courtiers*
GUILDENSTERN
OSRIC

A Gentleman

A Priest

MARCELLUS } *officers*
BARNARDO

FRANCISCO, *a soldier*

REYNALDO, *servant to Polonius*

Players

Two Clowns, grave-diggers

FORTINBRAS, *Prince of Norway*

A Norwegian Captain

English Ambassadors

GERTRUDE, *Queen of Denmark, and mother to Hamlet*

OPHELIA, *daughter to Polonius*

Lords, Ladies, Officers, Soldiers, Sailors, Messengers, and other Attendants

Ghost of Hamlet's Father

ACT I, SCENE i

1. **Elsinore.** Capital of Denmark
2. **unfold yourself.** Reveal who you are
3. **most carefully upon your hour.** Exactly at the time when you are supposed to come
4. **rivals.** Companions, partners
5. **liegemen.** Servants bound by oath
6. **Give you good night.** Good night to you.
7. **honest.** Faithful
8. **Holla.** Hello
9. **A piece of him.** Horatio is suffering from the excessive cold and is not feeling normal.

who is the ghost?
dead King Hamlet
appears to B.F. +
Horatio
not a good thing, but
a bad omen

[handwritten: Midnight]

[handwritten: single soldiers]

[handwritten: setting royal castle]

Act I

Enter BARNARDO *and* FRANCISCO, *two sentinels, meeting.*

BARNARDO.   Who's there?

FRANCISCO.   Nay, answer me. Stand and unfold yourself.[2]

◄ What is Francisco doing at the opening of the play?

BARNARDO.   Long live the King!

FRANCISCO.   Barnardo.

5   BARNARDO.   He.

FRANCISCO.   You come most carefully upon your hour.[3]

BARNARDO.   'Tis now strook twelf. Get thee to bed, Francisco.

FRANCISCO.   For this relief much thanks. 'Tis bitter cold,

And I am sick at heart.

◄ How does Francisco feel? Why might he feel this way?

10   BARNARDO.   Have you had quiet guard?

FRANCISCO.   Not a mouse stirring.

BARNARDO.   Well, good night.
If you do meet Horatio and Marcellus,
The rivals[4] of my watch, bid them make haste.

◄ For whom is Barnardo waiting?

Enter HORATIO *and* MARCELLUS.

FRANCISCO.   I think I hear them. Stand ho! Who is there?

15   HORATIO.   Friends to this ground.

MARCELLUS.   And liegemen[5] to the Dane.

FRANCISCO.   Give you good night.[6]

MARCELLUS.   O, farewell, honest[7] soldier.
Who hath reliev'd you?

FRANCISCO.   Barnardo hath my place.
Give you good night.   *Exit* FRANCISCO.

MARCELLUS.   Holla,[8] Barnardo!

BARNARDO.   Say—
What, is Horatio there?

HORATIO.   A piece of him.[9]

20   BARNARDO.   Welcome, Horatio, welcome, good Marcellus.

10. **Touching.** Concerning
11. **watch the minutes of this night.** Stand guard throughout the night
12. **approve our eyes.** Confirm what we have seen
13. **fortified.** Barnardo speaks metaphorically. Attempting to convince Horatio is like assailing a fort.
14. **yond same star . . . pole.** Polaris, the North Star, also known as the Pole Star. This star has long been used by mariners to guide their way.
15. **illume.** Illuminate
16. **beating.** Tolling
17. **In the same figure like.** With the same appearance as
18. **scholar.** Student
19. **Mark it.** Look at it carefully.
20. **harrows.** Digs into or disturbs, like a harrow, or plow
21. **usurp'st.** Takes possession of without the right to do so. The term *usurp* is used to describe the unjust seizure of power from a monarch or leader. It is therefore ironic that the term should be used here, given that the ghost is that of the rightful king of Denmark.
22. **Denmark.** King of Denmark. The ruler or lord of a country or territory was often referred to in Shakespeare's day by the name of the country or territory, just as today we speak of "the White House" when we mean the executive branch of government.
23. **sometimes.** In recent times
24. **I charge thee.** I demand of you

Words For Everyday Use	**en • treat** (en trēt´) *vt.*, beg
	ap • pa • ri • tion (ăp´ə rish´ən) *n.*, strange figure that appears unexpectedly, especially a ghost
	as • sail (ə sāl´) *adj.*, attack with arguments

HORATIO.   What, has this thing appear'd again tonight?

BARNARDO.   I have seen nothing.

MARCELLUS.   Horatio says 'tis but our fantasy,
And will not let belief take hold of him
25 Touching[10] this dreaded sight twice seen of us;
Therefore I have entreated him along,
With us to watch the minutes of this night,[11]
That if again this apparition come,
He may approve our eyes[12] and speak to it.

30 HORATIO.   Tush, tush, 'twill not appear.

BARNARDO.   Sit down a while,
And let us once again assail your ears,
That are so fortified[13] against our story,
What we have two nights seen.

HORATIO.   Well, sit we down,
And let us hear Barnardo speak of this.

35 BARNARDO.   Last night of all,
When yond same star that's westward from the pole[14]
Had made his course t' illume[15] that part of heaven
Where now it burns, Marcellus and myself,
The bell then beating[16] one—

Enter GHOST.

40 MARCELLUS.   Peace, break again! thee off! Look where it comes again!

BARNARDO.   In the same figure like[17] the King that's dead.

MARCELLUS.   Thou art a scholar,[18] speak to it, Horatio.

BARNARDO.   Looks 'a not like the King? Mark it,[19] Horatio.

HORATIO. Most like; it harrows[20] me with fear and wonder.

45 BARNARDO.   It would be spoke to.

MARCELLUS.   Speak to it, Horatio.

HORATIO.   What art thou that usurp'st[21] this time of night,
Together with that fair and warlike form
In which the majesty of buried Denmark[22]
Did sometimes[23] march? By heaven I charge thee[24] speak!

50 MARCELLUS.   It is offended.

◄ Why has Marcellus asked Horatio to come and stand watch with him?

◄ Does Horatio believe that Marcellus and Barnardo have actually seen a ghost?

◄ Whom does the ghost resemble?

◄ Why does Marcellus think that Horatio should speak to the ghost?

◄ What was the dead king like, according to Horatio?

25. **How now.** How are you now? A common expression similar to today's "How are you feeling?"

26. **on't.** Contraction of "on it," meaning "about it"

27. **sensible.** Sensory

28. **true avouch.** Truthful affirmation

29. **When he . . . Norway combated.** When he fought the ambitious king of Norway

30. **parle.** Parley, or negotiation. The word is here used ironically. The dead king was a man of action, not a negotiator. He negotiated with arms.

31. **smote the sledded Polacks.** Struck the Polish armies, who were fighting from sleds or sleighs

32. **jump at.** Exactly at

33. **In what particular thought to work I know not.** The line is ambiguous. It can mean "I don't know what the ghost intends" or "I don't know what to make of this."

34. **gross and scope of my opinion.** Overall or general meaning

35. **strange eruption to our state.** Unusual, sudden, negative occurrence in our general condition or in the nation

36. **observant watch.** Close vigil

37. **toils the subject.** Puts to work the subjects, or people

38. **mart.** Shopping

39. **impress.** Forced labor, or impressment. Ship builders are being forced to work even on Sundays.

40. **toward.** Afoot, about to happen

41. **make the night joint-laborer with the day.** Cause people to work day and night

42. **our last king.** The elder Hamlet, now deceased

43. **even but now.** Just now

44. **Fortinbras of Norway.** Fortinbras, the now-deceased king of Norway

45. **prick'd on by a most emulate pride.** Spurred on by an envious pride

Words For Everyday Use

mar • tial (mar´ shəl) *adj.*, soldierlike

bra • zen (brā´zən) *adj.*, made of brass (and, like it, bold)

BARNARDO.   See, it stalks away!

HORATIO.   Stay! Speak, speak, I charge thee speak!

Exit GHOST.

◄ *What does Horatio demand of the ghost? How does the ghost respond?*

MARCELLUS.   'Tis gone, and will not answer.

BARNARDO.   How now,[25] Horatio? you tremble and
look pale.
Is not this something more than fantasy?
55 What think you on't?[26] *a bout it*

HORATIO.   Before my God, I might not this believe
Without the sensible[27] and true avouch[28] *affirmation*
Of mine own eyes.

MARCELLUS.   Is it not like the King?

HORATIO.   As thou art to thyself.
60 Such was the very armor he had on
When he the ambitious Norway combated.[29]
So frown'd he once when in an angry parle[30] *negotiation*
He smote the sledded Polacks[31] on the ice.
'Tis strange.

◄ *What was the ghost wearing?*

65 MARCELLUS.   Thus twice before, and jump at[32] this
dead hour,
With martial stalk hath he gone by our watch.

HORATIO.   In what particular thought to work I know
not,[33] *what is going on?*.
But in the gross and scope of mine opinion,[34]
This bodes some strange eruption to our state.[35]

◄ *Of what, according to Horatio, might the appearance of this ghost be a warning?*

70 MARCELLUS.   Good now, sit down, and tell me, he that
knows,
Why this same strict and most observant watch[36] *vigil*
So nightly toils the subject[37] of the land,
And why such daily cast of brazen cannon,
And foreign mart[38] for implements of war,
75 Why such impress[39] of shipwrights, whose sore task
Does not divide the Sunday from the week,
What might be toward,[40] that this sweaty haste
Doth make the night joint-laborer with the day:[41]
Who is't that can inform me?

◄ *What is happening in Denmark at this time?*

HORATIO.   That can I,
80 At least the whisper goes so: our last king,[42] *elder Hamlet*
Whose image even but now[43] appear'd to us,
Was, as you know, by Fortinbras of Norway,[44]
Thereto prick'd on by a most emulate pride,[45]
Dar'd to the combat; in which our valiant Hamlet
85 (For so this side of our known world esteem'd him)

◄ *What was the dead king's name?*

46. **seal'd compact.** Contract bearing the king's seal
47. **heraldy.** Rules governing combat between noblemen
48. **Which he stood seized of.** That he owned
49. **moi'ty competent.** A like amount (of land)
50. **gaged.** Engaged, or bet
51. **comart / And carriage of the article.** *Comart*—joint bargain; *carriage of the article*—carrying out of the article or agreement
52. **young Fortinbras.** The son of Fortinbras, the former king of Norway, and nephew to the current king of Norway
53. **unimproved mettle.** Untested strength or ability
54. **skirts.** Outskirts
55. **Shark'd up . . . resolutes.** Like a shark, gathered up a group of men resolved on lawlessness
56. **For food . . . stomach in't.** Horatio is speaking metaphorically. An enterprise with stomach in it is one that requires courage. The lawless resolutes will serve as food and diet to this undertaking, meaning that they may well die in it.
57. **terms compulsatory.** Forced terms
58. **foresaid.** Aforesaid, previously mentioned
59. **head.** Source or cause
60. **post-haste and romage.** Fast work (like that of a rider carrying the post, or mail) and commotion (or rummaging about)
61. **e'en.** Even
62. **Well may it sort.** It may turn out. Barnardo is saying that it may well turn out that the ghost has appeared in arms because there is a threat of war.
63. **palmy.** Palm-filled. In ancient days, palm branches signified victory or triumph.
64. **the mightiest Julius.** Julius Cæsar, a Roman general, was assassinated by people who feared that he might proclaim himself emperor.
65. **Disasters.** Eruptions, solar flares or sun spots
66. **moist star.** Moon
67. **upon whose influence.** The moon controls the tides.
68. **Neptune's empire.** The sea. Neptune was the Roman god of the sea.
69. **sick . . . eclipse.** It was commonly believed that eclipses were signs of calamity to come.
70. **the like precurse.** The similar precursor
71. **omen.** The event itself
72. **Unto our climatures.** To our country
73. **soft.** An interjection meaning, at the same time, "hush" and "pay attention"
74. **cross it.** Cross its path, with a possible pun on "make the sign of the cross at it"
75. **blast.** Destroy

Words For Everyday Use

por • ten • tous (pôr tenʹtəs) *adj.*, warning of coming evil
mote (mōt) *n.*, speck
ten • ant • less (ten əntʹləs) *adj.*, empty of people (here, the dead)
har • bin • ger (härʹ bin jər) *n.*, something which comes before, announcing what is to come

Did slay this Fortinbras, who, by a seal'd compact[46]
Well ratified by law and heraldy,[47]
Did forfeit (with his life) all those his lands
Which he stood seiz'd of,[48] to the conqueror;
90 Against the which a moi'ty competent[49]
Was gaged[50] by our king, which had return'd
To the inheritance of Fortinbras,
Had he been vanquisher; as by the same comart
And carriage of the article[51] design'd,
95 His fell to Hamlet. Now, sir, young Fortinbras,[52]
Of unimproved mettle[53] hot and full,
Hath in the skirts[54] of Norway here and there
Shark'd up a list of lawless resolutes[55]
For food and diet to some enterprise
100 That hath a stomach in't,[56] which is no other,
As it doth well appear unto our state,
But to recover of us, by strong hand
And terms compulsatory,[57] those foresaid[58] lands
So by his father lost; and this, I take it,
105 Is the main motive of our preparations,
The source of this our watch, and the chief head[59]
Of this post-haste and romage[60] in the land.

> BARNARDO.   I think it be no other but e'en[61] so.
> Well may it sort[62] that this portentous figure
> 110 Comes armed through our watch so like the King
> That was and is the question of these wars.
>
> HORATIO.   A mote it is to trouble the mind's eye.
> In the most high and palmy[63] state of Rome,
> A little ere the mightiest Julius[64] fell,
> 115 The graves stood tenantless and the sheeted dead
> Did squeak and gibber in the Roman streets.
> As stars with trains of fire, and dews of blood,
> Disasters[65] in the sun; and the moist star[66]
> Upon whose influence[67] Neptune's empire[68] stands
> 120 Was sick almost to doomsday with eclipse.[69]
> And even the like precurse[70] of fear'd events,
> As harbingers preceding still the fates
> And prologue to the omen[71] coming on,
> Have heaven and earth together demonstrated
> 125 Unto our climatures[72] and countrymen.

Enter GHOST.
But soft,[73] behold! lo where it comes again!

It spreads his arms.

I'll cross it[74] though it blast[75] me. Stay, illusion!

◀ What did the previous king of Denmark win in battle from the king of Norway?

◀ What does the young Fortinbras intend to do, and why is Denmark preparing for war?

Here and through-out the text, passages that appear in the First Folio but not in the Second Quarto are enclosed by boxes.

◀ According to Horatio, what happened in ancient Rome before Julius Cæsar was assassinated?

76. **thou art privy to.** You are knowledgeable about
77. **partisan.** Weapon on a staff, the head of which bears, on one side, an ax, and on the other, a spear
78. **magestical.** Majestic
79. **the god of day.** Phoebus Apollo, associated in Greek and Roman mythology with the sun
80. **extravagant and erring.** Outside its proper bounds and wandering
81. **hies.** Flees
82. **probation.** Proof
83. **'gainst.** Just before
84. **no planets strike.** No planet exerts an evil influence (a reference to astrological belief)
85. **no fairy takes.** It was commonly believed that fairies stole away children.
86. **russet mantle.** Reddish cloak

Words For Everyday Use

ex • tort (eks tôrt´) *vt.,* to get something from someone by violence or threat

in • vul • ner • a • ble (in vul´nər ə bəl) *adj.,* not open to harm

ma • li • cious (mə lish´əs) *adj.,* ill-willed

sum • mons (sum´ əns) *n.,* official order to appear as a defendant before a court

con • fine (kän´ fīn) *n.,* bordered region

hal • lowed (hal´ ōd) *adj.,* holy

If thou hast any sound or use of voice,
Speak to me.
130 If there be any good thing to be done
That may to thee do ease, and grace to me,
Speak to me.
If thou art privy to[76] thy country's fate,
Which happily foreknowing may avoid,
135 O speak!
Or if thou hast uphoarded in thy life
Extorted treasure in the womb of earth,
For which, they say, your spirits oft walk in death,
Speak of it, stay and speak! [The cock crows.] Stop it,
    Marcellus.

140 MARCELLUS.   Shall I strike it with my partisan?[77] weapon

HORATIO.   Do, if it will not stand.

BARNARDO.   'Tis here!

HORATIO.   'Tis here!

MARCELLUS.   'Tis gone!   Exit GHOST.
We do it wrong, being so majestical,[78] majestic harm or
To offer it the show of violence,   not open to injury
145 For it is as the air, invulnerable,   ill-willed
And our vain blows malicious mockery.

BARNARDO.   It was about to speak when the cock crew.

HORATIO.   And then it started like a guilty thing
√ Upon a fearful summons. I have heard
150 The cock, that is the trumpet to the morn,
Doth with his lofty and shrill-sounding throat
Awake the god of day,[79] and at his warning,
Whether in sea or fire, in earth or air,
begin Th' extravagant and erring[80] spirit hies[81] flees
155 To his confine; and of the truth herein
This present object made probation.[82]

MARCELLUS.   It faded on the crowing of the cock.
Some say that ever 'gainst[83] that season comes
Wherein our Saviour's birth is celebrated,
160 This bird of dawning singeth all night long,
And then they say no spirit dare stir abroad,
The nights are wholesome, then no planets strike,[84] no planets
No fairy takes,[85] nor witch hath power to charm,   for evil force
So hallowed, and so gracious, is that time.

165 HORATIO.   So have I heard and do in part believe it. Red cloak
But look, the morn in russet mantle[86] clad
Walks o'er the dew of yon high eastward hill.

◄ What does Horatio ask of the ghost?

◄ What does Horatio think the ghost might know?

◄ According to popular belief, what happens to a roaming spirit when the cock crows at the break of day?

87. **dumb.** Silent

88. *Exeunt.* Latin for "they exit."

ACT I, SCENE ii

1. **the memory be green.** The death has occurred recently and thus the memory is still green, like a young plant.

2. **our sometime sister.** My former sister-in-law. Claudius uses the "royal we"; as King, he says "our," while a common person would say "my."

3. **imperial jointress.** Person who holds sovereign power jointly

4. **dole.** Grief

5. **supposal.** Supposition, valuation

6. **disjoint and out of frame.** In shambles or disarray, like a badly done work of carpentry

7. **Coleagued.** Joined

8. **writ.** Written

9. **impotent and bedred.** Lacking strength and bedridden

10. **his further gait.** His additional strides or movements

11. **lists.** Enlistments

Words For Everyday Use

im • part (im part´) *vt.,* tell

dis • cre • tion (dis kre´shən) *n.,* care to behave properly

aus • pi • cious (ôs pish´ əs) *adj.,* looking to a happy future

dirge (dʉrj) *n.,* funeral hymn

late (lāt) *adj.,* recently deceased

val • iant (val´ yənt) *adj.,* brave

sup • press (sə pres´) *vt.,* keep back or down

lev • y (le´ vē) *n.,* tax

Break we our watch up, and by my advice
Let us impart what we have seen tonight
170 Unto young Hamlet, for, upon my life,
This spirit, dumb[87] to us, will speak to him.
Do you consent we shall acquaint him with it,
As needful in our loves, fitting our duty?

MARCELLUS. Let's do't, I pray, and I this morning know
175 Where we shall find him most convenient. *Exeunt.*[88]

SCENE ii: A room of state in the castle

Flourish. Enter CLAUDIUS, KING OF DENMARK, GERTRUDE THE
QUEEN, POLONIUS *and his son* LAERTES, HAMLET, *others
including* VOLTEMAND *and* CORNELIUS.

KING.   Though yet of Hamlet our dear brother's death
The memory be green,[1] and that it us befitted
To bear our hearts in grief, and our whole kingdom
To be contracted in one brow of woe,
5 Yet so far hath discretion fought with nature
That we with wisest sorrow think on him
Together with remembrance of ourselves.
Therefore our sometime sister,[2] now our queen,
Th' imperial jointress[3] to this warlike state,
10 Have we, as 'twere with a defeated joy,
With an auspicious, and a dropping eye,
With mirth in funeral, and with dirge in marriage
In equal scale weighing delight and dole,[4]
Taken to wife; nor have we herein barr'd
15 Your better wisdoms, which have freely gone
With this affair along. For all, our thanks.
Now follows that you know young Fortinbras,
Holding a weak supposal[5] of our worth,
Or thinking by our late dear brother's death
20 Our state to be disjoint and out of frame,[6]
Coleagued[7] with this dream of his advantage,
He hath not fail'd to pester us with message
Importing the surrender of those lands
Lost by his father, with all bands of law,
25 To our most valiant brother. So much for him.
Now for ourself, and for this time of meeting,
Thus much the business is: we have here writ[8]
To Norway, uncle of young Fortinbras—
Who, impotent and bedred,[9] scarcely hears
30 Of this his nephew's purpose—to suppress
His further gait[10] herein, in that the levies,
The lists,[11] and full proportions are all made

◄ Whom does
Horatio want to tell
about the ghost, and
why?

◄ How long has it
been since the death
of the elder Hamlet?
What was the rela-
tionship between the
elder Hamlet and
King Claudius?

◄ Whom did
Claudius marry?
What was Claudius's
former relationship to
this person?

◄ Why has King
Claudius written to
young Fortinbras's
uncle?

12. **subject.** Subjects, the people who are subject to the King of Norway's authority

13. **delated.** Detailed

14. **let your haste commend your duty.** Let the speed with which you set about your task speak well of your dutifulness.

15. **We doubt it nothing.** I do not doubt it. Claudius, being king and therefore representative of the entire body of the people, uses the royal we when referring to himself.

16. **suit.** Request

17. **cannot speak . . . lose your voice.** Cannot ask anything reasonable of the Danish king (Claudius) and not be heard

18. **native.** Literally, of the same country; connected

19. **pardon.** Permission

20. **laborsome.** Much belabored, tireless

21. **cousin.** Relative. The word is a figure of speech. Hamlet is not literally Claudius's cousin, but his nephew.

22. **more than kin.** More than merely a relative. Claudius is now a double relative, both uncle and stepfather.

23. **less than kind.** The word kind, as used here, is ambiguous. It means both "affectionate" and "natural." Hamlet is saying that Claudius has been unkind to him and is not of the same kind, or type of creature, as Hamlet is. Hamlet views the marriage of Claudius to Queen Gertrude as unnatural.

24. **too much in the sun.** The word *sun,* as used here, is a pun. Hamlet dislikes being referred to as Claudius's son.

25. **nighted color.** Hamlet's dark mood and his black mourning clothes.

Words For Everyday Use

in • stru • men • tal (in strə men´ təl) *adj.*, useful

cor • o • na • tion (kôr ə nā´ shən) n., ceremony in which a sovereign is crowned

Out of his subject;[12] and we here dispatch
You, good Cornelius, and you, Voltemand,
35 For bearers of this greeting to old Norway,
Giving to you no further personal power
To business with the King, more than the scope
Of these delated[13] articles allow.   *Giving a paper.*
Farewell, and let your haste commend your duty.[14]

40 CORNELIUS, VOLTEMAND.   In that, and all things, will we
     show our duty.

KING.   We doubt it nothing;[15] heartily farewell.
                    Exeunt VOLTEMAND *and* CORNELIUS.
And now, Laertes, what's the news with you?
You told us of some suit,[16] what is't, Laertes?
You cannot speak of reason to the Dane
45 And lose your voice.[17] What wouldst thou beg, Laertes,
That shall not be my offer, not thy asking?
The head is not more native[18] to the heart,
The hand more instrumental to the mouth,
Than is the throne of Denmark to thy father.
50 What wouldst thou have, Laertes?

◄ How does King
Claudius feel toward
Laertes's father?

LAERTES.   My dread lord,
Your leave and favor to return to France,
From whence though willingly I came to Denmark
To show my duty in your coronation,
Yet now I must confess, that duty done,
55 My thoughts and wishes bend again toward France,
And bow them to your gracious leave and pardon.[19]

◄ What does
Laertes want?

KING.   Have you your father's leave? What says
Polonius?

POLONIUS.   H'ath, my lord, wrung from me my slow
leave
By laborsome[20] petition, and at last
60 Upon his will I seal'd my hard consent.
I do beseech you give him leave to go.

KING.   Take thy fair hour, Laertes, time be thine,
And thy best graces spend it at thy will!
But now, my cousin[21] Hamlet, and my son—

◄ What two terms
does Claudius use to
describe young
Hamlet? How does
Hamlet feel about
Claudius?

65 HAMLET.   [*Aside.*] A little more than kin,[22] and less
     than kind.[23]

KING.   How is it that the clouds still hang on you?

HAMLET.   Not so, my lord, I am too much in the sun.[24]

QUEEN.   Good Hamlet, cast thy nighted color[25] off,
And let thine eye look like a friend on Denmark.

◄ Hamlet's use of
the word *sun* is a
pun on what word
used by Claudius?
What does this pun
indicate about
Hamlet's feelings
toward Claudius?

26. **vailed lids.** Downcast eyes
27. **'tis common.** It is commonplace
28. **common.** Hamlet's uses the word in another sense, meaning "base," "vile," or "low." He is referring, most likely, to the marriage of Claudius and Gertrude.
29. **so particular with.** So unusual to
30. **suspiration.** Sigh
31. **havior of the visage.** Look on the face
32. **obsequious.** Having to do with obsequies, or ritual observances
33. **condolement.** Grief
34. **as common . . . to sense.** As common as the most ordinary thing that we perceive with our senses
35. **corse.** Corpse, dead body
36. **unprevailing.** Futile, ineffectual
37. **us.** Again, Claudius uses the royal form, referring to himself in the plural
38. **most immediate.** Most likely successor

- Hamlet dislikes Claudius
(his uncle) - doesn't want
to be called his son.
Hamlet is mourning for his
fr.
claud - but a natural
thing

I tell Hamlet that he
is next to the throne + he
loves him as a son

Words For Everyday Use	com • men • da • ble (kä men´ də bəl) *adj.*, praiseworthy
	ob • sti • nate (äb´ stə nət) *adj.*, stubborn, unyielding
	im • pi • ous (im pī´ əs) *adj.*, lacking reverence for God or for a parent

70   Do not for ever with thy vailed lids[26]
      Seek for thy noble father in the dust.
      Thou know'st 'tis common,[27] all that lives must die,
      Passing through nature to eternity.

HAMLET.   Ay, madam, it is common.[28]

QUEEN.   If it be,
75   Why seems it so particular with[29] thee?

HAMLET.   Seems, madam? nay, it is, I know not
      "seems."
      'Tis not alone my inky cloak, good mother,
      Nor customary suits of solemn black,
      Nor windy suspiration[30] of forc'd breath,
80   No, nor the fruitful river in the eye,
      Nor the dejected havior of the visage,[31]
      Together with all forms, moods, shapes of grief,
      That can denote me truly. These indeed seem,
      For they are actions that a man might play,
85   But I have that within which passes show,
      These but the trappings and the suits of woe.

KING.   'Tis sweet and commendable in your nature,
        Hamlet,
      To give these mourning duties to your father.
      But you must know your father lost a father,
90   That father lost, lost his, and the survivor bound
      In filial obligation for some term
      To do obsequious[32] sorrow. But to persever
      In obstinate condolement[33] is a course
      Of impious stubbornness, 'tis unmanly grief,
95   It shows a will most incorrect to heaven,
      A heart unfortified, or mind impatient,
      An understanding simple and unschool'd:
      For what we know must be, and is as common
      As any the most vulgar thing to sense,[34]
100   Why should we in our peevish opposition
      Take it to heart? Fie, 'tis a fault to heaven,
      A fault against the dead, a fault to nature,
      To reason most absurd, whose common theme
      Is death of fathers, and who still hath cried,
105   From the first corse[35] till he that died today,
      "This must be so." We pray you throw to earth
      This unprevailing[36] woe, and think of us[37]
      As of a father, for let the world take note
      You are the most immediate[38] to our throne,
110   And with no less nobility of love
      Than that which dearest father bears his son

◄ Why has Hamlet been dressing in black, sighing, crying, and otherwise showing grief? What does he have within himself?

◄ What does Claudius think of the fact that Hamlet continues to grieve for his dead father? What does Claudius want Hamlet to do?

◄ Who is next in line to the throne after Claudius?

39. **Wittenberg.** The University of Wittenberg, made famous as the school associated with Martin Luther, who initiated the Protestant Reformation by challenging the authority of the Pope and claiming that only through God's grace could one be saved

40. **retrograde.** Opposed, contrary

41. **in all my best.** To the best of my ability

42. **health . . . shall tell.** When the king drinks a toast to someone's health, a cannon shall be shot. This was, evidently, an old Danish custom.

43. **rouse.** Merriment

44. **bruit.** Proclaim

45. **too solid.** Because of the recent events and perhaps also because of his studies in philosophy and theology at Wittenberg, Hamlet detests things of this earth and longs for release into the world of the spirit. This is a much-debated line because Quarto 2 gives the word as *sallied,* which many editors have taken to be an alternate spelling of sullied, meaning "dirtied."

46. **canon.** Authoritative law of the church, especially as derived from scripture

47. **all the uses.** All the habits or customs

48. **things rank . . . possess it merely.** Hamlet compares the world to a garden taken over by rank, or rapidly growing, and gross, or overgrown, weeds.

49. **to this.** Compared to this (in other words, compared to Claudius)

50. **Hyperion.** In Greek mythology, a Titan often identified with the sun god. The identification of a king with the sun is traditional.

51. **satyr.** In Greek and Roman mythology, a creature, half-human, half-goat, that followed Dionysus, the god of wine, merriment, and debauchery

52. **beteem.** Allow

53. **increase of appetite . . . it fed on.** Her appetite, or desire, for him, increased the more she fed on, or associated with, him.

54. **Niobe.** In Greek myth, a mother whose children were killed. Niobe wept until she turned into a stone and continued weeping even after that.

55. **wants discourse.** Lacks the faculty

56. **Hercules.** In Greek mythology, a man possessed of extraordinary, superhuman strength

Words For Everyday Use

cour • ti • er (kôrt´ ē ər) *n.,* attendant at a royal court

ac • cord (ə kôrd´) *n.,* agreement

jo • cund (jäk´ ənd) *adj.,* cheerful

frail • ty (frāl´ tē) *n.,* weakness

Do I impart toward you. For your intent
In going back to school in Wittenberg,[39]
It is most retrograde[40] to our desire,
115 And we beseech you bend you to remain
Here in the cheer and comfort of our eye,
Our chiefest courtier, cousin, and our son.

QUEEN.   Let not thy mother lose her prayers, Hamlet,
I pray thee stay with us, go not to Wittenberg.

120 HAMLET.   I shall in all my best[41] obey you, madam.

KING.   Why, 'tis a loving and a fair reply.
Be as ourself in Denmark. Madam, come.
This gentle and unforc'd accord of Hamlet
Sits smiling to my heart, in grace whereof,
125 No jocund health that Denmark drinks today,
But the great cannon to the clouds shall tell[42]
And the King's rouse[43] the heaven shall bruit[44] again,
Respeaking earthly thunder. Come away.

Flourish. Exeunt all but HAMLET.

HAMLET.   O that this too too solid[45] flesh would melt,
130 Thaw, and resolve itself into a dew!
Or that the Everlasting had not fix'd
His canon[46] 'gainst self-slaughter! O God, God,
How weary, stale, flat, and unprofitable
Seem to me all the uses[47] of this world!
135 Fie on't, ah fie! 'tis an unweeded garden
That grows to seed, things rank and gross in nature
Possess it merely.[48] That it should come to this!
But two months dead, nay, not so much, not two.
So excellent a king, that was to this[49]
140 Hyperion[50] to a satyr,[51] so loving to my mother
That he might not beteem[52] the winds of heaven
Visit her face too roughly. Heaven and earth,
Must I remember? Why, she should hang on him
As if increase of appetite had grown
145 By what it fed on,[53] and yet, within a month—
Let me not think on't! Frailty, thy name is woman!—
A little month, or ere those shoes were old
With which she followed my poor father's body,
Like Niobe,[54] all tears—why, she, even she—
150 O God, a beast that wants discourse[55] of reason
Would have mourn'd longer—married with my uncle,
My father's brother, but no more like my father
Than I to Hercules.[56] Within a month
Ere yet the salt of most unrighteous tears
155 Had left the flushing in her galled eyes,

[Margin notes, handwritten:]
Hamlet wants t school!

◀ What does Hamlet want to do? What do Claudius and Gertrude think about this?

wants him to home

◀ Why does Claudius want to celebrate? In what way will he do so?

Hamlet says that he's going to obey his mother

◀ How is Hamlet feeling? What does he think of life in this world? To what does he compare the world?

◀ How long has Hamlet's father been dead? According to Hamlet, how does Claudius compare to Hamlet's dead father?

what dies his mother do?

◀ How does Hamlet regard his mother's marriage to Claudius? Why?

dislike marriage.

57. **post . . . dexterity.** Move so nimbly and quickly

58. **incestious.** Technically, the marriage of Claudius and Gertrude is not, of course, incest, but Hamlet considers it so because his father and Claudius were brothers. Marriage to one's dead brother's wife was not approved of by the church.

59. **change that name with you.** Be called your servant rather than the other way around

60. **what make you from.** What is the news from.

61. **teach you to drink deep.** A reference to the king's festivities, which Hamlet considers disgusting. Hamlet is bitterly saying that the one thing Denmark can add to Horatio's education is schooling in the art of drinking.

62. **followed hard upon.** Came soon after

63. **coldly furnish . . . tables.** Cold, leftover meats from the funeral feast were used for the marriage feast. This is a bitterly humorous exaggeration.

64. **dearest.** Worst, most costly

65. **Or ever.** Before

66. **methinks.** I think

Words For Everyday Use

tru • ant (troó ənt) *adj.,* staying away from school
dis • po • si • tion (dis´pə zish´ən) *adj.,* inclination, desire

She married—O most wicked speed: to post
With such dexterity[57] to incestious[58] sheets,
It is not, nor it cannot come to good,
But break my heart, for I must hold my tongue.

Enter HORATIO, MARCELLUS, *and* BARNARDO.

160 HORATIO.   Hail to your lordship!

HAMLET.   I am glad to see you well.
Horatio—or I do forget myself.

HORATIO.   The same, my lord, and your poor servant
ever.

HAMLET.   Sir, my good friend—I'll change that name
    with you.[59]
And what make you from Wittenberg, Horatio?
165 Marcellus?

MARCELLUS.   My good lord.

HAMLET.   I am very glad to see you. [*To* BARNARDO.]
    Good even, sir.—
But what, in faith, make you from[60] Wittenberg?

HORATIO.   A <u>truant</u> <u>disposition</u>, good my lord.

170 HAMLET.   I would not hear your enemy say so,
Nor shall you do my ear that violence
To make it truster of your own report
Against yourself. I know you are no truant.
But what is your affair in Elsinore?
175 We'll teach you to drink deep[61] ere you depart.

HORATIO.   My lord, I came to see your father's funeral.

HAMLET.   I prithee do not mock me, fellow studient,
I think it was to see my mother's wedding.

HORATIO.   Indeed, my lord, it followed hard upon.[62]

180 HAMLET.   Thrift, thrift, Horatio, the funeral bak'd
    meats
Did coldly furnish forth the marriage tables.[63]
Would I had met my dearest[64] foe in heaven
Or ever[65] I had seen that day, Horatio!
My father—methinks[66] I see my father.

185 HORATIO.   Where, my lord?

HAMLET.   In my mind's eye,
Horatio.

HORATIO.   I saw him once, 'a was a goodly king.

HAMLET.   'A was a man, take him for all in all,

◀ How did Hamlet
come to know
Horatio?

◀ What two events
happened very close
to one another?

◀ What is Hamlet's
tone here? How does
he feel about the
marriage having
occurred so soon
after the funeral?

◀ With what single
word does Hamlet
sum up his father's
qualities?

67. **yesternight.** Last night
68. **Season your admiration.** Hold back your astonishment
69. **attent.** Attentive
70. **at point exactly.** In every detail
71. **cap-a-pe.** Head to toe
72. **thrice.** Three times
73. **truncheon's.** Of a staff signifying high military office
74. **delivered.** Described
75. **address . . . motion.** Apply itself to making a gesture

I shall not look upon his like again.

HORATIO.   My lord, I think I saw him yesternight.[67]

190 HAMLET.   Saw, who?

HORATIO.   My lord, the King your father.

HAMLET.   The King my father?

HORATIO.   Season your admiration[68] for a while
With an attent[69] ear, till I may deliver,
Upon the witness of these gentlemen,
195 This marvel to you.

HAMLET.   For God's love let me hear!

HORATIO.   Two nights together had these gentlemen
Marcellus and Barnardo, on their watch,
In the dead waste and middle of the night
Been thus encount'red: a figure like your father,
200 Armed at point exactly,[70] cap-a-pe,[71]
Appears before them, and with solemn march
Goes slow and stately by them, thrice[72] he walk'd
By their oppress'd and fear-surprised eyes
Within his truncheon's[73] length, whilst they, distill'd
205 Almost to jelly with the act of fear,
Stand dumb and speak not to him. This to me
In dreadful secrecy impart they did,
And I with them the third night kept the watch,
Where, as they had delivered,[74] both in time,
210 Form of the thing, each word made true and good,
The apparition comes. I knew your father,
These hands are not more like.

HAMLET.   But where was this?

MARCELLUS.   My lord, upon the platform where we
    watch.

HAMLET.   Did you not speak to it?

HORATIO.   My lord, I did,
215 But answer made it none. Yet once methought
It lifted up it head and did address
Itself to motion[75] like as it would speak;
But even then the morning cock crew loud,
And at the sound it shrunk in haste away
220 And vanish'd from our sight.

HAMLET.   'Tis very strange.

HORATIO.   As I do live, my honor'd lord, 'tis true,
And we did think it writ down in our duty
To let you know of it.

◄ What surprising
news does Horatio
have for Hamlet?

◄ Is Horatio certain
that the ghost was
that of Hamlet's
father? How do you
know?

How do you know?

76. **beaver.** Visor on a helmet
77. **Very like.** That's likely
78. **tell.** Count to
79. **sable silver'd.** Black with streaks or touches of gray
80. **Perchance.** By chance, with luck
81. **warr'nt.** State with confidence
82. **tenable.** Held, kept
83. **hap.** Happen

Words For Everyday Use

coun • te • nance (koun′tə nəns) *n.*, facial expression
griz • zled (griź əld) *adj.*, streaked gray and black
re • quite (rē kwīt′) *vt.*, reward

HAMLET.   Indeed, indeed, sirs. But this troubles me.
225 Hold you the watch tonight?

MARCELLUS, BARNARDO.   We do, my lord.

HAMLET.   Arm'd, say you?

MARCELLUS, BARNARDO.   Arm'd, my lord.

HAMLET.   From top to toe?

MARCELLUS, BARNARDO.   My lord, from head to foot.

HAMLET.   Then saw you not his face.

230 HORATIO.   O yes, my lord, he wore his beaver[76] up.

HAMLET.   What, look'd he frowningly?

HORATIO.   A <u>countenance</u> more
In sorrow than in anger.

HAMLET.   Pale, or red?   *pale*

HORATIO.   Nay, very <u>pale</u>.   *eyes fixed*

HAMLET.   And <u>fix'd his eyes</u> upon you?

HORATIO.   Most constantly.

HAMLET.   I would I had been there.

235 HORATIO.   It would have much amaz'd you.

HAMLET.   Very like,[77] very like. Stay'd it long?

HORATIO.   While one with moderate haste might tell[78]
   a hundreth.

MARCELLUS, BARNARDO.   Longer, longer.

HORATIO.   Not when I saw't.

HAMLET.   His beard was <u>grisl'd</u>, no?   *silver beard*

240 HORATIO.   It was, as I have seen it in his life,
A sable silver'd.[79]

HAMLET.   I will watch tonight,
Perchance[80] 'twill walk again.

HORATIO.   I warr'nt[81] it will.

HAMLET.   If it assume my noble father's person,
I'll speak to it though hell itself should gape
245 And bid me hold my peace. I pray you all,
If you have hitherto conceal'd this sight,
Let it be tenable[82] in your silence still,
And whatsomever else shall hap[83] tonight,
Give it an understanding but no tongue.
250 I will <u>requite</u> your loves. So fare you well.
Upon the platform 'twixt aleven and twelf

◄ According to Horatio, what expression did the ghost have?

◄ What does Hamlet vow that he will do?

84. **doubt.** Suspect

ACT I, SCENE iii

1. **necessaries are inbark'd.** Supplies are on board the ship
2. **as the winds . . . assistant.** At every opportunity, when the proper winds are blowing and ships are available to carry the message
3. **favor.** Interest; in this case, romantic
4. **fashion and a toy in blood.** Passing behavior and an idle amusement of youthful passion
5. **violet.** Wild, short-lived flower that grows in the springtime by the banks of rivers and streams. These flowers will have a further symbolic significance later in the play. See act IV, scene v, lines 184–187.
6. **primy.** Of the prime, or early time; also, perhaps, stimulated
7. **suppliance.** Pastime
8. **crescent.** At the beginning of its development (like the crescent moon)
9. **alone.** Only
10. **thews.** Sinews, muscles
11. **this temple waxes.** The body grows. The body was traditionally referred to as the "temple of the soul," and "waxes" continues the metaphor of the moon, referring to its apparent growth from crescent to full.
12. **service.** Furnishings
13. **cautel.** Deceit
14. **subject to his birth.** Hamlet is a prince and likely to be king. Just as the people are subject to a king, so the king is subject to the conditions required by his station in life, including his choice of wife.
15. **unvalued persons.** People of lower station
16. **circumscrib'd/Unto.** Bounded within
17. **main voice.** General agreement or assent

III, Laertes – bye to his sister –

H, seeing Ophelia –

Laertes speaks against his sister + H. ① King & could never be serious in his relationship.

Words For Everyday Use	**tri • fling** (trī´ fliŋ) *n.*, frivolous play
	for • ward (fôr´ wərd) *adj.*, too bold; too soon
	be • smirch (bē smurch´) *vt.*, make dirty; bring dishonor to

she promises to be careful

I'll visit you.

ALL.   Our duty to your honor.

HAMLET.   Your loves, as mine to you; farewell.

                              Exeunt all but HAMLET.

My father's spirit—in arms! All is not well,
255 I doubt[84] some foul play. Would the night were come!
Till then sit still, my soul. Foul deeds will rise,
Though all the earth o'erwhelm them, to men's eyes.

                                          Exit.

◄ What does
Hamlet make of the
fact that the ghost
has appeared?

SCENE iii: Polonius's quarters in the castle

Enter LAERTES *and* OPHELIA, *his sister.*

LAERTES.   My necessaries are inbark'd.[1] Farewell.
And, sister, as the winds give benefit
And convey is assistant,[2] do not sleep,
But let me hear from you.

◄ What is Laertes
getting ready to do?

OPHELIA.   Do you doubt that?

5   LAERTES.   For Hamlet, and the trifling of his favor,[3]
Hold it a fashion and a toy in blood,[4]
A violet[5] in the youth of primy[6] nature,
Forward, not permanent, sweet, not lasting,
The perfume and suppliance[7] of a minute—
10   No more.

◄ What advice does
Laertes give his sister,
Ophelia, with regard
to Hamlet?

OPHELIA.   No more but so?

LAERTES.   Think it no more:
For nature crescent[8] does not grow alone[9]
In thews[10] and bulk, but as this temple waxes,[11]
The inward service[12] of the mind and soul
Grows wide withal. Perhaps he loves you now,
15   And now no soil nor cautel[13] doth besmirch
The virtue of his will, but you must fear,
His greatness weigh'd, his will is not his own,
For he himself is subject to his birth:[14]
He may not, as unvalued persons[15] do,
20   Carve for himself, for on his choice depends
The safety and health of this whole state,
And therefore must his choice be circumscrib'd
Unto[16] the voice and yielding of that body
Whereof he is the head. Then if he says he loves
25   It fits your wisdom so far to believe it
As he in his particular act and place
May give his saying deed, which is no further
Than the main voice[17] of Denmark goes withal.
Then weigh what loss your honor may sustain

◄ What reason
does Laertes give his
sister for not taking
Hamlet's romantic
overtures seriously?

18. **credent.** Believing
19. **list.** Heed
20. **chariest.** Most cautious, shy, or modest
21. **canker galls.** Blight disfigures or irritates
22. **buttons.** Buds
23. **blastments.** Blights
24. **Youth . . . near.** Even when there is no one else around to rebel against, young people feel compelled to rebel and so do so against themselves.
25. **ungracious.** Devoid of grace, which is defined by Protestant Reformers, following Luther, as salvation God extends to sinners despite their unworthiness. The concept of grace plays a central role in this play. See the introduction to this text.
26. **the primrose path.** The road to hell has been traditionally described as outwardly attractive (adorned with primroses), whereas the road to salvation has been described as stony or steep.
27. **reaks not his own rede.** Reckons not (or attends not to) his own advice
28. **Occasion . . . leave.** Circumstances make possible a second leave-taking.
29. **you are stay'd for.** The ship is waiting for you.
30. **character.** Write (with a pun on character in the sense of personal qualities)
31. **unproportion'd.** Overly emotional or excessive
32. **their adoption tried.** Their worthiness to become friends tested
33. **dull thy palm.** Make your hand insensitive (by shaking lots of hands)

Words For Everyday Use

chaste (chāst) *adj.*, pure
im • por • tu • ni • ty (im´pôr tōōn´i tē) *n.*, persistent demand
prod • i • gal (präd´i gəl) *adj.*, carelessly wasteful
ca • lum • ni • ous (kə lum´nē əs) *adj.*, slanderous
im • mi • nent (im´ə nənt) *adj.*, close to happening

li • ber • tine (lib´ ər tēn) *n.*, one who leads an immoral life
dal • li • ance (dal´yəns) *n.*, playing at love
pre • cept (prē´sept) *n.*, principle
un • fledged (un flejd´) *adj.*, not yet feathered, like a bird; thus, immature
cen • sure (sen´shər) *n.*, disapproval

30   If with too credent[18] ear you list[19] his songs,
    Or lose your heart, or your chaste treasure open
    To his unmast'red importunity.
    Fear it, Ophelia, fear it, my dear sister,
    And keep you in the rear of your affection,
35   Out of the shot and danger of desIre.
    The chariest[20] maid is prodigal enough
    If she unmask her beauty to the moon.
    Virtue itself scapes not calumnious strokes.
    The canker galls[21] the infants of the spring
40   Too oft before their buttons[22] be disclos'd,
    And in the morn and liquid dew of youth
    Contagious blastments[23] are most imminent.
    Be wary then, best safety lies in fear:
    Youth to itself rebels, though none else near.[24]

45   **OPHELIA.**   I shall the effect of this good lesson keep
    As watchman to my heart. But, good my brother,
    Do not, as some ungracious[25] pastors do,
    Show me the steep and thorny way to heaven,
    Whiles, like a puff'd and reckless libertine,
50   Himself the primrose path[26] of dalliance treads,
    And reaks not his own rede.[27]

    LAERTES.   O, fear me not.
    Enter POLONIUS.

    I stay too long—but here my father comes.
    A double blessing is a double grace,
    Occasion smiles upon a second leave.[28]

55   **POLONIUS.**   Yet here, Laertes? Aboard, aboard, for
      shame!
    The wind sits in the shoulder of your sail,
    And you are stay'd for.[29] There—[*laying his hand on*
      LAERTES' *head*] my blessing with thee!
    And these few precepts in thy memory
    Look thou character.[30] Give thy thoughts no tongue,
60   Nor any unproportion'd[31] thought his act.
    Be thou familiar, but by no means vulgar:
    Those friends thou hast, and their adoption tried,[32]
    Grapple them unto thy soul with hoops of steel,
    But do not dull thy palm[33] with entertainment
65   Of each new-hatch'd, unfledg'd courage. Beware
    Of entrance to a quarrel, but being in,
    Bear't that th' opposed may beware of thee.
    Give every man thy ear, but few thy voice,
    Take each man's censure, but reserve thy judgment.

◄ What does Laertes tell Ophelia that she might lose if she gives herself over to Hamlet's affections?

◄ What does Ophelia tell her brother to do?

34. **Costly . . . buy.** Wear the most expensive clothes that you can afford
35. **of a most select . . . in that.** Are at the forefront of that (fashion)
36. **husbandry.** Thrift
37. **season.** Bring to ripeness or fullness
38. **tend.** Attend, wait
39. **touching.** Regarding
40. **Marry.** Indeed; originally, by Mary (the mother of Christ)
41. **well bethought.** Thoughtful
42. **audience.** Company; to give someone audience is to allow them to come before you
43. **bounteous.** Bountiful
44. **put on.** Told to
45. **behooves.** Fits
46. **tenders.** Tentative expressions or offers
47. **Unsifted.** Untried

70 Costly thy habit as thy purse can buy,[34]
But not express'd in fancy, rich, not gaudy,
For the apparel oft proclaims the man,
And they in France of the best rank and station
Are of a most select and generous chief in that.[35]
75 Neither a borrower nor a lender be,
For loan oft loses both itself and friend,
And borrowing dulleth th' edge of husbandry.[36]
This above all: to thine own self be true, ✱
And it must follow, as the night the day,
80 Thou canst not then be false to any man.
Farewell, my blessing season[37] this in thee!

◄ What does Polonius regard as the most important advice that he can give to Laertes?

LAERTES.   Most humbly do I take my leave, my lord.

POLONIUS.   The time invests you, go, your servants tend.[38]

LAERTES.   Farewell, Ophelia, and remember well
85 What I have said to you.

OPHELIA.   'Tis in my memory lock'd,
And you yourself shall keep the key of it.

LAERTES.   Farewell.   *Exit* LAERTES.

POLONIUS.   What is't, Ophelia, he hath said to you?

OPHELIA.   So please you, something touching[39] the
Lord Hamlet.

90 POLONIUS.   Marry,[40] well bethought.[41]
'Tis told me, he hath very oft of late
Given private time to you, and you yourself
Have of your audience[42] been most free and
bounteous[43]
If it be so—as so 'tis put on[44] me,
95 And that in way of caution—I must tell you,
You do not understand yourself so clearly
As it behooves[45] my daughter and your honor.
What is between you? Give me up the truth.

doesn't trust Hamlet—young—only have set on minds

OPHELIA.   He hath, my lord, of late made many
tenders[46]
100 Of his affection to me.

◄ What does Ophelia reveal to her father?

POLONIUS.   Affection, puh! You speak like a green girl,
Unsifted[47] in such perilous circumstance.
Do you believe his tenders, as you call them?

OPHELIA.   I do not know, my lord, what I should think.

105 POLONIUS.   Marry, I will teach you: think yourself a
baby

48. **tenders for true pay.** Polonius makes a pun on the word *tenders,* which can mean either offers or payments.

49. **sterling.** Real money; the sterling was an English silver penny.

50. **Tender yourself more dearly.** Value yourself more highly.

51. **tender.** Render, make

52. **fashion.** Ophelia uses the word in the sense of "manner" or "style." Again, Polonius puns, using the word in the sense of "passing fancy"

53. **Go to.** Interjection, similar to the modern phrase "come on," expressing surprise that another person would believe such a thing

54. **countenance.** Authoritative appearance

55. **springes to catch woodcocks.** Traps for capturing easily caught birds

56. **how prodigal . . . vows.** Ironic statement given Polonius's wordiness

57. **extinct.** Extinguished

58. **scanter . . . presence.** Don't make yourself so freely available.

59. **Set your . . . rate.** Require more before you allow someone to make entreaties toward you.

60. **larger.** Longer

61. **in few.** In a few words, in short

62. **his vows . . . beguile.** His promises are go-betweens, dressed up to look better than they are; they are out-and-out spokesmen for immoral requests, speaking like holy lovers' vows the better to deceive

63. **slander . . . leisure.** Bring a bad name on any moment's free time

64. **charge.** Command

ACT I, SCENE iv

1. **shrowdly.** Sharply

2. **eager.** Biting, bitter

3. **lacks of.** Is a little before

Words For Everyday Use

par • ley (pär´ lē) *vi.,* meet for conversation   **be • guile** (bə gīl´) *vt.,* deceive
te • ther (te´ thər) *n.,* leash
sanc • ti • fied (saŋk´ tə fīd) *adj.,* holy

That you have ta'en these tenders for true pay,[48]
Which are not sterling.[49] Tender yourself more dearly,[50]
Or (not to crack the wind of the poor phrase,
Wringing it thus) you'll tender[51] me a fool.

110 OPHELIA.   My lord, he hath importun'd me with love
In honorable fashion.

POLONIUS.   Ay, fashion[52] you may call it. Go to,[53] go
to.

OPHELIA.   And hath given countenance[54] to his
speech, my lord,
With almost all the holy vows of heaven.

115 POLONIUS.   Ay, springes to catch woodcocks.[55] I do
know,
When the blood burns, how prodigal the soul
Lends the tongue vows.[56] These blazes, daughter,
Giving more light than heat, extinct[57] in both
Even in their promise, as it is a-making,
120 You must not take for fire. From this time
Be something scanter of your maiden presence,[58]
Set your entreatments at a higher rate[59]
Than a command to parley. For Lord Hamlet,
Believe so much in him, that he is young,
125 And with a larger[60] tether may he walk
Than may be given you. In few,[61] Ophelia,
Do not believe his vows, for they are brokers,
Not of that dye which their investments show,
But mere implorators of unholy suits,
130 Breathing like sanctified and pious bonds,
The better to beguile.[62] This is for all:
I would not, in plain terms, from this time forth
Have you so slander any moment leisure[63]
As to give words or talk with the Lord Hamlet.
135 Look to't, I charge[64] you. Come your ways.

OPHELIA.   I shall obey, my lord.   Exeunt.

SCENE iv: The guard platform of the castle

Enter HAMLET, HORATIO, and MARCELLUS.

HAMLET.   The air bites shrowdly,[1] it is very cold.

HORATIO.   It is a nipping and an eager[2] air.

HAMLET.   What hour now?

HORATIO.   I think it lacks of[3] twelf.

[Margin notes]

◀ Does Ophelia believe that Hamlet's feelings toward her are genuine? How do you know?

◀ What does Polonius tell Ophelia that she must do with regard to Hamlet? What does Ophelia agree to do?

◀ Where are Hamlet, Horatio, and Marcellus? For what are they waiting?

[Handwritten annotations: "Ophelia obeys her dad's wishes to avoid Hamlet.", "(nite Time)", "Waiting for the ghost"]

4. **held his wont.** Was accustomed
5. **two pieces.** Two cannons
6. **takes his rouse.** Carouses, makes merry
7. **Keeps wassail.** Drinks
8. **swaggering up-spring reels.** Drunken dances
9. **draughts.** Drafts
10. **Rhenish.** Rhine wine
11. **triumph of his pledge.** His success in drinking down the cup in a single gulp. The word *triumph* is used ironically because it usually refers to a great military victory.
12. **to the manner born.** Born into the place that has this custom
13. **More honor'd . . . observance.** It would do a person more honor to forego than to observe this custom.
14. **traduc'd and tax'd.** Mocked and taken to task
15. **clip.** Call
16. **with swinish . . . addition.** Dirty their description of us by calling us pigs
17. **pith and marrow.** Essence
18. **mole.** Spot or blemish, like a mole on the skin, with a pun on mole in the sense of a burrowing beast
19. **his.** Its
20. **o'ergrowth of some complexion.** Enlargement of a natural attribute
21. **pales.** Sharp stakes placed in the ground to form a fence as part of a fortification (compare the modern word impale)
22. **o'er-leavens.** Causes to grow too much (Yeast is used to leaven bread, or cause it to grow in size.)
23. **plausive.** Pleasing
24. **livery.** Uniform of a servant. (The one defect is like the uniform that nature makes the person wear. The person becomes a servant to this defect.)
25. **fortune's star.** Elizabethans commonly believed in astrology, the pseudoscience that claims people's fortunes, or fates, to be governed by the motions of the stars.
26. **general censure.** Common estimation
27. **dram of eale.** Small amount of something. (Scholars are unsure about the exact meaning of *eale*. The word may be a misprint of "ale," in which case Hamlet would be referring again to the custom that initiated his speech.
28. **of a doubt.** Call into question. (The small defect, like a small amount of ale, can undermine the entire noble substance of a person, turning the person into the subject of popular gossip and scandal.)

Words For Everyday Use

bray (brā) *vt.*, make a loud, harsh cry like a donkey

MARCELLUS.   No, it is strook.

5 HORATIO.   Indeed? I heard it not. It then draws near
      the season
   Wherein the spirit held his wont[4] to walk.
      A flourish of trumpets, and two pieces[5] goes off within.
   What does this mean, my lord?

   HAMLET.   The King doth wake tonight and takes his
   rouse[6]
   Keeps wassail,[7] and the swagg'ring up-spring reels;[8]
10 And as he drains his draughts[9] of Rhenish[10] down,
   The kettle-drum and trumpet thus bray out
   The triumph of his pledge.[11]

   HORATIO.   Is it a custom?

   HAMLET.   Ay, marry, is't,
   But to my mind, though I am native here
15 And to the manner born,[12] it is a custom
   More honor'd in the breach than the observance.[13]

   This heavy-headed revel east and west
   Makes us traduc'd and tax'd[14] of other nations.
   They clip[15] us drunkards, and with swinish phrase
20 Soil our addition,[16] and indeed it takes
   From our achievements, though perform'd at height,
   The pith and marrow[17] of our attribute.
   So, oft it chances in particular men,
   That for some vicious mole[18] of nature in them,
25 As in their birth, wherein they are not guilty
   (Since nature cannot choose his[19] origin),
   By their o'ergrowth of some complexion[20]
   Oft breaking down the pales[21] and forts of reason,
   Or by some habit, that too much o'er-leavens[22]
30 The form of plausive[23] manners—that these men,
   Carrying, I say, the stamp of one defect,
   Being nature's livery,[24] or fortune's star,[25]
   His virtues else, be they as pure as grace,
   As infinite as man may undergo,
35 Shall in the general censure[26] take corruption
   From that particular fault: the dram of eale[27]
   Doth all the noble substance of a doubt[28]
   To his own scandal.

   Enter GHOST.

   HORATIO.   Look, my lord, it comes!

   HAMLET.   Angels and ministers of grace defend us!
40 Be thou a spirit of health, or goblin damn'd,
   Bring with thee airs from heaven, or blasts from hell,

◄ What does
Hamlet think of the
custom being kept by
King Claudius?

◄ According to
Hamlet, what can
happen as a result of
a person's being
born with one per-
sonality defect, or
"mole of nature"?

a celebration going on in the castle

ghost appears.

29. **questionable shape.** Form that makes me curious
30. **canoniz'd bones.** Bones that have been consecrated, or given holy burial
31. **cerements.** Grave-clothes
32. **interr'd.** Buried
33. **op'd.** Opened
34. **complete steel.** Full armor
35. **impartment.** Communication, something to impart
36. **courteous.** Well-mannered, in the manner of people of the court
37. **set my life at a pin's fee.** Count my life worth the price of a pin. Note that from the very beginning, Hamlet discounts earthly life as being of little value and thinks of himself as an immortal creature.
38. **tempt you toward the flood.** Tempts you into the sea (in which you might drown).
39. **beetles o'er his base.** Looks over the base (of the cliff) like bushy eyebrows
40. **sovereignty of reason.** Reason is viewed as a sovereign, or king, who rules the body.
41. **The very place.** The cliff
42. **toys.** Idle imaginings
43. **fadoms.** Fathoms; nautical measurements equaling six feet

Words For Everyday Use

se • pul • cher (sep'əl kər) *n.*, burial vault

Be thy intents wicked, or charitable,
Thou com'st in such a questionable shape[29]
That I will speak to thee. I'll call thee Hamlet,
45 King, father, royal Dane. O, answer me!
    Let me not burst in ignorance, but tell
    Why thy canoniz'd bones,[30] hearsed in death,
    Have burst their cerements;[31] why the sepulcher,
    Wherein we saw thee quietly interr'd,[32]
50 Hath op'd[33] his ponderous and marble jaws
    To cast thee up again. What may this mean,
    That thou, dead corse, again in complete steel[34]
    Revisits thus the glimpses of the moon,
    Making night hideous, and we fools of nature
55 So horridly to shake our disposition
    With thoughts beyond the reaches of our souls?
    Say why is this? wherefore? what should we do?

                    GHOST *beckons* HAMLET.

HORATIO.   It beckons you to go away with it,
As if it some impartment[35] did desire
60 To you alone.

MARCELLUS.   Look with what courteous[36] action
It waves you to a more removed ground,
But do not go with it.

HORATIO.   No, by no means.

HAMLET.   It will not speak, then I will follow it.

HORATIO.   Do not, my lord.

HAMLET.   Why, what should be the fear?
65 I do not set my life at a pin's fee,[37]
And for my soul, what can it do to that,
Being a thing immortal as itself?
It waves me forth again, I'll follow it.

HORATIO.   What if it tempt you toward the flood,[38] my
        lord,
70 Or to the dreadful summit of the cliff
That beetles o'er his base[39] into the sea,
And there assume some other horrible form
Which might deprive your sovereignty of reason,[40]
And draw you into madness? Think of it.
75 The very place[41] puts toys[42] of desperation,
Without more motive, into every brain
That looks so many fadoms[43] to the sea
And hears it roar beneath.

HAMLET.   It waves me still.—

44. **artere.** Artery; Elizabethans believed that the arteries carried the "vital spirits" that empowered bodies and gave them life.
45. **Nemean lion's.** Belonging to a lion from Greek mythology that Hercules killed as one of his twelve labors
46. **lets.** Hinders
47. **Have after.** Follow him.
48. **issue.** Outcome

ACT I, SCENE V

1. **Mark.** Listen to
2. **for a certain term.** For a while. According to conventional Catholic belief, criticized in the Europe of Shakespeare's day, those whose sins were not sufficient to send them to hell might have to spend time in purgatory, a place of torment where they would pay for their sins before going to heaven.

Go on, I'll follow thee.

80 MARCELLUS.   You shall not go, my lord.

HAMLET.   Hold off your hands.

HORATIO.   Be rul'd, you shall not go.

HAMLET.   My fate cries out,
And makes each petty artere[44] in this body
As hardy as the Nemean lion's[45] nerve.
Still am I call'd. Unhand me, gentlemen.
85 By heaven, I'll make a ghost of him that lets[46] me!
I say away!—Go on, I'll follow thee.

                 Exeunt GHOST *and* HAMLET.

HORATIO.   He waxes desperate with imagination.

MARCELLUS.   Let's follow. 'Tis not fit thus to obey him.

HORATIO.   Have after.[47] To what issue[48] will this come?

90 MARCELLUS.   Something is rotten in the state of
     Denmark.

HORATIO.   Heaven will direct it.

MARCELLUS.   Nay, let's follow him.   *Exeunt.*

      SCENE V: **Another part of the guard platform**

Enter GHOST *and* HAMLET.

HAMLET.   Whither wilt thou lead me? Speak, I'll go no
     further.

GHOST.   Mark[1] me.

HAMLET.   I will.

GHOST.   My hour is almost come
When I to sulph'rous and tormenting flames
Must render up myself.

HAMLET.   Alas, poor ghost!

5 GHOST.   Pity me not, but lend thy serious hearing
To what I shall unfold.

HAMLET.   Speak, I am bound to hear.

GHOST.   So art thou to revenge, when thou shalt hear.

HAMLET.   What?

GHOST.   I am thy father's spirit,
10 Doom'd for a certain term[2] to walk the night,
And for the day confin'd to fast in fires,
Till the foul crimes done in my days of nature

[margin notes:]

Marc. + Horatio tell Hamlet

◄ Why does Hamlet threaten to make ghosts of his friends?

not to got wil the ghost

◄ In what does Horatio put his faith? What is Marcellus's response?

they are concerned for his safety —

◄ Is this ghost about to surrender himself to heaven or hell? How do you know?

◄ Why must Hamlet's father's spirit walk the night and spend his days in flames?

3. **But that I am forbid.** If I were not forbidden
4. **harrow up.** Dig into and turn up, like a harrow, or plow
5. **spheres.** Eye sockets
6. **porpentine.** Porcupine
7. **eternal blazon.** Description of afterlife (In heraldry, a blazon was an emblem on a shield)
8. **List.** Listen
9. **Lethe wharf.** Banks of Lethe, the mythical river of forgetfulness in the underworld
10. **stung.** Bit
11. **forged process.** False tale
12. **Rankly abus'd.** Grossly deceived
13. **Ay.** Aye, yes
14. **adulterate.** Given to adultery
15. **most seeming virtuous.** Seemingly virtuous
16. **decline.** Sink down

Words
For
Everyday
Use

wretch (rech) *n.*, despised person

Are burnt and purg'd away. But that I am forbid[3]
To tell the secrets of my prison-house,
15 I could a tale unfold whose lightest word
Would harrow up[4] thy soul, freeze thy young blood,
Make thy two eyes like stars start from their spheres,[5]
Thy knotted and combined locks to part,
And each particular hair to stand an end,
20 Like quills upon the fearful porpentine.[6]
But this eternal blazon[7] must not be
To ears of flesh and blood. List,[8] list, O, list!
If thou didst ever thy dear father love—

HAMLET.   O God!

25 GHOST.   Revenge his foul and most unnatural murther.

HAMLET.   Murther!

GHOST.   Murther most foul, as in the best it is,
But this most foul, strange, and unnatural.

HAMLET.   Haste me to know't, that I with wings as
    swift
30 As meditation, or the thoughts of love,
May sweep to my revenge.

GHOST.   I find thee apt,
And duller shouldst thou be than the fat weed
That roots itself in ease on Lethe wharf,[9]
Wouldst thou not stir in this. Now, Hamlet, hear:
35 'Tis given out that, sleeping in my orchard,
A serpent stung[10] me, so the whole ear of Denmark
Is by a forged process[11] of my death
Rankly abus'd;[12] but know, thou noble youth,
The serpent that did sting thy father's life
40 Now wears his crown.

HAMLET.   O my prophetic soul!
My uncle?

GHOST.   Ay,[13] that incestuous, that adulterate[14] beast,
With witchcraft of his wits, with traitorous gift
O wicked wit and gifts that have the power
45 So to seduce!—won to his shameful lust
The will of my most seeming virtuous[15] queen.
O Hamlet, what a falling-off was there
From me, whose love was of that dignity
That it went hand in hand even with the vow
50 I made to her in marriage, and to decline[16]
Upon a <u>wretch</u> whose natural gifts were poor
To those of mine!

◄ How did Hamlet's
father die?

◄ What does
Hamlet vow to do?

◄ According to the
ghost, who killed
him? What relation-
ship does the killer
have to Hamlet's
father? to Hamlet?

17. **sate.** Become satiated, or so full as to no longer have any appetite for
18. **methinks.** I think
19. **scent.** Smell
20. **my secure hour.** Time when I felt safe and at ease
21. **hebona.** Poisonous herbs, perhaps henbane
22. **leprous distillment.** Distilled, or concentrated, liquid causing effects like those of leprosy
23. **posset.** Thicken in clumps
24. **eager.** Sour, acidic
25. **tetter.** Rash
26. **bark'd about.** Covered the skin like bark
27. **Most lazar-like.** Like that on a leper (from the name of Lazarus, a leper in the Bible)
28. **dispatch'd.** Deprived, bereft
29. **even in . . . sin.** While in a sinful and unconfessed state
30. **Unhous'led.** Without having received the Eucharist
31. **unanel'd.** Unanointed (that is, without having received last rites)
32. **to my account.** To judgment
33. **hast nature in thee.** Would behave like my natural-born child
34. **luxury.** Lust
35. **Taint not thy mind.** Remain pure in thought
36. **contrive . . . aught.** Conspire at all against your mother
37. **glow-worm.** Firefly
38. **matin.** Morning; matins are morning prayers.
39. **gins . . . fire.** Begins to lose the light of his ineffectual, that is, cold, fire
40. **couple hell.** Join with hell. (Hamlet calls, in turn, on heaven, earth, and hell.)
41. **sinows.** Sinews; muscles, that is, strength
42. **this distracted globe.** Ambiguous phrase meaning, perhaps, "in my disordered head," "in this disordered world," and "in this theater" (the Globe Theater, Shakespeare's playhouse)

Words For Everyday Use

ra • di • ant (rā´dē ənt) *adj.,* shining
ce • les • ti • al (sə les´chəl) *adj.,* heavenly
vial (vīl) *n.,* small glass bottle

en • mi • ty (en´mə tē) *n.,* hostility

But virtue, as it never will be moved,
Though lewdness court it in a shape of heaven,
55   So lust, though to a radiant angel link'd,
Will sate[17] itself in a celestial bed
And prey on garbage.
But soft, methinks[18] I scent[19] the morning air,
Brief let me be. Sleeping within my orchard,
60   My custom always of the afternoon,
Upon my secure hour[20] thy uncle stole,
With juice of cursed hebona[21] in a vial,
And in the porches of my ears did pour
The leprous distillment,[22] whose effect
65   Holds such an enmity with blood of man
That swift as quicksilver it courses through
The natural gates and alleys of the body,
And with a sudden vigor it doth posset[23]
And curd, like eager[24] droppings into milk,
70   The thin and wholesome blood. So did it mine,
And a most instant tetter[25] bark'd about,[26]
Most lazar-like,[27] with vile and loathsome crust
All my smooth body.
Thus was I, sleeping, by a brother's hand
75   Of life, of crown, of queen, at once dispatch'd,[28]
Cut off even in the blossoms of my sin,[29]
Unhous'led,[30] disappointed, unanel'd,[31]
No reck'ning made, but sent to my account[32]
With all my imperfections on my head.
80   O, horrible, O, horrible, most horrible!
If thou hast nature in thee,[33] bear it not,
Let not the royal bed of Denmark be
A couch for luxury[34] and damned incest.
But howsomever thou pursues this act,
85   Taint not thy mind,[35] nor let thy soul contrive
Against thy mother aught.[36] Leave her to heaven,
And to those thorns that in her bosom lodge
To prick and sting her. Fare thee well at once!
The glow-worm[37] shows the matin[38] to be near,
90   And gins to pale his uneffectual fire.[39]
Adieu, adieu, adieu! remember me.   *Exit.*

HAMLET.   O all you host of heaven! O earth! What
      else?
And shall I couple hell?[40] O fie, hold, hold, my heart,
And you, my sinews,[41] grow not instant old,
95   But bear me stiffly up. Remember thee!
Ay, thou poor ghost, whiles memory holds a seat
In this distracted globe.[42] Remember thee!

◄ Why must the ghost be brief?

◄ How did Claudius murder his brother, the king?

◄ What was the elder Hamlet unable to do before he died? Why must he suffer torment after his death?

◄ What does the ghost want Hamlet to do? How does he instruct Hamlet to act toward his mother?

43. **fond.** Foolish
44. **saws.** Old sayings
45. **forms.** Conventional behaviors or impressions
46. **pressures.** Impressions
47. **baser.** Lesser
48. **villain.** Originally, a villain was a serf bound to a lord's land. To call Claudius a villain is to distinguish him as much as is possible from a rightful king
49. **tables.** Writing tablets
50. **meet.** Fitting
51. **secure him.** Make him safe
52. **Hillo . . . come.** Hamlet answers Marcellus's call as though calling a falcon. (Trained falcons were used by princes and other nobles for hunting.)
53. **wonderful.** Not "great," as in the modern sense, but in the root sense of "full of wonder" or "causing amazement"
54. **There's never.** There was never
55. **arrant knave.** Out-and-out rogue

Words For Everyday Use

per • ni • cious (pər nish´əs) *adj.*, causing great harm

Yea, from the table of my memory
I'll wipe away all trivial fond[43] records,
100 All saws[44] of books, all forms,[45] all pressures[46] past
That youth and observation copied there,
And thy commandement all alone shall live
Within the book and volume of my brain,
Unmix'd with baser[47] matter. Yes, by heaven!
105 O most pernicious woman!
O villain,[48] villain, smiling, damned villain!
My tables[49]—meet[50] it is I set it down
That one may smile, and smile, and be a villain!
At least I am sure it may be so in Denmark.

◀ What does Hamlet vow that he will do?

He writes.

110 So, uncle, there you are. Now to my word:
It is "Adieu, adieu! remember me."
I have sworn't.

HORATIO.   [*Within.*] My lord, my lord!

MARCELLUS.   [*Within.*]   Lord Hamlet!

Enter HORATIO *and* MARCELLUS.

HORATIO.   Heavens secure him![51]

HAMLET.   So be it!

115 MARCELLUS.   Illo, ho, ho, my lord!

HAMLET.   Hillo, ho, ho, boy! Come, bird, come.[52]

MARCELLUS.   How is't, my noble lord?

HORATIO.   What news, my lord?

HAMLET.   O, wonderful![53]

HORATIO.   Good my lord, tell it.

HAMLET.   No, you will reveal it.

120 HORATIO.   Not I, my lord, by heaven.

MARCELLUS.   Nor I, my lord.

HAMLET.   How say you then, would heart of man once
    think it?—
But you'll be secret?

HORATIO, MARCELLUS.   Ay, by heaven, my lord.

HAMLET.   There's ne'er[54] a villain dwelling in all
    Denmark
But he's an arrant knave.[55]

125 HORATIO.   There needs no ghost, my lord, come from
    the grave
To tell us this.

◀ Who is a villain even though he smiles and smiles?

[handwritten margin note:] Hamlet is angry—but will focus his life on 1 event—avenge his father's murder

56. **Saint Patrick.** The patron saint of purgatory
57. **O'ermaster't.** Overcome it
58. **poor.** Small
59. **Upon my sword.** Hamlet asks them to swear on his sword because it is in the shape of a cross. It was a chivalric convention to swear oaths in this way.
60. **truepenny.** Trustworthy person (like a real, as opposed to a false or counterfeit penny). Some scholars have suggested that Hamlet's delay in taking revenge later in the play is due to his doubt about the ghost's truthfulness, but this comment undermines that interpretation.
61. **in the cellarage.** Below (in the cellar)

HAMLET.   Why, right, you are in the right,
And so, without more circumstance at all,
I hold it fit that we shake hands and part,
You, as your business and desire shall point you,
130 For every man hath business and desire,
Such as it is, and for my own poor part,
I will go pray.

HORATIO.   These are but wild and whirling words, my
    lord.

HAMLET.   I am sorry they offend you, heartily,
135 Yes, faith, heartily.

HORATIO.   There's no offense, my lord.

HAMLET.   Yes, by Saint Patrick,[56] but there is, Horatio,
And much offense too. Touching this vision here,
It is an honest ghost, that let me tell you.
For your desire to know what is between us,
140 O'ermaster't[57] as you may. And now, good friends,
As you are friends, scholars, and soldiers,
Give me one poor[58] request.

HORATIO.   What is't, my lord, we will.

HAMLET.   Never make known what you have seen
    tonight.

145 HORATIO, MARCELLUS.   My lord, we will not.

HAMLET.   Nay, but swear't.

HORATIO.   In faith,
My lord, not I.

MARCELLUS.   Nor I, my lord, in faith.

HAMLET.   Upon my sword.[59]

MARCELLUS.   We have sworn, my lord, already.

HAMLET.   Indeed, upon my sword, indeed.
                    GHOST cries under the stage.

GHOST.   Swear.

150 HAMLET.   Ha, ha, boy, say'st thou so? Art thou there,
    truepenny?[60]
Come on, you hear this fellow in the cellarage,[61]
Consent to swear.

HORATIO.   Propose the oath, my lord.

HAMLET.   Never to speak of this that you have seen,
Swear by my sword.

155 GHOST.   [Beneath.] Swear.

◄ Does Hamlet
believe the ghost?
How do you know?

◄ What does
Hamlet ask of
Horatio and
Marcellus?

62. *Hic et ubique?* Latin for "here and everywhere?"
63. **hither.** Here
64. **Canst . . . so fast.** Can you travel into the earth so quickly and securely? (The word *fast* had both meanings.)
65. **pioner.** Soldier who digs trenches
66. **as a stranger . . . welcome.** Hamlet puns on the word *strange,* saying welcome the ghost as you would a stranger or guest.
67. **your philosophy.** One's own philosophy of life
68. **put an antic disposition on.** Pretend to be insane
69. **encumb'red.** Folded
70. **doubtful.** Knowing
71. **list.** Wished
72. **aught.** Anything
73. **I do . . . to you.** I entrust myself to you.
74. **friending.** Friendship
75. **still your fingers on your lips.** Keep your fingers to your lips (remain silent).
76. **out of joint.** Disjointed, disturbed

Words
For
Everyday
Use

per • turbed (pər tʉrbed´) *adj.,* troubled

HAMLET.   *Hic et ubique?*[62] Then we'll shift our ground.
Come hither,[63] gentlemen,
And lay your hands again upon my sword.
Swear by my sword
160 Never to speak of this that you have heard.

GHOST.   [*Beneath.*] Swear by his sword.

HAMLET.   Well said, old mole, canst work i' th' earth so
     fast?[64]
A worthy pioner![65] Once more remove, good friends.

HORATIO.   O day and night, but this is wondrous strange!

165 HAMLET.   And therefore as a stranger give it welcome.[66]
There are more things in heaven and earth, Horatio,
Than are dreamt of in your philosophy.[67]
But come—
Here, as before, never, so help you mercy,
170 How strange or odd some'er I bear myself—
As I perchance hereafter shall think meet
To put an antic disposition on[68]—
That you, at such times seeing me, never shall,
With arms encumb'red[69] thus, or this headshake,
175 Or by pronouncing of some doubtful[70] phrase
As "Well, well, we know," or "We could, and if we
     would,"
Or "If we list[71] to speak," or "There be, and if they
     might,"
Or such ambiguous giving out, to note
That you know aught[72] of me—this do swear,
180 So grace and mercy at your most need help you.

GHOST.   [*Beneath.*] Swear.   *They swear.*

HAMLET.   Rest, rest, perturbed spirit! So, gentlemen,
With all my love I do commend me to you,[73]
And what so poor a man as Hamlet is
185 May do t' express his love and friending[74] to you,
God willing, shall not lack. Let us go in together,
And still your fingers on your lips,[75] I pray.
The time is out of joint[76]—O cursed spite,
That ever I was born to set it right!
190 Nay, come, let's go together.   *Exeunt.*

◀ What pretense
does Hamlet say that
he will make? Why
might he do this?

◀ What does
Hamlet ask Horatio
and Marcellus to do?

◀ What does
Hamlet feel that he
has to set right?

Responding to the Selection

How would you feel if you were Hamlet and had heard news such as that delivered by the ghost? What would you do if you were in Hamlet's position?

Reviewing the Selection

Recalling and Interpreting

1. **R:** What have Barnardo and Marcellus seen twice before during their watch?
2. **I:** Why does Marcellus ask Horatio to join in the watch?
3. **R:** What has young Fortinbras of Norway recently done?
4. **I:** Why are the people of Denmark preparing for war?
5. **R:** According to Horatio, what happened in Rome shortly before Julius Caesar was assassinated?
6. **I:** What possible explanation occurs to Barnardo for the appearance of the ghost at this time?
7. **R:** Who has recently died? What has this person's widow done?
8. **I:** How does Hamlet feel about these events? How do you know?
9. **R:** What requests do Claudius and Gertrude make of Hamlet?
10. **I:** Does Hamlet intend to honor these requests? Why, or why not?
11. **R:** What advice does Laertes give to his sister Ophelia before departing for France?
12. **I:** What view of Hamlet, or perhaps of young men generally, does Laertes's advice imply?
13. **R:** Why does Polonius detain his son shortly after chiding him for not already being aboard the ship?
14. **I:** What sort of man is Polonius?
15. **R:** What does Polonius tell his daughter that she must do, and why?
16. **I:** Is Polonius right to require his daughter to do this? Give reasons to support your answer.
17. **R:** What does the ghost reveal to Hamlet? What does it ask Hamlet to do?
18. **I:** Why does Hamlet decide to put on an "antic disposition," or pretend to be insane?

Synthesizing

19. What unnatural events have occurred recently in Denmark? What does Hamlet vow to set right? What factors in Hamlet's character lead to this decision?

20. Hamlet wonders aloud whether the ghost is a heavenly or diabolical spirit. Which do you think it is? Why? Give evidence from the text to support your answer.

Understanding Literature (QUESTIONS FOR DISCUSSION)

1. **Central Conflict and Inciting Incident.** A **central conflict** is the primary struggle dealt with in the plot of a story or drama. The **inciting incident** is the event that introduces the central conflict. What central conflict is introduced in act I of *Hamlet?* What incident introduces this conflict?

2. **Mood. Mood,** or **atmosphere,** is the emotion created in the reader by part or all of a literary work. What is the predominant mood of the opening of *Hamlet?* What descriptions, events, and pieces of dialogue create this mood?

3. **Irony. Irony** is a difference between appearance and reality. How would you describe Claudius's manner in scene ii of act I? What is ironic about the way in which Claudius presents himself?

4. **Foil.** A **foil** is a character whose attributes, or characteristics, contrast with, and therefore throw into relief, the attributes of another character. Throughout this play, Fortinbras will be presented as a foil to Hamlet. In act I, however, we learn of several similarities between the two young men. What are the similarities between Hamlet and Fortinbras?

5. **Theme.** A **theme** is a main idea in a literary work. One theme that recurs throughout *Hamlet* is that of salvation and the means by which it is either achieved or lost. Why is the ghost of Hamlet's father doomed to walk the earth during the night and to spend its days in flames? Another theme of the play is revenge. On whom is Hamlet asked to take revenge, and why? Is it right for Hamlet to undertake this revenge? Do you believe that he can do so and still behave morally? Why, or why not?

ACT II, SCENE i

1. **marvell's.** Marvelously
2. **inquire.** Inquiries
3. **Danskers.** Danes (people from Denmark)
4. **encompassment.** Encircling
5. **come you . . . touch it.** Come close to the topic that you are interested in (Laertes's behavior) without asking specifically about that topic
6. **Take you.** Assume, or pretend to have
7. **put on him . . . you please.** Make up whatever you wish to
8. **rank.** Stinking, disgusting
9. **gaming.** Gambling
10. **Drabbing.** Consorting with women of ill repute
11. **incontinency.** Lewd behavior
12. **quaintly.** Cleverly
13. **taints of liberty.** Minor faults that a person with lots of freedom falls into

Words For Everyday Use

wan • ton (wän´tən) *adj.*, undisciplined

Act II

Enter old POLONIUS *with his man* REYNALDO.

POLONIUS.   Give him this money and these notes,
Reynaldo.

REYNALDO.   I will, my lord.

POLONIUS.   You shall do marvell's[1] wisely, good
Reynaldo,
Before you visit him, to make inquire[2]
5   Of his behavior.

REYNALDO.   My lord, I did intend it.

POLONIUS.   Marry, well said, very well said. Look you, sir,
Inquire me first what Danskers[3] are in Paris,
And how, and who, what means, and where they keep,
What company, at what expense; and finding
10   By this encompassment[4] and drift of question
That they do know my son, come you more nearer
Than your particular demands will touch it.[5]
Take you[6] as 'twere some distant knowledge of him,
As thus, "I know his father and his friends,
15   And in part him." Do you mark this, Reynaldo?

REYNALDO.   Ay, very well, my lord.

POLONIUS.   "And in part him—but," you may say; "not
well.
But if't be he I mean, he's very wild,
Addicted so and so," and there put on him
20   What forgeries you please:[7] marry, none so rank[8]
As may dishonor him, take heed of that,
But, sir, such wanton, wild, and usual slips
As are companions noted and most known
To youth and liberty.

REYNALDO.   As gaming,[9] my lord.

25   POLONIUS.   Ay, or drinking, fencing, swearing, quarreling,
Drabbing[10]—you may go so far.

REYNALDO.   My lord, that would dishonor him.

POLONIUS.   Faith, as you may season it in the charge:
You must not put another scandal on him,
30   That he is open to incontinency[11]—
That's not my meaning. But breathe his faults so
quaintly[12]
That they may seem the taints of liberty,[13]

14. **unreclaimed.** Untamed
15. **Of general assault.** Such as might attack or overcome most anyone
16. **fetch of wit.** Ingenious strategy
17. **sallies.** Taints
18. **a thing . . . working.** Something soiled from use or contact
19. **Your party in converse.** The person with whom you are conversing
20. **sound.** Sound out, question
21. **prenominate.** Aforementioned
22. **Having ever . . . guilty.** Having ever seen the youth of whom you speak engaged in (and therefore guilty of) the aforementioned reprehensible actions
23. **closes.** Finishes, ends his conversation
24. **in this consequence.** In this way
25. **addition.** Title or mode of address
26. **leave.** Leave off
27. **o'ertook in's rouse.** Overtaken (encountered) by drunkenness
28. *Videlicet.* Namely; that is (From the Latin *videre licet,* "it is permitted to see")
29. **carp.** Type of fish, known for its subtlety in avoiding capture
30. **windlasses.** Roundabout maneuvers, literally, circles made to intercept one's quarry during a hunt
31. **assays of bias.** Indirect trials
32. **lecture.** Lesson
33. **Shall you my son.** Shall you find out my son.
34. **have me.** Understand me

Words For Everyday Use

in • di • rec • tion (inˊdə rekˊshən) *n.,* roundabout means

The flash and outbreak of a fiery mind,
A savageness in unreclaimed[14] blood,
35 Of general assault.[15]

REYNALDO.   But, my good lord—

POLONIUS.   Wherefore should you do this?

REYNALDO.   Ay, my lord,
I would know that.

POLONIUS.   Marry, sir, here's my drift,
And I believe it is a fetch of wit:[16]
You laying these slight sallies[17] on my son,
40 As 'twere a thing a little soil'd wi' th' working.[18]
Mark you,
Your party in converse,[19] him you would sound,[20]
Having ever seen in the prenominate[21] crimes
The youth you breathe of guilty,[22] be assur'd
45 He closes[23] with you in this consequence:[24]
"Good sir," or so, or "friend," or "gentleman,"
According to the phrase or the addition[25]
Of man and country.

REYNALDO.   Very good, my lord.

POLONIUS.   And then, sir, does 'a this—'a does—what was
    I about to say?
50 By the mass, I was about to say something.
Where did I leave?[26]

REYNALDO.   At "closes in the consequence."

POLONIUS.   At "closes in the consequence," ay, marry.
He closes thus: "I know the gentleman.
I saw him yesterday, or th' other day,
55 Or then, or then, with such or such, and as you say,
There was 'a gaming, there o'ertook in 's rouse,[27]
There falling out at tennis"; or, perchance,
"I saw him enter such a house of sale,"
Videlicet,[28] a brothel, or so forth. See you now,
60 Your bait of falsehood take this carp[29] of truth,
And thus do we of wisdom and of reach,
With windlasses[30] and with assays of bias[31]
By indirections find directions out;
So by my former lecture[32] and advice
65 Shall you my son.[33] You have me,[34] have you not?

REYNALDO.   My lord, I have.

POLONIUS.   God bye ye, fare ye well.

REYNALDO.   Good my lord.

◄ What is
Polonius's plan to
find out whether his
son has been behav-
ing properly?

35. **Observe . . . in yourself.** The sentence has two possible interpretations. It can mean either "behave as he behaves" (so that you can win his trust and so observe truly what he is like) or "observe his behavior personally." The former is more likely given Polonius's next statement.

36. **let him ply.** See that he goes on with

37. **How now.** What's up? or What's with you?

38. **affrighted.** Frightened

39. **With.** By

40. **closet.** Room

41. **doublet.** Jacket

42. **unbraced.** Unfastened

43. **fouled.** Messed up

44. **down-gyved.** Fallen down so that they resemble fetters (A gyve is a fetter, or shackle, such as might be attached to a ball and chain.)

45. **purport.** Meaning

46. **As.** As if

47. **thrice.** Three times

48. **bended.** Turned, directed

49. **ecstasy.** Madness

50. **fordoes.** Undoes, or destroys

Words For Everyday Use

pe • ru • sal (pə rōō´zəl) *n.*, study
pi • te • ous (pit´ē əs) *adj.*, exciting pity or compassion

POLONIUS. Observe his inclination in yourself.[35]

REYNALDO. I shall, my lord.

70 **POLONIUS.** And let him ply[36] his music.

REYNALDO. Well, my lord.

POLONIUS. Farewell. *Exit* REYNALDO.

Enter OPHELIA.

How now,[37] Ophelia, what's the matter?

OPHELIA. O my lord, my lord, I have been so affrighted![38]

POLONIUS. With[39] what, i' th' name of God?

OPHELIA. My lord, as I was sewing in my closet,[40]
75 Lord Hamlet, with his doublet[41] all unbrac'd,[42]
No hat upon his head, his stockins fouled,[43]
Ungart'red, and down-gyved[44] to his ankle,
Pale as his shirt, his knees knocking each other,
And with a look so piteous in purport[45]
80 As if he had been loosed out of hell
To speak of horrors—he comes before me.

POLONIUS. Mad for thy love?

OPHELIA. My lord, I do not know,
But truly I do fear it.

POLONIUS. What said he?

OPHELIA. He took me by the wrist, and held me hard,
85 Then goes he to the length of all his arm,
And with his other hand thus o'er his brow,
He falls to such perusal of my face
As[46] 'a would draw it. Long stay'd he so.
At last, a little shaking of mine arm,
90 And thrice[47] his head thus waving up and down,
He rais'd a sigh so piteous and profound
As it did seem to shatter all his bulk
And end his being. That done, he lets me go,
And with his head over his shoulder turn'd,
95 He seem'd to find his way without his eyes,
For out a' doors he went without their helps,
And to the last bended[48] their light on me.

POLONIUS. Come, go with me. I will go seek the King.
This is the very ecstasy[49] of love,
100 Whose violent property fordoes[50] itself,
And leads the will to desperate undertakings
As oft as any passions under heaven

◄ Why does Polonius tell Reynaldo to let Laertes "ply his music"?

◄ What has frightened Ophelia?

◄ What do Polonius and Ophelia believe has driven Hamlet mad?

◄ What evidence does Ophelia have that Hamlet is crazy with love for her?

◄ To whom does Polonius plan to report Hamlet's actions?

[Handwritten margin notes: "Hamlet came to see Ophelia clothes messed pale"; "he shook his head 3 times + gave out a cry +"; "walked out of the room"]

51. **hard.** Stern
52. **coted.** Observed
53. **beshrow.** Curse
54. **proper.** Natural
55. **cast beyond ourselves.** Seek beyond what we actually know or understand
56. **kept close.** Kept close to the chest, kept secret
57. **might move . . . utter love.** Might cause more sorrow if hidden than cause anger if told

ACT II, SCENE ii

1. **Moreover that.** In addition to the fact that
2. **sending.** Sending for you
3. **Sith.** Since
4. **nor.** Neither
5. **So much . . . of himself.** So removed from self-awareness (To be mad is to be incapable of understanding what one is doing)
6. **of so young days.** From your youth
7. **sith so neighbored to.** Since [you are] so intimately acquainted with
8. **havior.** Behavior
9. **voutsafe your rest.** Vouchsafe, or agree, to stay
10. **aught.** Anything
11. **he more adheres.** He is more attached emotionally
12. **gentry.** Courtesy

Words For Everyday Use

dis • cre • tion (di skresh´ən) *n.,* good judgment
trans • for • ma • tion (trans´fər mā´ shən) *n.,* change of form or appearance

en • treat (en trēt´) *vt.,* beg
ex • pend (eks pend´) *vt.,* spend; use up

That does afflict our natures. I am sorry—
What, have you given him any hard[51] words of late?

105 OPHELIA.   No, my good lord, but as you did command
I did repel his letters, and denied
His access to me.

POLONIUS.   That hath made him mad.
I am sorry that with better heed and judgment
I had not coted[52] him. I fear'd he did but trifle
110 And meant to wrack thee, but beshrow[53] my jealousy!
By heaven, it is as proper[54] to our age
To cast beyond ourselves[55] in our opinions,
As it is common for the younger sort
To lack discretion. Come, go we to the King.
115 This must be known, which, being kept close,[56] might move
More grief to hide than hate to utter love.[57]
Come.   *Exeunt.*

SCENE II: **A room in the castle**

Flourish. Enter KING *and* QUEEN, ROSENCRANTZ *and*
GUILDENSTERN *with others.*

KING.   Welcome, dear Rosencrantz and Guildenstern!
Moreover that[1] we much did long to see you,
The need we have to use you did provoke
Our hasty sending.[2] Something have you heard
5 Of Hamlet's transformation; so call it,
Sith[3] nor[4] th' exterior nor the inward man
Resembles that it was. What it should be
More than his father's death, that thus hath put him
So much from th' understanding of himself,[5]
10 I cannot dream of. I entreat you both
That, being of so young days[6] brought up with him,
And sith so neighbored to[7] his youth and havior,[8]
That you voutsafe your rest[9] here in our court
Some little time, so by your companies
15 To draw him on to pleasures, and to gather
So much as from occasion you may glean,
Whether aught[10] to us unknown afflicts him thus,
That, open'd, lies within our remedy.

QUEEN.   Good gentlemen, he hath much talk'd of you
20 And sure I am two men there is not living
To whom he more adheres.[11] If it will please you
To show us so much gentry[12] and good will
As to expend your time with us a while

Handwritten margin notes:

not being to see ask Hamlet

◄ To what cause does Polonius attribute Hamlet's madness? What mistake in judgment does Polonius think that he has made? How has Polonius's opinion of Hamlet changed?

Hell tells O. must report to Hamlet to King

2 months have passed.

2 friends who indicate that H. is acting strange

◄ Why has Claudius sent for Rosencrantz and Guildenstern? What does he want them to do?

Gert think has to work w/ her 2 friends? dead

13. **dread.** To be dreaded, commanding respect
14. **in the full bent.** To the greatest extent, like a bow that is bent as far as one can bend it
15. **still hast.** Always have
16. **liege.** Lord
17. **very.** Actual or true
18. **grace.** Honor, with a pun on the grace, or prayer, that is said before a meal
19. **head.** Beginning, foremost part

Words For Everyday Use

en • treat • y (en trē´tē) *n.*, begging favors
be • seech (bē sēch´) *vt.*, beg
dis • tem • per (dis tem´pər) *n.*, disturbance

For the supply and profit of our hope,
25 Your visitation shall receive such thanks
As fits a king's remembrance.

ROSENCRANTZ.   Both your Majesties
Might, by the sovereign power you have of us,
Put your dread[13] pleasures more into command
Than to <u>entreaty</u>.

GUILDENSTERN.   But we both obey
30 And here give up ourselves, in the full bent,[14]
To lay our service freely at your feet,
To be commanded.

KING.   Thanks, Rosencrantz and gentle Guildenstern.

QUEEN.   Thanks, Guildenstern and gentle Rosencrantz.
35 And I <u>beseech</u> you instantly to visit
My too much changed son. Go some of you
And bring these gentlemen where Hamlet is.

GUILDENSTERN.   Heavens make our presence and our
    practices
Pleasant and helpful to him!

QUEEN.   Ay, amen!
                    Exeunt ROSENCRANTZ *and* GUILDENSTERN
                        with some ATTENDANTS

Enter POLONIUS.

40 POLONIUS.   Th' embassadors from Norway, my good
    lord,
Are joyfully return'd.

KING.   Thou still hast[15] been the father of good news.

POLONIUS.   Have I, my lord? I assure my good liege[16]
I hold my duty as I hold my soul,
45 Both to my God and to my gracious king;
And I do think, or else this brain of mine
Hunts not the trail of policy so sure
As it hath us'd to do, that I have found
The very[17] cause of Hamlet's lunacy.

50 KING.   O, speak of that, that do I long to hear.

POLONIUS.   Give first admittance to th' embassadors;
My news shall be the fruit to that great feast.

KING.   Thyself do grace[18] to them, and bring them in.
                        Exit POLONIUS.
He tells me, my dear Gertrude, he hath found
55 The head[19] and source of all your son's <u>distemper</u>.

◄ What do
Rosencrantz and
Guildenstern agree
to do?

◄ What does
Queen Gertrude
want Rosencrantz
and Guildenstern to
do immediately?
Why is she so
insistent?

◄ What does
Polonius believe that
he has discovered?

[Handwritten margin notes:]
to help Gert. find out what is wrong?

So they isps on Hamlet

King's thanks + recognition

Pol. tells the K.+G. the cause of Hamlet's madness

20. **main.** Primary or chief concern
21. **sift him.** Examine him carefully, as one sifts grain
22. **Upon our first.** When we first spoke
23. **levies.** Enlistments of soldiers
24. **Whereat.** At which [he]
25. **borne in hand.** Led by the hand, or deceived
26. **arrests . . . Fortinbras.** Orders that Fortinbras stop
27. **in fine.** Finally
28. **give th' assay of.** Make the attempt to raise
29. **crowns.** Units of money
30. **On such regards.** With such considerations
31. **allowance.** Permission
32. **It likes us.** We like it
33. **our more considered time.** In my leisure time, when I have time to consider
34. **brevity . . . flourishes.** Wit is described, metaphorically, as a person with brevity as his soul and tediousness as his less important limbs

Words For Everyday Use

sup • press (sə pres´) *vt.*, abolish by authority

com • mis • sion (kə mish´ən) *n.*, authorization

ex • pos • tu • late (eks päs´chə lāt´) *vt.*, reason with or about

brev • i • ty (brev´ə tē) *n.*, quality of being concise

QUEEN. I doubt it is no other but the main,[20]
His father's death and our o'erhasty marriage.

Enter POLONIUS *with* VOLTEMAND *and* CORNELIUS, *the*
Embassadors.

KING. Well, we shall sift him.[21]—Welcome, my good
    friends!
Say, Voltemand, what from our brother Norway?

60 VOLTEMAND. Most fair return of greetings and desires.
Upon our first,[22] he sent out to <u>suppress</u>
His nephew's levies,[23] which to him appear'd
To be a preparation 'gainst the Polack;
But better look'd into, he truly found
65 It was against your Highness. Whereat[24] griev'd,
That so his sickness, age, and impotence
Was falsely borne in hand,[25] sends out arrests
On Fortinbras,[26] which he, in brief, obeys,
Receives rebuke from Norway, and in fine,[27]
70 Makes vow before his uncle never more
To give th' assay of[28] arms against your Majesty.
Whereon old Norway, overcome with joy,
Gives him threescore thousand crowns[29] in annual fee,
And his <u>commission</u> to employ those soldiers,
75 So levied, as before, against the Polack,
With an entreaty, herein further shown,

                                 Giving a paper.

That it might please you to give quiet pass
Through your dominions for this enterprise,
On such regards[30] of safety and allowance[31]
80 As therein are set down.

KING.   It likes us[32] well,
And at our more considered time[33] we'll read,
Answer, and think upon this business.
Meantime, we thank you for your well-took labor.
Go to your rest, at night we'll feast together.
85 Most welcome home!

                 Exeunt EMBASSADORS *and* ATTENDANTS.

POLONIUS.   This business is well ended.
My liege, and madam, to <u>expostulate</u>
What majesty should be, what duty is,
Why day is day, night night, and time is time,
Were nothing but to waste night, day, and time;
90 Therefore, since <u>brevity</u> is the soul of wit,
And tediousness the limbs and outward flourishes,[34]
I will be brief. Your noble son is mad:

◄ What does the
queen fear to be the
cause of Hamlet's
madness?

◄ Has Claudius's
diplomatic mission
to Norway been
successful? In what
way?

◄ What does the
king of Norway
request of Claudius?

◄ Does Claudius
immediately agree to
the king of
Norway's request?
Why, or why not?

35. **But let that go.** Even Polonius seems to recognize, here, that he has said nothing, defining the state of true madness as the state of being mad.

36. **More . . . art.** More content with less attempt to make it sound artful

37. **figure.** Figure of speech, or rhetorical flourish. After swearing that he uses no art in his speech, Polonius immediately makes a failed attempt to speak in a fancy, ornamented manner.

38. **Perpend.** Consider, think on this

39. **beautified.** Beautiful

40. **stay.** Wait, stay your tongue

41. **faithful.** I.e., to the letter as written

42. **ill at these numbers.** Bad at writing metrical verse (words whose beats, or stresses, can be counted)

43. **reckon.** Count, explain

44. **this machine.** The body. The idea that the body was a mere machine, or mechanism, inhabited by a soul was to figure largely in late Renaissance and Enlightenment philosophy. The use of the term is typical of Hamlet, who generally speaks with disdain of that which is not spiritual.

45. **more above.** In addition

46. **solicitings . . . fell out.** Requests as they occurred

47. **mine.** My

48. **As of.** As I would think of

**Words
For
Everyday
Use**

sur • mise (sər mīz´) *vi.,* imagine

Mad call I it, for to define true madness,
What is't but to be nothing else but mad?
95 But let that go.[35]

QUEEN.   More matter with less art.[36]

POLONIUS.   Madam, I swear I use no art at all.
That he's mad, 'tis true, 'tis true 'tis pity,
And pity 'tis 'tis true—a foolish figure,[37]
But farewell it, for I will use no art.
100 Mad let us grant him then, and now remains
That we find out the cause of this effect,
Or rather say, the cause of this defect,
For this effect defective comes by cause:
Thus it remains, and the remainder thus.
105 Perpend.[38] *Consider this*
I have a daughter—have while she is mine—
Who in her duty and obedience, mark,
Hath given me this. Now gather, and surmise.
                    Reads the salutation of the letter.
"To the celestial and my soul's idol, the most
110 beautified[39] Ophelia"—
That's an ill phrase, a vile phrase, "beautified" is a vile
phrase. But you shall hear. Thus:
"In her excellent white bosom, these, etc."

QUEEN.   Came this from Hamlet to her?

115 POLONIUS.   Good madam, stay[40] awhile. I will be
faithful.[41]
                        Reads the letter.
"Doubt thou the stars are fire,
Doubt that the sun doth move
Doubt truth to be a liar
But never doubt I love.
120 O dear Ophelia, I am ill at these numbers.[42] I have not
art to reckon[43] my groans, but that I love thee best, O
most best, believe it. Adieu.
        Thine evermore, most dear lady
            whilst this machine[44] is to him, Hamlet."
125 This in obedience hath my daughter shown me,
And more above,[45] hath his solicitings,
As they fell out[46] by time, by means, and place,
All given to mine[47] ear.

KING.   But how hath she
Receiv'd his love?

POLONIUS.   What do you think of me?

130 KING.   As of[48] a man faithful and honorable.

(margin annotations)
◄ What does Gertrude ask Polonius to do?

◄ What does Hamlet's letter to Ophelia seem to reveal?

Pol. reads a letter H. wrote to O. that expresses his love + feeling for her

words I cannot explain myself

How did she respond?

49. **fain.** Wish to

50. **play'd . . . table-book.** Simply absorbed the information, as a writing desk or a diary might

51. **round.** The use of this word is humorous because Polonius evidently means "directly," but he does nothing directly. Instead, he tries to undertake everything in an indirect manner.

52. **bespeak.** Address

53. **out of thy star.** Beyond your fortunes (The stars were believed to govern people's fortunes.)

54. **from his resort.** From his visits

55. **watch.** Waking state (i.e., he stopped sleeping regularly)

56. **declension.** Downfall, with a pun on declension in the sense of a grammatical list of the forms of a verb

57. **try it.** Test this hypothesis

58. **together.** At a time

59. **lobby.** Room in the upper part of the castle

60. **loose . . . to him.** Polonius speaks of his daughter as though she were an animal that might be loosed from its tether.

61. **arras.** Tapestry, curtain

Words For Everyday Use

pre • script (prē´skript) *n.*, direction

to • ken (tō´kən) *n.*, gift as symbol of the giver's affection

POLONIUS.   I would fain[49] prove so. But what might
        you think
When I had seen this hot love on the wing—
As I perceiv'd it (I must tell you that)
Before my daughter told me—what might you,
135 Or my dear Majesty your queen here, think,
If I had play'd the desk or table-book[50]
Or given my heart a winking, mute and dumb,
Or look'd upon this love with idle sight,
What might you think? No, I went round[51] to work,
140 And my young mistress thus I did bespeak:[52]
"Lord Hamlet is a prince out of thy star;[53]
This must not be"; and then I prescripts gave her,
That she should lock herself from his resort,[54]
Admit no messengers, receive no tokens.
145 Which done, she took the fruits of my advice;
And he repell'd, a short tale to make,
Fell into a sadness, then into a fast,
Thence to a watch,[55] thence into a weakness,
Thence to a lightness, and by this declension,[56]
150 Into the madness wherein now he raves,
        And all we mourn for.

KING.   Do you think 'tis this?

QUEEN.   It may be, very like.

POLONIUS.   Hath there been such a time—I would fain
        know that—
That I have positively said, "'Tis so,"
155 When it prov'd otherwise?

KING.   Not that I know.

POLONIUS.   [Points to his head and shoulder.] Take this
        from this, if this be otherwise.
If circumstances lead me, I will find
Where truth is hid, though it were hid indeed
Within the center.

KING.   How may we try it[57] further?

160 POLONIUS.   You know sometimes he walks four hours
        together[58]
Here in the lobby.[59]

QUEEN.   So he does indeed.

POLONIUS.   At such a time I'll loose my daughter to
        him.[60]
Be you and I behind an arras[61] then
Mark the encounter: if he love her not

◀ According to
Polonius, how did
Hamlet come to his
present state of
madness?

◀ What does
Polonius propose to
do to find out whether
Hamlet has, indeed,
been driven crazy by
his unrequited love
for Ophelia?

62. **thereon.** As a result, for that reason
63. **carters.** People to carry goods to market in carts
64. **beseech.** Request of
65. **board him.** Stop, intercept. (The term is metaphorical. Polonius speaks of Hamlet as though he were a ship that Polonius might board, like a pirate.)
66. **Excellent.** Very
67. **fishmonger.** A seller of fish (The profession of fishmonger was a lower-class occupation.)
68. **Then I would . . . a man.** If you are not a fish seller, then I might well wish that you had a profession that was that honorable.
69. **sun breed . . . dog.** Elizabethans believed in the theory of spontaneous generation, whereby the mere presence of the sun bred maggots (wormlike insect larvae) in meat
70. **good kissing carrion.** Flesh good enough for the sun to kiss and cause it to become pregnant with maggots
71. **Let her . . . may conceive.** Do not let Ophelia walk in the sun for, like the dead dog, she may conceive a child, and that might not be a blessing. The word "sun" may be, in this case, a reference to Hamlet. (See act I, scene ii, line 67.)
72. **the matter.** The substance (what the book is about); Hamlet answers as if Polonius meant an argument between people.
73. **thick amber . . . gum.** Resins from trees

Words For Everyday Use

ex • trem • i • ty (eks strem´ə tē) *n.*, extreme danger
slan • der (slan´dər) *n.*, statement harmful to someone's reputation
purge (pʉrj) *vt.*, get rid of, here as tears

165 And be not from his reason fall'n thereon,[62]
Let me be no assistant for a state,
But keep a farm and carters.[63]

KING.   We will try it.

Enter HAMLET *reading on a book.*

QUEEN. But look where sadly the poor wretch comes
    reading.

POLONIUS. Away, I do beseech[64] you, both away.
170 I'll board him[65] presently.   *Exeunt* KING *and* QUEEN.
                  O, give me leave,
How does my good Lord Hamlet?

HAMLET. Well, God-a-mercy.

POLONIUS. Do you know me, my lord?

HAMLET. Excellent[66] well, you are a fishmonger.[67]

175 POLONIUS. Not I, my lord.

HAMLET. Then I would you were so honest a man.[68]

POLONIUS. Honest, my lord?

HAMLET. Ay, sir, to be honest, as this world goes, is to
be one man pick'd out of ten thousand.

180 POLONIUS. That's very true, my lord.

HAMLET. For if the sun breed maggots in a dead dog,[69]
being a good kissing carrion[70]—Have you a daughter?

POLONIUS. I have, my lord.

HAMLET. Let her not walk i' th' sun. Conception is a
185 blessing, but as your daughter may conceive,[71] friend,
look to't.

POLONIUS. [*Aside.*] How say you by that? still harping
on my daughter. Yet he knew me not at first, 'a said I
was a fishmonger. 'A is far gone. And truly in my youth
190 I suff'red much extremity for love— very near this. I'll
speak to him again.—What do you read, my lord?

HAMLET. Words, words, words.

POLONIUS. What is the matter,[72] my lord?

HAMLET. Between who?

195 POLONIUS. I mean, the matter that you read, my lord.

HAMLET. Slanders, sir; for the satirical rogue says here
that old men have gray beards, that their faces are
wrinkled, their eyes purging thick amber and plumtree
gum,[73] and that they have a plentiful lack of wit,

◄ What does
Hamlet call Polonius?

◄ According to
Hamlet, what does
the sun do?

◄ Why, according
to Hamlet, should
Ophelia not be
allowed to walk in
the sun?

◄ What does
Polonius mean by his
question? What is
Hamlet's answer?

74. **honesty.** Honorable
75. **there is method in 't.** It shows some design or reason
76. **walk out of the air.** Go inside
77. **pregnant.** Full of suggested meaning
78. **suddenly.** At once, immediately
79. **withal.** With
80. **indifferent.** Average, ordinary
81. **button.** Ornamental button at the top of a cap (i.e., "We are not at the height of fortune.")
82. **privates.** Intimate friends
83. **strumpet.** One who gives her favors indiscriminately, without rhyme or reason

Words For Everyday Use

te • di • ous (tē´dē əs) *adj.*, tiresome; boring

200 together with most weak hams; all which, sir, though I
most powerfully and potently believe, yet I hold it not
honesty[74] to have it thus set down, for yourself, sir, shall
grow old as I am, if like a crab you could go backward.

POLONIUS. [*Aside*.] Though this be madness, yet there is
205 method in't.[75]—Will you walk out of the air,[76] my lord?

HAMLET. Into my grave.

POLONIUS. Indeed that's out of the air. [*Aside*.] How
pregnant[77] sometimes his replies are! a happiness that
often madness hits on, which reason and sanity could
210 not so prosperously be deliver'd of. I will leave him, and
suddenly[78] contrive the means of meeting between him
and my daughter.—My lord, I will take my leave of you.

HAMLET. You cannot take from me any thing that I
will not more willingly part withal[79]—except my life,
215 except my life, except my life.

POLONIUS. Fare you well, my lord.

HAMLET. These tedious old fools!

Enter GUILDENSTERN *and* ROSENCRANTZ.

POLONIUS. You go to seek the Lord Hamlet, there he is.

ROSENCRANTZ. [*To* POLONIUS.] God save you, sir!

Exit POLONIUS.

220 GUILDENSTERN. My honor'd lord!

ROSENCRANTZ. My most dear lord!

HAMLET. My excellent good friends! How dost thou,
Guildenstern? Ah, Rosencrantz! Good lads, how do
you both?

225 ROSENCRANTZ. As the indifferent[80] children of the earth.

GUILDENSTERN. Happy, in that we are not over-happy,
on Fortune's cap we are not the very button.[81]

HAMLET. Nor the soles of her shoe?

ROSENCRANTZ. Neither, my lord.

230 HAMLET. Then you live about her waist, or in the
middle of her favors?

GUILDENSTERN. Faith, her privates we.[82]

HAMLET. In the secret parts of Fortune? O, most true,
she is a strumpet.[83] What news?

235 ROSENCRANTZ. None, my lord, but the world's grown
honest.

◄ What "method" is there in Hamlet's "madness" in the preceding lines? Of whom is Hamlet making fun? What does Polonius mean by his question? In what way does Hamlet willfully misinterpret Polonius?

◄ Polonius recognizes that Hamlet's "madness" contains some sense, but does he therefore conclude that Hamlet is sane and rational? Explain.

◄ With what two things does Hamlet say he would gladly part?

Hamlet is pleased to see them until he finds out that King told them to spy on Hamlet

84. **Then . . . near.** Hamlet implies that nothing but the threat of impending doomsday could make people suddenly become honest.

85. **more in particular.** More closely, in more detail

86. **'tis none to you.** It is not prison to you

87. **bounded.** Enclosed

88. **the very substance . . . of a dream.** Ambitious people are so insubstantial that they are made up not of dreams but of the shadows of dreams.

89. **are our beggars . . . beggars' shadows.** If to have no ambition is to be substantial, then beggars are substantial and have bodies. If to have ambition is to be insubstantial, then heroes slain in war are insubstantial, no more than the shadows of beggars.

90. **fay.** Faith, with a pun on fay in the sense of fairy. Throughout this playful interchange with Rosencrantz and Guildenstern, Hamlet toys with metaphors based on the insubstantial world of fairies. A fairy would be small enough to be "bounded in a nutshell."

91. **wait upon you.** Act as your servants

92. **No such matter.** I don't want that.

93. **I am most dreadfully attended.** I have terrible servants.

94. **the beaten way of friendship.** Well-worn path, with a possible pun on the word *beaten* in the sense of "beaten upon," suggesting that friendship is often abused

95. **what make you at.** Why do you come to

96. **Beggar that I am.** Harkening back to the previous conversation

97. **too dear a halfpenny.** Too costly at a halfpenny, not worth much

98. **justly.** Truthfully

HAMLET. Then is doomsday near.[84] But your news is not true. Let me question more in particular.[85] What have you, my good friends, deserv'd at the hands of
240 Fortune, that she sends you to prison hither?

GUILDENSTERN. Prison, my lord?

HAMLET. Denmark's a prison.

ROSENCRANTZ. Then is the world one.

HAMLET. A goodly one, in which there are many
245 confines, wards, and dungeons, Denmark being one o' th' worst.

ROSENCRANTZ. We think not so, my lord.

HAMLET. Why then 'tis none to you;[86] for there is nothing either good or bad, but thinking makes it so. To
250 me it is a prison.

ROSENCRANTZ. Why then your ambition makes it one. 'Tis too narrow for your mind.

HAMLET. O God, I could be bounded[87] in a nutshell, and count myself a king of infinite space—were it not
255 that I have bad dreams.

GUILDENSTERN. Which dreams indeed are ambition, for the very substance of the ambitious is merely the shadow of a dream.[88]

HAMLET. A dream itself is but a shadow.

260 ROSENCRANTZ. Truly, and I hold ambition of so airy and light a quality that it is but a shadow's shadow.

HAMLET. Then are our beggars bodies, and our monarchs and outstretch'd heroes the beggars' shadows.[89] Shall we to th' court? for, by my fay,[90] I cannot reason.

265 ROSENCRANTZ, GUILDENSTERN. We'll wait upon you.[91]

HAMLET. No such matter.[92] I will not sort you with the rest of my servants; for to speak to you like an honest man, I am most dreadfully attended.[93] But in the beaten way of friendship,[94] what make you at[95] Elsinore?

270 ROSENCRANTZ. To visit you, my lord, no other occasion.

HAMLET. Beggar that I am,[96] I am even poor in thanks —but I thank you, and sure, dear friends, my thanks are too dear a halfpenny.[97] Were you not sent for? is it your own inclining? is it a free visitation? Come, come,
275 deal justly[98] with me. Come, come—nay, speak.

GUILDENSTERN. What should we say, my lord?

◄ To what does Hamlet compare Denmark and the world as a whole?

◄ According to Hamlet, what makes something good or bad?

◄ What keeps Hamlet from counting himself "a king of infinite space"?

◄ What two meanings might "the beaten way of friendship" have?

99. **color.** Hide or disguise, as by color applied to the face
100. **conjure you.** Require of you
101. **consonancy.** Closeness, harmoniousness
102. **what more dear.** Anything more valuable
103. **even.** Fair
104. **have an eye of you.** Shall keep my eyes on you
105. **prevent your discovery.** Keep you from disclosing what business you are on for the king and queen
106. **molt.** Lose feathers
107. **of late.** Recently
108. **custom of exercises.** Usual activities
109. **frame.** Anything that is built
110. **sterile promontory.** Barren rock or land jutting into the sea
111. **canopy . . . firmament.** According to the Ptolemaic astronomy current in Shakespeare's day, the earth was the center of the universe. Around the earth were several spheres containing the planets, stars, and the sun.
112. **fretted.** Decorated, like a carved ceiling
113. **piece of work.** Fine creation
114. **faculties.** Abilities, both mental and physical
115. **moving.** Movement
116. **express.** Quick, agile
117. **nor woman . . . say so.** Hamlet says that he is not delighted by people and rejects the implication that he has any romantic interests at all.
118. **lenten.** Meager. Lent is the season of fasting and penance that precedes Easter. During Lent, the theaters in Elizabethan England were closed.
119. **players.** Actors
120. **coted.** Passed

Words For Everyday Use

mirth (murth) *n.,* joy
dis • po • si • tion (dis pə zish´ən) *n.,* temperament
pes • ti • lent (pes´tə lənt) *adj.,* likely to cause death through contagion
ap • pre • hen • sion (ap rē hen´shən) *n.,* understanding
par • a • gon (par´ə gän) *n.,* highest model
quin • tes • sence (kwin tes´əns) *n.,* pure, concentrated essence

HAMLET. Any thing but to th' purpose. You were sent for, and there is a kind of confession in your looks, which your modesties have not craft enough to color.[99]
280 I know the good King and Queen have sent for you.

ROSENCRANTZ. To what end, my lord?

HAMLET. That you must teach me. But let me conjure you,[100] by the rights of our fellowship, by the consonancy[101] of our youth, by the obligation of our
285 ever-preserv'd love, and by what more dear[102] a better proposer can charge you withal, be even[103] and direct with me, whether you were sent for or no!

◀ What does Hamlet ask Rosencrantz and Guildenstern?

ROSENCRANTZ. [*Aside to* GUILDENSTERN.] What say you?

HAMLET. [*Aside.*] Nay then I have an eye of you![104]—
290 If you love me, hold not off.

GUILDENSTERN. My lord, we were sent for.

HAMLET. I will tell you why, so shall my anticipation prevent your discovery,[105] and your secrecy to the King and Queen molt[106] no feather. I have of late[107] but
295 wherefore I know not—lost all my mirth, forgone all custom of exercises;[108] and indeed it goes so heavily with my disposition, that this goodly frame,[109] the earth, seems to me a sterile promontory;[110] this most excellent canopy, the air, look you, this brave o'erhanging firma-
300 ment,[111] this majestical roof fretted[112] with golden fire, why, it appeareth nothing to me but a foul and pestilent congregation of vapors. What a piece of work[113] is a man, how noble in reason, how infinite in faculties,[114] in form and moving[115] how express[116] and
305 admirable, in action how like an angel, in apprehension, how like a god! the beauty of the world; the paragon of animals; and yet to me what is this quintessence of dust? Man delights not me— nor women neither, though by your smiling you seem to say so.[117]

◀ What does Hamlet say that he thinks of the earth? of the air? of human beings?

310 **ROSENCRANTZ.** My lord, there was no such stuff in my thoughts.

HAMLET. Why did ye laugh then, when I said, "Man delights not me"?

ROSENCRANTZ. To think, my lord, if you delight not in
315 man, what lenten[118] entertainment the players[119] shall receive from you. We coted[120] them on the way, and hither are they coming to offer you service.

◀ Who has arrived at Elsinore?

HAMLET. He that plays the king shall be welcome—

121. **foil and target.** Sword and shield

122. **gratis.** For nothing

123. **humorous.** Someone ruled by one of his humors. The Elizabethans still maintained a theory, advanced by the ancient Greek physician Galen, that people had four humors, or bodily fluids, that governed their personalities—choler, or yellow bile (angry, irritable, or choleric personality), phlegm (sluggish, dull, or phlegmatic personality), black bile (sad or melancholic personality), and blood (cheerful or sanguine personality). A humorous character would be one dominated by a single exaggerated trait.

124. **tickled a' th' sere.** Easily triggered (The sear is the catch that holds the hammer of a gun until the trigger releases it.)

125. **were wont.** Used

126. **tragedians.** Actors in tragedies

127. **of the city.** What city, precisely, is meant here is open to speculation

128. **Their residence . . . both ways.** They would have enjoyed a greater reputation and greater profits if they had stayed at home in the city.

129. **inhibition.** Prohibition from playing (as though the theaters of the city had been closed)

130. **late.** Recent

131. **innovation.** Disturbance, insurrection

132. **wonted.** Usual, accustomed

133. **aery.** Nest

134. **eyases.** Hawks. The discussion here refers to the innovation, which occurred around the time of the writing of *Hamlet*, of employing companies of child actors in the theater. These popular child actors became quite controversial because their employment threatened available work for the established companies, in which children were used only to play female parts.

135. **cry out . . . question.** Make themselves heard above all others

136. **tyrannically.** Excessively (This may, as well, be a reference to the royal support of these child actors.)

137. **these.** Child actors

138. **berattle the common stages.** Abuse or put down the public theaters

139. **many . . . goose-quills.** Gallants (the sort of men who wear swords) are afraid of being considered unfashionable by writers (those who use goose-quill pens.)

140. **thither.** There (to the public theaters)

141. **escoted.** Supported

142. **quality.** Profession (of acting)

143. **Will they . . . own succession.** Later on, when these children grow up and become ordinary adult players (which will happen if they do not have other means for providing for themselves), will they not say that the playwrights that use them did them wrong to make them argue against using adult actors?

144. **tarre.** Provoke

145. **no money . . . argument.** No money offered by theater companies for a new play

146. **went to cuffs.** Were willing to fight

147. **carry it away.** Emerge victorious

148. **Hercules and his load.** The company of the Globe Theater, whose emblem was a depiction of Hercules carrying the globe of the world on his shoulders

| Words For Everyday Use | **blank verse** (blaŋk´ vʉrs´) *n.*, unrhymed verse having five iambic feet typical of Elizabethan drama |

his Majesty shall have tribute on me, the adventurous
320 knight shall use his foil and target,[121] the lover shall
not sigh gratis,[122] the humorous[123] man shall end his
part in peace, the clown shall make those laugh whose
lungs are tickle a' th' sere,[124] and the lady shall say her
mind freely, or the <u>blank verse</u> shall halt for't. What
325 players are they?

ROSENCRANTZ.   Even those you were wont[125] to take
such delight in, the tragedians[126] of the city.[127]

HAMLET.   How chances it they travel? Their residence,
both in reputation and profit, was better both ways.[128]

330 ROSENCRANTZ.   I think their inhibition[129] comes by the
means of the late[130] innovation.[131]

HAMLET.   Do they hold the same estimation they did
when I was in the city? Are they so follow'd?

ROSENCRANTZ.   No indeed are they not.

335 HAMLET.   How comes it? do they grow rusty?

ROSENCRANTZ.   Nay, their endeavor keeps in the
wonted[132] pace; but there is, sir, an aery[133] of children,
little eyases,[134] that cry out on the top of question,[135]
and are most tyrannically[136] clapp'd for't. These[137] are
340 now the fashion, and so berattle the common stages[138]—
so they call them—that many wearing rapiers are afraid
of goose-quills[139] and dare scarce come thither.[140]

HAMLET.   What, are they children? Who maintains 'em?
How are they escoted?[141] Will they pursue the quality[142]
345 no longer than they can sing? Will they not say after-
wards, if they should grow themselves to common players
(as it is most like, if their means are no better), their
writers do them wrong, to make them exclaim against
their own succession?[143]

350 ROSENCRANTZ.   Faith, there has been much to do on
both sides, and the nation holds it no sin to tarre[144]
them to controversy. There was for a while no money
bid for argument,[145] unless the poet and the player
went to cuffs[146] in the question.

355 HAMLET.   Is't possible?

GUILDENSTERN.   O, there has been much throwing
about of brains.

HAMLET.   Do the boys carry it away?[147]

ROSENCRANTZ.   Ay, that they do, my lord—Hercules and
360 his load[148] too.

child actor

◄ *According to Rosencrantz, why are the newly arrived actors no longer popular in the city?*

149. **make mouths.** Make faces
150. **ducats.** Coins
151. **in little.** In miniature. Miniature portraits were quite fashionable in Shakespeare's time.
152. **'Sblood.** By God's blood (an oath)
153. **appurtenance.** Proper accompaniment
154. **comply . . . garb.** Treat you in this manner
155. **extent.** Extension (of welcoming signs)
156. **like entertainment.** Like a favorable reception
157. **mad north-north-west.** When the wind is blowing from the north-north-west
158. **southerly.** From the south
159. **I know . . . handsaw.** I can make discriminations. This is a fine example of Hamlet's verbal wit. At the same time that he is proclaiming his general sanity, he uses an example that draws that sanity into question. His intent, of course, is to confuse Rosencrantz and Guildenstern, but also to warn them to stay out of his affairs.
160. **that great baby.** Polonius
161. **clouts.** Clothes
162. **Happily.** Perhaps
163. **twice a child.** Because of senility
164. **Roscius.** A famous Roman actor. Hamlet is making fun of Polonius's typical way of speaking whereby he builds up to everything with a long-winded introduction in the manner of Roscius.
165. **Buzz, buzz.** Hamlet suggests that Polonius is like a busy bee.
166. **on his ass.** Polonius has just said that "The actors are come hither . . . Upon my honor." Hamlet's reply equates Polonius's honor with a jackass.
167. **Seneca.** Roman writer of tragedies
168. **Plautus.** Roman writer of comedies
169. **the law . . . liberty.** The sense of this line is obscure. It may refer to plays that follow the rules of dramatic structure and those that do not, or it may refer to plays performed within some legal jurisdiction and those performed outside of that jurisdiction.

HAMLET. It is not very strange, for my uncle is King of Denmark, and those that would make mouths[149] at him while my father liv'd, give twenty, forty, fifty, a hundred ducats[150] a-piece for his picture in little.[151]
365 'Sblood,[152] there is something in this more than natural, if philosophy could find it out. *A flourish for the* PLAYERS.

◄ *What does Hamlet think of public opinion? How do you know?*

GUILDENSTERN. There are the players.

HAMLET. Gentlemen, you are welcome to Elsinore. Your hands, come then: th' appurtenance[153] of welcome
370 is fashion and ceremony. Let me comply with you in this garb,[154] lest my extent[155] to the players, which, I tell you, must show fairly outwards, should more appear like entertainment[156] than yours. You are welcome; but my uncle-father and aunt-mother are deceiv'd.

375 GUILDENSTERN. In what, my dear lord?

HAMLET. I am but mad north-north-west.[157] When the wind is southerly[158] I know a hawk from a hand-saw.[159]

Enter POLONIUS.

◄ *What does Hamlet say about his so-called madness?*

POLONIUS. Well be with you, gentlemen!

HAMLET. [*Aside to them.*] Hark you, Guildenstern, and
380 you too—at each ear a hearer—that great baby[160] you see there is not yet out of his swaddling-clouts.[161]

ROSENCRANTZ. Happily[162] he is the second time come to them, for they say an old man is twice a child.[163]

HAMLET. I will prophesy, he comes to tell me of the
385 players, mark it. [*Aloud.*] You say right, sir, a' Monday morning, 'twas then indeed.

POLONIUS. My lord, I have news to tell you.

HAMLET. My lord, I have news to tell you. When Roscius[164] was an actor in Rome—

390 POLONIUS. The actors are come hither, my lord.

HAMLET. Buzz, buzz![165]

POLONIUS. Upon my honor—

HAMLET. "Then came each actor on his ass"[166]—

POLONIUS. The best actors in the world, either for
395 tragedy, comedy, history, pastoral, pastoral-comical, historical-pastoral, tragical-historical, tragical-comical-historical-pastoral, scene individable, or poem unlimited; Seneca[167] cannot be too heavy, nor Plautus[168] too light, for the law of writ and the liberty:[169] these are the only men.

170. **Jephthah.** Jephthah, whose story is told in Judges 11 in the Bible, made a vow to God that if he were successful in a war with the Amorites, he would, on returning home, sacrifice the first thing that came out of his door. Jephthah overcame the Amorites but, on returning home, his only daughter ran out to meet him. The daughter asked permission to spend two months in the wilderness "bewailing her virginity" before she was sacrificed in fulfillment of Jephthah's promise. Hamlet may be comparing Polonius to Jephthah because both doomed their daughters to not having normal, full lives.

171. **passing.** Surpassingly

172. **pious chanson.** Holy ballad

173. **valanc'd.** Bearded (A valance is a draped fringe.)

174. **beard.** Challenge (To beard someone was to pluck his beard.)

175. **chopine.** A high-heeled shoe

176. **your voice . . . ring.** In Shakespeare's day, a gold coin contained a picture of the monarch with a ring, or circle, around it. If the coin were cracked so that the crack extended within the ring, then the coin was uncurrent, or no longer of value. Boys were used to play women's parts in the theatre until their voices cracked (changed). Hamlet is using the metaphor of the cracked ring to express his hope that the boy, having grown a bit, has not become so old that he no longer has the voice to play female parts.

177. **falc'ners.** In Shakespeare's day it was common for nobles to train falcons to hunt.

178. **straight.** Right away

179. **the million.** The general run of people

180. **'twas caviary to the general.** It was like feeding caviar to ordinary people, who would not appreciate it.

181. **cried in the top of.** Were louder than

182. **well digested.** Well organized

183. **modesty.** Restraint

184. **cunning.** Skill (in using rhetorical flourishes)

185. **sallets.** Salads (tasty bits)

Words For Everyday Use

a • bridge • ment (ə brij´mənt) *n.*, reduction, or curtailment; interruption

al • ti • tude (al´tə to͞od´) *n.*, height

sa • vo • ry (sā´vər ē) *adj.*, pleasing to taste; appetizing

in • dict (in dīt´) *vt.*, charge with committing a crime

af • fec • tion (ə fek´shən) *n.*, fond or tender feeling

400 HAMLET.   O Jephthah,[170] judge of Israel, what a
treasure hadst thou!

POLONIUS.   What a treasure had he, my lord?

HAMLET.   Why—
   "One fair daughter, and no more
405   The which he loved passing[171] well."

POLONIUS.   [*Aside.*] Still on my daughter.

HAMLET.   Am I not i' th' right, old Jephthah?

POLONIUS.   If you call me Jephthah, my lord, I have a
daughter that I love passing well.

410 HAMLET.   Nay, that follows not.

POLONIUS.   What follows then, my lord?

HAMLET.   Why—
   "As by lot, God wot,"
and then, you know,
415   "It came to pass, as most like it was"—
the first row of the pious chanson[172] will show you
more, for look where my <u>abridgment</u> comes.

Enter the PLAYERS, *four or five.*

◄ In what sense is Hamlet "abridged" when the players arrive?

You are welcome, masters, welcome all. I am glad to see
thee well. Welcome, good friends. O, old friend! why,
420 thy face is valanc'd[173] since I saw thee last; com'st thou
to beard[174] me in Denmark? What, my young lady and
mistress! by' lady, your ladyship is nearer to heaven than
when I saw you last, by the <u>altitude</u> of a chopine.[175]
Pray God your voice, like a piece of uncurrent gold, be
425 not crack'd within the ring.[176] Masters, you are all welcome. We'll e'en to't like French falc'ners[177]—fly at any
thing we see; we'll have a speech straight.[178] Come give
us a taste of your quality, come, a passionate speech.

◄ For what does Hamlet ask?

FIRST PLAYER.   What speech, my good lord?

430 HAMLET.   I heard thee speak me a speech once, but it was
never acted, or if it was, not above once; for the play, I
remember, pleas'd not the million,[179] 'twas caviary to
the general,[180] but it was—as I receiv'd it, and others,
whose judgments in such matters cried in the top of[181]
435 mine—an excellent play, well digested[182] in the scenes, set
down with as much modesty[183] as cunning.[184] I remember one said there were no sallets[185] in the lines to make
the matter <u>savory</u>, nor no matter in the phrase that might
<u>indict</u> the author of <u>affection</u>, but call'd it an honest
440 method, as wholesome as sweet, and by very much more

◄ What excellent characteristics did the play recalled by Hamlet have?

186. **more handsome than fine.** More honestly and plainly attractive than fancy

187. **Aeneas . . . Dido.** Aeneas, the hero of the *Aeneid*, an epic poem by the Roman writer Virgil, was a Trojan prince who fled the burning of his city by the Greeks. He was wooed by Dido, the queen of Carthage. Hamlet asks that the actor give a speech from a play in which Aeneas tells Dido about the killing of Priam, the elderly Trojan king.

188. **Pyrrhus.** Pyrrhus, the son of Achilles, took revenge for the death of his father, Achilles. His situation thus parallels Hamlet's.

189. **Hyrcanian beast.** Tiger from Hyrcania, mentioned in the *Aeneid*

190. **sable.** Black

191. **the ominous horse.** The Greeks built a wooden horse, placed soldiers within it, and left the horse outside the gates of the city of Troy. After the Trojans brought the horse inside, the Greeks climbed out of it and sacked the city.

192. **heraldy.** Signs

193. **total gules.** Completely red

194. **trick'd.** Decorated

195. **Bak'd . . . streets.** Pyrrhus's body is covered with the blood of Trojans. The hot streets have baked the blood onto his body so that it resembles a paste.

196. **o'er-sized.** Made to look bigger

197. **coagulate.** Coagulated

198. **carbuncles.** Glowing precious stones

199. **Anon.** Soon

200. **antique.** Ancient

201. **Repugnant to.** Refusing

202. **fell.** Terrible

203. **senseless.** Devoid of sense, unknowing

204. **Ilium.** The citadel or tower of the city of Troy. Ilium was another name for Troy.

205. **Stoops to his base.** Falls to the ground. (his = modern-day its)

206. **declining.** Falling

207. **milky.** White (because of his gray hair)

208. **reverent.** Worthy of reverence

209. **as a painted tyrant.** Like a picture of a tyrant (The word painted, however, has a double meaning, given the painting of Pyrrhus's body with blood.)

210. **a neutral . . . matter.** Someone unconcerned with his purpose or intent

211. **against.** Before

212. **rack.** Clouds

213. **orb.** Sphere, globe

214. **anon.** Soon

215. **rend the region.** Split the air

216. **Cyclops.** One-eyed giants from classical mythology who worked as black-smiths for Vulcan, the god of blacksmiths, of fire, and of volcanoes

217. **Mars.** Roman god of war

218. **for proof eterne.** For everlasting strength

Words For Everyday Use	
parch • ing (pärch´iŋ) *adj.*, drying up with heat	
gore (gôr) *n.*, blood from a wound	
venge • ance (ven´jəns) *n.*, desire to punish another in payment for a wrong	

handsome than fine.[186] One speech in't I chiefly lov'd,
'twas Aeneas' tale to Dido,[187] and thereabout of it espe-
cially when he speaks of Priam's slaughter. If it live in
your memory, begin at this line—let me see, let me see:
445 "The rugged Pyrrhus,[188] like th' Hyrcanian beast[189]—"
'Tis not so, it begins with Pyrrhus:
"The rugged Pyrrhus, he whose sable[190] arms,
Black as his purpose, did the night resemble
When he lay couched in th' ominous horse[191]
450 Hath now this dread and black complexion smear'd
With heraldy[192] more dismal: head to foot
Now is he total gules,[193] horridly trick'd[194]
With blood of fathers, mothers, daughters, sons,
Bak'd and impasted with the <u>parching</u> streets,[195]
455 That lend a tyrannous and a damned light
To their lord's murther. Roasted in wrath and fire,
And thus o'er-sized[196] with coagulate[197] <u>gore</u>,
With eyes like carbuncles,[198] the hellish Pyrrhus
Old grandsire Priam seeks."
460 So proceed you.

POLONIUS.   'Fore God, my lord, well spoken, with good
accent and good discretion.

FIRST PLAYER.   "Anon[199] he finds him
Striking too short at Greeks. His antique[200] sword,
Rebellious to his arm, lies where it falls,
465 Repugnant to[201] command. Unequal match'd,
Pyrrhus at Priam drives, in rage strikes wide,
But with the whiff and wind of his fell[202] sword
Th' unnerved father falls. Then senseless[203] Ilium,[204]
Seeming to feel this blow, with flaming top
470 Stoops to his base,[205] and with a hideous crash
Takes prisoner Pyrrhus' ear; for lo his sword,
Which was declining[206] on the milky[207] head
Of reverent[208] Priam, seem'd i' th' air to stick.
So as a painted tyrant[209] Pyrrhus stood
475 And, like a neutral to his will and matter,[210]
Did nothing.
But as we often see, against[211] some storm,
A silence in the heavens, the rack[212] stand still,
The bold winds speechless, and the orb[213] below
480 As hush as death, anon[214] the dreadful thunder
Doth rend the region;[215] so after Pyrrhus' pause,
A roused <u>vengeance</u> sets him new a-work,
And never did the Cyclops'[216] hammers fall
On Mars's[217] armor forg'd for proof eterne[218]

◀ For what speech
does Hamlet ask?

219. **strumpet.** Unreliable, disreputable woman
220. **Fortune.** Fortune was often personified as a woman.
221. **general synod.** Together in council
222. **fellies.** Pieces of the rim
223. **wheel.** Fortune was often pictured as a wheel whose turning signified the change from good fortune to bad or vice versa.
224. **nave.** Rim
225. **hill of heaven.** In classical mythology, the gods were said to hold councils on top of Mount Olympus.
226. **he's for.** He would prefer
227. **bawdry.** Sexual license
228. **or he sleeps.** Or perhaps he is asleep and hasn't heard this good speech.
229. **Hecuba.** Priam's queen
230. **mobled.** Ruffled around the head. The wearing of ruffled collars was the fashion in Elizabethan England but not in ancient Troy. In Elizabethan theaters, however, it was conventional for actors to wear modern (Elizabethan) and not period costumes.
231. **bisson rheum.** Blinding tears
232. **clout.** Cloth
233. **late.** Not long before
234. **diadem.** Royal crown
235. **lank.** Thin
236. **o'er-teemed.** Worn out
237. **milch.** Milky, flowing with tears
238. **burning eyes of heaven.** Burning in the sense of "angry" and "fiery" as the sun and the stars are
239. **passion.** Deep sorrow
240. **in 's.** In his
241. **bestow'd.** Lodged, taken care of
242. **abstract.** Summary
243. **were.** Had
244. **use.** Treat
245. **their desert.** What they deserve
246. **God's bodkin.** Swearing by the little body of God (the Eucharistic wafer), an oath
247. **scape.** Escape

Words For Everyday Use

mince (mins) *vt.,* cut or chop into little pieces
clam • or (klam´ər) *n.,* loud outcry; uproar
ep • i • taph (ep´ə taf´) *n.,* inscription on a gravestone

485 With less remorse than Pyrrhus' bleeding sword
Now falls on Priam.
Out, out, thou strumpet[219] Fortune![220] All you gods,
In general synod[221] take away her power!
Break all the spokes and fellies[222] from her wheel,[223]
490 And bowl the round nave[224] down the hill of heaven[225]
As low as to the fiends!"

POLONIUS.   This is too long.

HAMLET.   It shall to the barber's with your beard.
Prithee say on, he's for[226] a jig or a tale of bawdry,[227] or
495 he sleeps.[228] Say on, come to Hecuba.[229]

FIRST PLAYER.   "But who, ah woe, had seen the
mobled[230] queen"—

HAMLET.   "The mobled queen"?

POLONIUS.   That's good, "mobled queen" is good.

FIRST PLAYER.   "Run barefoot up and down, threat'ning
the flames
500 With bisson rheum,[231] a clout[232] upon that head
Where late[233] the diadem[234] stood, and for a robe,
About her lank[285] and all o'er-teemed[236] loins,
A blanket, in the alarm of fear caught up
Who this had seen, with tongue in venom steep'd,
505 'Gainst Fortune's state would treason have pronounc'd.
But if the gods themselves did see her then,
When she saw Pyrrhus make malicious sport
In <u>mincing</u> with his sword her husband's limbs,
The instant burst of <u>clamor</u> that she made,
510 Unless things mortal move them not at all,
Would have made milch[237] the burning eyes of heaven,[238]
And passion[239] in the gods."

POLONIUS.   Look whe'er he has not turn'd his color
and has tears in 's[240] eyes. Prithee no more.

515 HAMLET.   'Tis well, I'll have thee speak out the rest of
this soon. Good my lord, will you see the players well
bestow'd?[241] Do you hear, let them be well us'd, for
they are the abstract[242] and brief chronicles of the time.
After your death you were[243] better have a bad <u>epitaph</u>
520 than their ill report while you live.

POLONIUS.   My lord, I will use[244] them according to
their desert.[245]

HAMLET.   God's bodkin,[246] man, much better: use every
man after his desert, and who shall scape[247] whipping?

◄ What emotion
does the actor
express when he tells
about Hecuba
watching the murder
of her husband?

◄ What does
Hamlet say of
actors?

◄ According to
Hamlet, what does
every person deserve,
and what should
every man be given?

248. **the Murther of Gonzago.** Play about the killing of a nobleman
249. **mock him not.** A humorous line. Hamlet suggests that Polonius is so ludicrous that professional actors would feel compelled to make fun of him.
250. **peasant slave.** Serf, someone who has no freedom
251. **monstrous.** Unnatural
252. **conceit.** Artfulness
253. **wann'd.** Became pale
254. **aspect.** Appearance
255. **cue.** Theatrical term designating anything that motivates speech or action
256. **muddy-mettled.** Having a spirit that is soiled or unclear as to its intent
257. **John-a-dreams.** A sleeping person
258. **Unpregnant of.** Not delivering forth or acting upon
259. **pate.** Head

Words
For
Everyday
Use

rogue (rōg) *n.*, idle person of little worth or repute
vis • age (vis´ij) *n.*, face; features
dis • trac • tion (di strak´shən) *n.*, confusion; diversion
cleave (klēv) *vt.*, divide or split

525 Use them after your own honor and dignity—the less they
deserve, the more merit is in your bounty. Take them in.

POLONIUS.   Come, sirs.   *Exit.*

HAMLET.   Follow him, friends, we'll hear a play tomorrow.
                        Exeunt all the PLAYERS *but the First.*
Dost thou hear me, old friend? Can you play "The
530 Murther of Gonzago"?[248]

FIRST PLAYER.   Ay, my lord.

HAMLET.   We'll ha't tomorrow night. You could for need
study a speech of some dozen lines, or sixteen lines,
which I would set down and insert in't, could you not?

535 FIRST PLAYER.   Ay, my lord.

HAMLET.   Very well. Follow that lord, and look you
mock him not.[249]   *Exit* FIRST PLAYER.
My good friends, I'll leave you till night. You are welcome to Elsinore.

540 ROSENCRANTZ.   Good my lord!

HAMLET.   Ay so, God buy to you.
                        Exeunt ROSENCRANTZ *and* GUILDENSTERN.
                        Now I am alone.
O, what a rogue and peasant slave[250] am I!
Is it not monstrous[251] that this player here,
But in a fiction, in a dream of passion,
545 Could force his soul so to his own conceit[252]
That from her working all the visage wann'd[253]
Tears in his eyes, distraction in his aspect,[254]
A broken voice, an' his whole function suiting
With forms to his conceit? And all for nothing,
550 For Hecuba!
What's Hecuba to him, or he to Hecuba
That he should weep for her? What would he do
Had he the motive and the cue[255] for passion
That I have? He would drown the stage with tears,
555 And cleave the general ear with horrid speech,
Make mad the guilty, and appall the free,
Confound the ignorant, and amaze indeed
The very faculties of eyes and ears. Yet I,
A dull and muddy-mettled[256] rascal, peak
560 Like John-a-dreams,[257] unpregnant of[258] my cause,
And can say nothing; no, not for a king,
Upon whose property and most dear life
A damn'd defeat was made. Am I a coward?
Who calls me villain, breaks my pate[259] across,

◄ What does
Hamlet want the
players to perform?
In what way does he
intend to modify
the play?

◄ What makes
Hamlet's comment
about not mocking
Polonius funny?

◄ To whom does
Hamlet compare
himself? Why is
Hamlet upset with
himself? What does
he feel that he
should be doing?

◄ What question
about his own char-
acter does Hamlet
consider?

260. **gives me . . . lungs.** A reference, perhaps, to a gesture made by moving the hand from the throat to the chest in indication that the other person is lying
261. **does me this.** Any of the foregoing list of actions would be enough to move a person who was not a coward to demand satisfaction in the form of apology or a duel.
262. **'swounds.** By God's wounds (an oath)
263. **pigeon-liver'd . . . gall.** It was believed that pigeons were timid because their livers did not secrete gall, also known as choler or yellow bile, the humor believed to cause people to be irritable and quick to anger.
264. **ere.** Before
265. **fatted . . . kites.** Fattened all the kites (birds of prey) in the air
266. **offal.** Entrails
267. **kindless.** Devoid of natural feeling
268. **unpack . . . a-cursing.** Cry about my condition and then curse
269. **drab.** Loose woman
270. **scullion.** Kitchen worker, one who did the lowest or dirtiest work
271. **About.** Turn around
272. **very cunning.** Realistic portrayal
273. **tent . . . quick.** Probe him to his deepest part
274. **blench.** Flinch
275. **Abuses.** Deludes
276. **relative.** Relevant

Words For Everyday Use

mal • e • fac • tion (mal´ə fak´shən) *n.*, wrongdoing; crime

565   Plucks off my beard and blows it in my face,
      Tweaks me by the nose, gives me the lie i' th' throat
      As deep as to the lungs?[260] Who does me this?[261]
      Hah, 'swounds,[262] I should take it; for it cannot be
      But I am pigeon-liver'd, and lack gall[263]
570   To make oppression bitter, or ere[264] this
      I should 'a' fatted all the region kites[265]
      With this slave's offal.[266] Bloody, bawdy villain!
      Remorseless, treacherous, lecherous, kindless[267] villain!
      Why, what an ass am I! This is most brave,
575   That I, the son of a dear father murthered,
      Prompted to my revenge by heaven and hell,
      Must like a whore unpack my heart with words,
      And fall a-cursing[268] like a very drab,[269]
      A scullion.[270] Fie upon't, foh!
580   About,[271] my brains! Hum—I have heard
      That guilty creatures sitting at a play
      Have by the very cunning[272] of the scene
      Been strook so to the soul, that presently
      They have proclaim'd their malefactions:
585   For murther, though it have no tongue, will speak
      With most miraculous organ. I'll have these players
      Play something like the murther of my father
      Before mine uncle. I'll observe his looks,
      I'll tent him to the quick.[273] If 'a do blench,[274]
590   I know my course. The spirit that I have seen
      May be a dev'l, and the dev'l hath power
      T' assume a pleasing shape, yea, and perhaps,
      Out of my weakness and my melancholy,
      As he is very potent with such spirits,
595   Abuses[275] me to damn me. I'll have grounds
      More relative[276] than this—the play's the thing
      Wherein I'll catch the conscience of the king.   *Exit.*

◄ What conclusion does Hamlet come to about himself?

◄ To what does Hamlet compare himself and why?

◄ What action has Hamlet decided to take? Why does he think that he needs to take this action?

◄ What might be true of the ghost, according to Hamlet?

Responding to the Selection

Act II presents events that occur some time after the ghost has appeared to Hamlet. At the end of the preceding act, Hamlet vowed to take revenge, saying "thy commandment all alone shall live / Within the book and volume of my brain." Has Hamlet kept his word in this matter? What has he done in response to the experience with the ghost? What do you think, in general, of Hamlet's response? How do you feel about his actions toward Ophelia? toward Polonius?

Reviewing the Selection

Recalling and Interpreting

1. **R:** What does Polonius send Reynaldo to do?

2. **I:** What do Polonius's instructions to Reynaldo reveal about Polonius's character? about what he thinks his son capable of? about what Polonius himself might have been like as a youth?

3. **R:** Why does Ophelia come to see her father in the middle of act II, scene i? How do both Polonius and Ophelia interpret Hamlet's visit?

4. **I:** Do you agree with Polonius and Ophelia's assessment? Is Hamlet's scene in Ophelia's chamber a sign that he has been driven crazy by love for her, or is it a sign of something else? If something else, then what?

5. **R:** What is the relationship between Rosencrantz and Guildenstern and Hamlet? Why do Claudius and Gertrude bring Rosencrantz and Guildenstern to court?

6. **I:** What similarity exists between the action of the king and queen with regard to Hamlet and the action of Polonius, in the preceding scene, with regard to Laertes?

7. **R:** What is the news from Norway? What does Norway request of Claudius?

8. **I:** In the matter of Fortinbras, does Claudius behave in a wise, kingly manner? Explain.

9. **R:** What suggestion does Polonius make to the king and queen to explain Hamlet's madness? What stratagem does Polonius suggest they employ to test his theory?

10. **I:** What do you think of Polonius's method of testing his hypothesis? Is it moral to do what Polonius suggests that they do?

11. **R:** What does Hamlet call Polonius in scene ii, line 400? Earlier in the scene, what does he tell Polonius that he should do in regard to his daughter?

12. **I:** What reason might Hamlet have for calling Polonius what he does in scene ii, line 400?

13. **R:** What does Hamlet tell Rosencrantz and Guildenstern that Denmark is like? About what does he demand that they be truthful with him?

14. **I:** What is Hamlet's mood in act II? Why does Hamlet not treat his old companions with genuine warmth and welcome?

15. **R:** When speaking to Rosencrantz and Guildenstern, what does Hamlet tell them that the earth and the air are like to him? How does he say that he feels about men and women?

16. **I:** Do you believe that Hamlet really has the opinions that he shares with Rosencrantz and Guildenstern? If so, what is Hamlet's state of mind? If Hamlet does not have these opinions, why does he say these things?

17. **R:** What speech does Hamlet ask the player to recite? How does Hamlet react to hearing the speech?

18. **I:** Why does Hamlet ask that this particular speech be recited? Why does Hamlet react as he does on hearing it?

Synthesizing

19. What do you believe to be Hamlet's state of mind in act II? Give evidence from the text to support your opinion.

20. Why does Hamlet think it necessary to pretend madness? Why does he think it necessary to stage a play to test Claudius? Why does Hamlet delay taking his revenge?

Understanding Literature

1. Foil. A **foil** is a character whose attributes, or characteristics, contrast with and therefore throw into relief the attributes of another character. In what way are Pyrrhus, in the player's speech, and the player himself foils for Hamlet? How do they differ from him?

2. Soliloquy. A **soliloquy** is a speech given by a character who is, or believes himself to be, alone. In this speech the character reveals his or her thoughts to the audience. What opinions does Hamlet express about himself in the soliloquy that ends act II? Why does he think about himself in this manner? Do you agree with Hamlet's assessment of himself? Why, or why not? What does Hamlet resolve to do?

3. Psychodrama. A **psychodrama** is a play that deals with the state of mind of its central character. The term is generally used to describe twentieth-century plays and films that deal with madness or other extreme psychological states. Nonetheless, one can legitimately call *Hamlet* a psychodrama. The Elizabethans believed in an ancient Greek medical theory, called the theory of humors, that described human personality as being determined by the combination of four humors, or fluids produced by the body. These humors were blood, phlegm, yellow bile, and black bile. An excess of blood was believed to create a **sanguine,** or cheerful and lusty personality. An excess of phlegm was said to create a **phlegmatic,** or sluggish, dull personality. An excess of yellow bile, or choler, was said to create a **choleric,** or angry, irritable personality. An excess of black bile was said to create a **melancholic,** or depressive personality. Using this theory of humors, analyze Hamlet's personality. Which humor does Hamlet display in abundance? What evidence can you give from acts I and II to support the theory that Hamlet is meant to typify this type of personality?

4. Protagonist and Antagonist. The **protagonist,** or **main character,** is the central figure in a literary work. An **antagonist** is a character who is working against a protagonist. Who is the protagonist of this play? Who is the major antagonist? In what respects does Hamlet sometimes act as his own antagonist?

ACT III, SCENE i

1. **circumstance.** Roundabout discussion
2. **forward.** Inclined
3. **Niggard of question.** Miserly or stingy in his questioning
4. **assay . . . pastime.** Attempt to interest him in any pastime
5. **o'erraught.** Overreached, passed
6. **edge.** Sharpness, keenness (of desire)

Words For Everyday Use

tur • bu • lent (tʉr´byo͞o lənt) *adj.,* wildly agitated or disturbed; stormy

sound • ed (sound´əd) *adj.,* willing to speak honest feelings

dis • po • si • tion (dis´pə zish´ ən) *n.,* one's nature or temperament

en • treat (en trēt´) *vt.,* ask earnestly; plead

Act III

Enter KING, QUEEN, POLONIUS, OPHELIA, ROSENCRANTZ,
GUILDENSTERN, LORDS.

KING.   An' can you by no drift of circumstance[1]
Get from him why he puts on this confusion,
Grating so harshly all his days of quiet
With turbulent and dangerous lunacy?

5   ROSENCRANTZ.   He does confess he feels himself
        distracted,
But from what cause 'a will by no means speak.

GUILDENSTERN.   Nor do we find him forward[2] to be
        sounded,
But with a crafty madness keeps aloof
When we would bring him on to some confession
10   Of his true state.

QUEEN.   Did he receive you well?

ROSENCRANTZ.   Most like a gentleman.

GUILDENSTERN.   But with much forcing of his disposition.

ROSENCRANTZ.   Niggard of question,[3] but of our demands
Most free in his reply.

QUEEN.   Did you assay him
15   To any pastime?[4]

ROSENCRANTZ.   Madam, it so fell out that certain
        players
We o'erraught[5] on the way; of these we told him,
And there did seem in him a kind of joy
To hear of it. They are here about the court,
20   And as I think, they have already order
This night to play before him.

POLONIUS.   'Tis most true,
And he beseech'd me to entreat your Majesties
To hear and see the matter.

KING.   With all my heart, and it doth much content me
25   To hear him so inclin'd.
Good gentlemen, give him a further edge[6]
And drive his purpose into these delights.

ROSENCRANTZ.   We shall, my lord.
                    Exeunt ROSENCRANTZ *and* GUILDENSTERN.

◄ Why is Claudius
happy that Hamlet is
interested in hearing
the players?

7. **closely.** In secret
8. **Affront.** Meet
9. **espials.** Spies
10. **as he is behav'd.** By observing his behavior
11. **no.** Not
12. **wonted.** Customary
13. **to both your honors.** And so do honor to you both
14. **Gracious.** Your grace
15. **That show . . . color.** That the act may provide a pretext for
16. **loneliness.** Being alone
17. **plast'ring art.** Makeup
18. **most painted.** Deceptive, false
19. **burthen.** Burden
20. **Whether 'tis nobler . . . to suffer.** Whether it is more noble to endure, privately, or within one's own mind
21. **slings.** Devices for throwing stones
22. **take arms against a sea.** Using a weapon to fight against the sea was a traditional metaphor for any futile effort. In an ancient Irish legend, the crazed hero Cuchulain draws his sword, charges into the waves, and drowns.
23. **is heir to.** Inherits (just by being born)
24. **To die . . . dream.** When one sleeps, one's activity does not end but rather is extended into dreams. If death is like a sleep, then perhaps there is, in death, something that corresponds to dreaming. This is the thought that Hamlet considers here.
25. **rub.** Difficulty, obstacle, or impediment

Words For Everyday Use

vis • age (vis´ij) *n.*, face; features
con • sum • ma • tion (kän´sə mā´shən) *n.*, completion; fulfillment
de • vout • ly (di vout´lē) *adv.*, earnestly; sincerely

KING.   Sweet Gertrude, leave us two,
For we have closely[7] sent for Hamlet hither,
30   That he, as 'twere by accident, may here
Affront[8] Ophelia. Her father and myself, lawful espials,[9]
We'll so bestow ourselves that, seeing unseen,
We may of their encounter frankly judge,
And gather by him, as he is behav'd,[10]
35   If't be th' affliction of his love or no[11]
That thus he suffers for.

QUEEN.   I shall obey you.
And for your part, Ophelia, I do wish
That your good beauties be the happy cause
Of Hamlet's wildness. So shall I hope your virtues
40   Will bring him to his wonted[12] way again,
To both your honors.[13]

OPHELIA.   Madam, I wish it may.   *Exit* QUEEN.

POLONIUS.   Ophelia, walk you here.—Gracious,[14] so
     please you,
We will bestow ourselves. [*To* OPHELIA.] Read on this
     book,
That show of such an exercise may color[15]
45   Your loneliness.[16] We are oft to blame in this—
'Tis too much prov'd—that with devotion's visage
And pious action we do sugar o'er
The devil himself.

KING.   [*Aside.*] O, 'tis too true!
How smart a lash that speech doth give my conscience!
50   The harlot's cheek, beautied with plast'ring art,[17]
Is not more ugly to the thing that helps it
Than is my deed to my most painted[18] word.
O heavy burthen![19]

POLONIUS.   I hear him coming. Withdraw, my lord.
                         Exeunt KING *and* POLONIUS.

Enter HAMLET.

55   HAMLET. To be, or not to be, that is the question:
Whether 'tis nobler in the mind to suffer[20]
The slings[21] and arrows of outrageous fortune,
Or to take arms against a sea[22] of troubles,
And by opposing, end them. To die, to sleep—
60   No more, and by a sleep to say we end
The heart-ache and the thousand natural shocks
That flesh is heir to;[23] 'tis a consummation
Devoutly to be wish'd. To die, to sleep—
To sleep, perchance to dream[24]—ay, there's the rub,[25]

26. **shuffled . . . coil.** Evaded life by ridding ourselves of our bodies as a snake sheds its skin, or coil
27. **respect.** Consideration
28. **of so long life.** Last as long as it does (In other words, "There's the consideration that makes us prolong the calamity of our lives.")
29. **contumely.** Rudeness or insulting behavior
30. **of th' unworthy takes.** Receives from unworthy people
31. **quietus.** Discharge (as of a debt)
32. **bare bodkin.** Mere dagger
33. **fardels.** Bundles, burdens
34. **bourn.** Boundary
35. **native hue.** Natural color or inclination
36. **pitch.** Consequence, scope
37. **moment.** Import
38. **With this regard.** Because of this consideration
39. **Nymph.** Young woman (from the young nature goddesses of classical mythology)
40. **orisons.** Prayers (Polonius has previously given Ophelia a book, presumably a book of prayers.)
41. **this many a day.** All this time
42. **remembrances.** Things by which one is remembered, love tokens
43. **aught.** Anything
44. **givers prove unkind.** The phrase is directed at Hamlet, but it is Ophelia who is being unkind here. She refuses to admit (perhaps because her father is watching) that she was the one who put an end to seeing Hamlet, under her father's orders.
45. **honest.** Chaste, virginal, with a pun on honest in the sense of being just
46. **fair.** Physically attractive

Words For Everyday Use

in • so • lence (in´sə ləns) *n.*, boldly disrespectful, impudent manner

res • o • lu • tion (rez´ə lo͞o´shən) *n.*, firm determination

a • wry (ə rī´) *adv.*, away from the correct course

65 For in that sleep of death what dreams may come,
    When we have shuffled off this mortal coil,[26]
    Must give us pause, there's the respect[27]
    That makes calamity of so long life:[28]
    For who would bear the whips and scorns of time,
70 Th' oppressor's wrong, the proud man's contumely,[29]
    The pangs of despis'd love, the law's delay,
    The <u>insolence</u> of office, and the spurns
    That patient merit of th' unworthy takes,[30]
    When he himself might his quietus[31] make
75 With a bare bodkin;[32] who would fardels[33] bear,
    To grunt and sweat under a weary life,
    But that the dread of something after death,
    The undiscover'd country, from whose bourn[34]
    No traveler returns, puzzles the will,
80 And makes us rather bear those ills we have,
    Than fly to others that we know not of?
    Thus conscience does make cowards of us all,
    And thus the native hue[35] of <u>resolution</u>
    Is sicklied o'er with the pale cast of thought,
85 And enterprises of great pitch[36] and moment[37]
    With this regard[38] their currents turn <u>awry</u>,
    And lose the name of action.—Soft you now,
    The fair Ophelia. Nymph,[39] in thy orisons[40]
    Be all my sins rememb'red.

    OPHELIA.   Good my lord,
90 How does your honor for this many a day?[41]

    HAMLET.   I humbly thank you, well, well, well.

    OPHELIA.   My lord, I have remembrances[42] of yours
    That I have longed long to redeliver.
    I pray you now receive them.

    HAMLET.   No, not I,
95 I never gave you aught.[43]

    OPHELIA.   My honor'd lord, you know right well you did,
    And with them words of so sweet breath compos'd
    As made these things more rich. Their perfume lost,
    Take these again, for to the noble mind
100 Rich gifts wax poor when givers prove unkind.[44]
    There, my lord.

    HAMLET.   Ha, ha! are you honest?[45]

    OPHELIA.   My lord?

    HAMLET.   Are you fair?[46]

105 **OPHELIA.**   What means your lordship?

◄ According to Hamlet, what keeps people from killing themselves to escape the burdens of this life?

◄ What, according to Hamlet, keeps people from taking action?

◄ What does Hamlet deny?

◄ What does Hamlet ask Ophelia, and why does she respond as she does?

47. **admit no discourse to.** Not allow conversation with. Hamlet is being ironic. He is obviously hurt by the fact that Ophelia has stopped allowing him to see her, but here he says that a woman who wants to remain chaste should not allow conversation with her beauty. It is very likely that Hamlet is accusing Ophelia of being unchaste, of having a lover, an accusation that he makes explicitly later in the play.

48. **sometime.** In the past

49. **the power . . . proof.** Hamlet is saying that he used to think it paradoxical that true beauty would lead to lack of chastity, but events have led him to think otherwise, that beauty leading to bawdiness is the normal way of the world. Again, the implication is that Ophelia has been unchaste.

50. **I did love you once.** This is a much-debated line. It may be that Hamlet is saying, simply, that at one time he loved Ophelia, or it may be that he is making a veiled reference to a time when he and Ophelia had conjugal relations.

51. **virtue . . . of it.** Because of our basically sinful natures (our old stock), which came about as a result of Adam's eating the fruit of the tree in the garden of Eden, we cannot, by grafting virtue onto ourselves, bear fruit that will not taste of our sinfulness. (inoculate = graft a limb onto a tree; relish = taste)

52. **nunn'ry.** Nunnery, a cloister, or place in which women who have offered their lives to God live in chaste seclusion from the world

53. **indifferent honest.** Reasonably chaste

54. **at my beck.** At my command. Note that Hamlet himself describes revenge-fulness and ambition as sinful.

55. **crawling . . . heaven.** The image recalls Hamlet's earlier description of the body as a snakeskin, or coil, and his earlier reference to the Biblical story of the fall.

56. **arrant knaves.** Erring, wandering rogues

57. **to a nunn'ry.** Where she might escape the temptation to sin that is part of human nature

58. **calumny.** Slander upon her reputation

59. **wilt needs.** Much depends on whether this phrase is interpreted as meaning "will have to" or "will desire to." Both readings are possible.

60. **monsters.** Beasts with horns (i.e., cuckolds). In act I, Hamlet has learned that his mother made his father into a cuckold. Here he suggests that Ophelia would do the same.

61. **make your . . . ignorance.** Pretend that what is really wantonness in you merely appears to be so because of your innocence of such matters.

62. **moe.** More

Words For Everyday Use

dow • ry (dou´rē) *n.*, property that a woman brings to her marriage

HAMLET. That if you be honest and fair, your honesty should admit no discourse to[47] your beauty.

OPHELIA. Could beauty, my lord, have better commerce than with honesty?

110 **HAMLET.** Ay, truly, for the power of beauty will sooner transform honesty from what it is to a bawd than the force of honesty can translate beauty into his likeness. This was sometime[48] a paradox, but now the time gives it proof.[49] I did love you once.[50]

◄ According to Hamlet, what effect does beauty have on a person's honesty, or faithfulness?

115 **OPHELIA.** Indeed, my lord, you made me believe so.

HAMLET. You should not have believ'd me, for virtue cannot so inoculate our old stock but we shall relish of it.[51] I lov'd you not.

OPHELIA. I was the more deceiv'd.

◄ What does Hamlet deny?

120 **HAMLET.** Get thee to a nunn'ry,[52] why wouldst thou be a breeder of sinners? I am myself indifferent honest,[53] but yet I could accuse me of such things that it were better my mother had not borne me: I am very proud, revengeful, ambitious, with more offenses at my beck[54]

125 than I have thoughts to put them in, imagination to give them shape, or time to act them in. What should such fellows as I do crawling between earth and heaven?[55] We are arrant knaves,[56] believe none of us. Go thy ways to a nunn'ry.[57] Where's your father?

◄ What does Hamlet think of people in general? What reason does he give Ophelia for entering a nunnery?

130 **OPHELIA.** At home, my lord.

HAMLET. Let the doors be shut upon him, that he may play the fool no where but in 's own house. Farewell.

OPHELIA. O, help him, you sweet heavens!

HAMLET. If thou dost marry, I'll give thee this plague

135 for thy <u>dowry</u>: be thou as chaste as ice, as pure as snow, thou shalt not escape calumny.[58] Get thee to a nunn'ry, farewell. Or if thou wilt needs[59] marry, marry a fool, for wise men know well enough what monsters[60] you make of them. To a nunn'ry, go, and quickly too. Farewell.

140 **OPHELIA.** Heavenly powers, restore him!

HAMLET. I have heard of your paintings, well enough. God hath given you one face, and you make yourselves another. You jig and amble, and you lisp, you nickname God's creatures and make your wantonness your igno-

145 rance.[61] Go to, I'll no more on't, it hath made me mad. I say we will have no moe[62] marriage. Those that are

◄ What are Hamlet's feelings about marriage? When Hamlet says that one who is already married shall die, to whom is he referring?

63. **expectation.** Because Hamlet was expected to become king
64. **music.** Musical
65. **out of time.** Not in rhythm
66. **blown youth.** Youth that has blossomed
67. **blasted with ecstasy.** Blighted by madness
68. **his melancholy . . . brood.** In extreme sadness, or melancholy, Hamlet broods upon something as a bird sits on her eggs.
69. **doubt.** Suspect
70. **disclose.** Outcome
71. **tribute.** At the time when the play is set, England is a subject country and must make payments, or tribute, to Denmark.
72. **Haply.** Perhaps
73. **From fashion of himself.** Apart from his usual nature
74. **round.** Direct, but with a secondary meaning of indirect (roundabout) that emphasizes Polonius's habitual circuitousness
75. **in the ear.** In earshot
76. **find him not.** Cannot uncover or disclose what he is hiding

Tell Ophelia that to pretend she is praying. Hamlet enters to speak. Gives a thoay on his thoughts committing suicide. He sees Ophelia + she wants to return some gifts to Hamlet.

| Words For Everyday Use | **var • i • a • ble** (ver´ ē ə bəl) *adj.*, changeable; varied |

married already (all but one) shall live, the rest shall
keep as they are. To a nunn'ry, go. *Exit.*

OPHELIA. O, what a noble mind is here o'erthrown!
150 The courtier's, soldier's, scholar's, eye, tongue, sword,
Th' expectation[63] and rose of the fair state
The glass of fashion and the mould of form,
Th' observ'd of all observers, quite, quite down!
And I, of ladies most deject and wretched,
155 That suck'd the honey of his music[64] vows,
Now see that noble and most sovereign reason
Like sweet bells jangled out of time,[65] and harsh;
That unmatch'd form and stature of blown youth[66]
Blasted with ecstasy.[67] O, woe is me
160 T' have seen what I have seen, see what I see!
OPHELIA withdraws.

Enter KING *and* POLONIUS.

KING. Love? his affections do not that way tend,
Nor what he spake, though it lack'd form a little,
Was not like madness. There's something in his soul
O'er which his melancholy sits on brood,[68]
165 And I do doubt[69] the hatch and the disclose[70]
Will be some danger; which for to prevent,
I have in quick determination
Thus set it down: he shall with speed to England
For the demand of our neglected tribute.[71]
170 Haply[72] the seas, and countries different,
With variable objects, shall expel
This something-settled matter in his heart,
Whereon his brains still beating puts him thus
From fashion of himself.[73] What think you on't?

175 **POLONIUS.** It shall do well; but yet do I believe
The origin and commencement of his grief
Sprung from neglected love. *OPHELIA comes forward.*
How now, Ophelia?
You need not tell us what Lord Hamlet said,
We heard it all. My lord, do as you please,
180 But if you hold it fit, after the play
Let his queen-mother all alone entreat him
To show his grief. Let her be round[74] with him,
And I'll be plac'd (so please you) in the ear[75]
Of all their conference. If she find him not,[76]
185 To England send him, or confine him where
Your wisdom best shall think.

KING. It shall be so.
Madness in great ones must not unwatch'd go. *Exeunt.*

Margin notes:

◄ How does Ophelia respond to Hamlet's harsh rejection?

◄ Does Claudius believe that Hamlet is crazy? Explain.

◄ Why and on what pretext does Claudius decide to send Hamlet to England?

◄ What plan does Polonius have for discovering the true cause of Hamlet's distraction?

Handwritten notes: H. goes England, knows something else is afflicting his soul. King asks Gert. to leave. So that he + Pol. can observe mtg between Hamlet + Ophelia

ACT III, SCENE ii

1. **had as lief.** Would as soon
2. **use all.** Act in all ways
3. **robustious, periwig-pated.** Rough, bewigged
4. **passion.** A speech expressing deep emotion, such as grief or sorrow
5. **totters.** Tatters
6. **groundlings.** Theater goers who stood on the ground in front of the stage and paid very little for their tickets; common people
7. **are capable of.** Can understand
8. **Termagant.** A supposed Moslem deity or violent person
9. **Herod.** Ruler of Judea in the time of Christ and stock ranting figure in plays
10. **from.** Contrary to
11. **mirror . . . nature.** This is often taken to be an expression of the Aristotelian theory of mimesis, or art as imitation. In Shakespeare, however, mirrors are often associated with idealized representation. Thus a play represents reality, but that reality is heightened by the playwright's choices—his deliberate abstracting and marshalling of particulars.
12. **come tardy off.** Be done badly
13. **unskillful.** Those who lack skill in making judgments
14. **in your allowance.** In what you will allow, or admit
15. **nature's journeymen.** Ordinary hired workmen, as opposed to skilled craftsmen
16. **abominably.** In a bestial manner, like animals
17. **indifferently.** Reasonably well
18. **clowns.** Rude, common persons
19. **of.** Some of

Words For Everyday Use

be • get (bē get´) *vt.*, bring into being
tem • per • ance (tem´pər əns) *n.*, self-restraint; moderation
war • rant (wôr´ənt) *vt.*, deserve
dis • cre • tion (di skresh´ən) *n.*, good judgment
ju • di • cious (jōō dish´əs) *adj.*, showing wise judgment
pro • fane • ly (prō fān´lē) *adv.*, showing disrespect for sacred things

H. gives some last minute instructions to the players.

SCENE ii

Enter HAMLET *and three of the* PLAYERS.

HAMLET. Speak the speech, I pray you, as I pronounc'd
it to you, trippingly on the tongue, but if you mouth it,
as many of our players do, I had as lief[1] the towncrier
spoke my lines. Nor do not saw the air too much with
5   your hand, thus, but use all[2] gently, for in the very tor-
rent, tempest, and, as I may say, whirlwind of your passion, you must acquire and <u>beget</u> a <u>temperance</u> that may
give it smoothness. O, it offends me to the soul to hear a
robustious, periwig-pated fellow[3] tear a passion[4] to
10   totters,[5] to very rags, to spleet the ears of the
groundlings,[6] who for the most part are capable of[7]
nothing but inexplicable dumb shows and noise. I
would have such a fellow whipt for o'erdoing
Termagant,[8] it out-Herods[9] Herod, pray you avoid it.

15   **FIRST PLAYER.** I <u>warrant</u> your honor.

HAMLET. Be not too tame neither, but let your own
<u>discretion</u> be your tutor. Suit the action to the word,
the word to the action, with this special observance,
that you o'erstep not the modesty of nature: for any
20   thing so o'erdone is from[10] the purpose of playing,
whose end, both at the first and now, was and is, to
hold as 'twere the mirror up to nature:[11] to show virtue
her feature, scorn her own image, and the very age and
body of the time his form and pressure. Now this over-
25   done, or come tardy off,[12] though it makes the unskillful[13] laugh, cannot but make the <u>judicious</u> grieve; the
censure of which one must in your allowance[14] o'erweigh
a whole theatre of others. O, there be players that I have
seen play—and heard others praise, and that highly—not
30   to speak it <u>profanely</u>, that, neither having th' accent of
Christians nor the gait of Christian, pagan, nor man,
have so strutted and bellow'd that I have thought some
of Nature's journeymen[15] had made men, and not made
them well, they imitated humanity so abominably.[16]

35   **FIRST PLAYER.** I hope we have reform'd that indifferently[17] with us, sir.

HAMLET. O, reform it altogether. And let those that
play your clowns[18] speak no more than is set down for
them, for there be of[19] them that will themselves laugh
40   to set on some quantity of barren spectators to laugh

◀ What does
Hamlet want the
actors to avoid
doing?

*He confides
in Horatio
about his
plan.*

*Horatio
agrees to
watch the
King's reaction*

◀ According to
Hamlet, what is "the
purpose of playing"?

20. **uses it.** So acts
21. **just.** 1. Truthful; 2. well-made
22. **conversation.** Interactions
23. **cop'd withal.** Dealt with
24. **let . . . pomp.** Let people who fawn and use sweet words act like dogs, licking the hands of the powerful
25. **pregnant.** Telling, revealing
26. **thrift.** Profit
27. **distinguish her election.** Choose for herself which men to pick out
28. **seal'd . . . herself.** Placed a seal on you, marking you as her (his soul's) property, as a king's property is marked with his seal
29. **buffets.** Blows
30. **blood.** Passion
31. **co-meddled.** Commingled
32. **Something . . . this.** But I've said too much about this
33. **prithee.** Pray of thee, request
34. **the very . . . soul.** With your utmost powers of observation

too, though in the mean time some necessary question
of the play be then to be consider'd. That's villainous,
and shows a most pitiful ambition in the fool that uses
it.[20] Go make you ready.   *Exeunt* PLAYERS.

Enter POLONIUS, GUILDENSTERN, *and* ROSENCRANTZ.

45   How now, my lord? Will the King hear this piece of
     work?

POLONIUS.   And the Queen too, and that presently.

HAMLET.   Bid the players make haste.   *Exit* POLONIUS.
Will you two help to hasten them?

50   ROSENCRANTZ.   Ay, my lord.   *Exeunt they two.*

HAMLET.   What ho, Horatio!

Enter HORATIO.

HORATIO.   Here, sweet lord, at your service.

HAMLET.   Horatio, thou art e'en as just[21] a man
As e'er my conversation[22] cop'd withal.[23]

55   HORATIO.   O my dear lord—

HAMLET.   Nay, do not think I flatter,
For what advancement may I hope from thee
That no revenue hast but thy good spirits
To feed and clothe thee? Why should the poor be
     flatter'd?
No, let the candied tongue lick absurd pomp,[24]
60   And crook the pregnant[25] hinges of the knee
Where thrift[26] may follow fawning. Dost thou hear?
Since my dear soul was mistress of her choice
And could of men distinguish her election[27]
Sh' hath seal'd thee for herself,[28] for thou hast been

◄ *What characteris-
tics in Horatio does
Hamlet admire?*

65   As one in suff'ring all that suffers nothing,
A man that Fortune's buffets[29] and rewards
Hast ta'en with equal thanks; and blest are those
Whose blood[30] and judgment are so well co-meddled[31]
That they are not a pipe for Fortune's finger
70   To sound what stop she please. Give me that man
That is not passion's slave, and I will wear him
In my heart's core, ay, in my heart of heart,
As I do thee. Something too much of this.[32]
There is a play tonight before the King,
75   One scene of it comes near the circumstance
Which I have told thee of my father's death.
I prithee,[33] when thou seest that act afoot
Even with the very comment of thy soul[34]

◄ *What does
Hamlet want Horatio
to do?*

35. **occulted.** Hidden

36. **unkennel.** Drive from its den

37. **Vulcan's stithy.** The forge of Vulcan, blacksmith of the gods in classical mythology

38. **In censure . . . seeming.** In estimation of his appearance

39. **be.** Pretend to be

40. **the chameleon's dish.** The air, supposedly all that chameleons needed to live upon

41. **Julius . . . me.** At the time when Shakespeare wrote Hamlet, his play *Julius Cæsar* was in production. This speech is a sort of advertisement for the other play and a kind of in joke. In *Cæsar*, the character Brutus, like Hamlet, has a mortal action (killing Cæsar) unwillingly thrust upon him. It is likely that the same actors who were to play Polonius and Hamlet were also playing, respectively, Cæsar and Brutus.

42. **capital a calf.** The word *capital* is a pun. It can mean "excellent" or "involving death," but it also refers to the fact that Cæsar was killed on the steps of the Roman capitol. A calf was often the animal of choice for sacrifice.

43. **metal more attractive.** A more magnetic metal; Hamlet is saying he is drawn more powerfully to sit by Ophelia than by his mother.

Words For Everyday Use

riv • et (riv´it) *vi.*, fix or hold the attention

Observe my uncle. If his occulted[35] guilt
80   Do not itself unkennel[36] in one speech,
It is a damned ghost that we have seen,
And my imaginations are as foul
As Vulcan's stithy.[37] Give him heedful note
For I mine eyes will <u>rivet</u> to his face,
85   And after we will both our judgments join
In censure of his seeming.[38]

HORATIO.   Well, my lord.
If 'a steal aught the whilst this play is playing
And scape detecting, I will pay the theft.

Sound a flourish. Danish march. Enter Trumpets and Kettle drums, KING, QUEEN, POLONIUS, OPHELIA, ROSENCRANTZ, GUILDENSTERN, *and other* LORDS *attendant, with his* GUARD *carrying torches.*

HAMLET.   They are coming to the play. I must be[39] idle;
90   Get you a place.

KING.   How fares our cousin Hamlet?

HAMLET.   Excellent, i' faith, of the chameleon's dish:[40] I eat the air, promise-cramm'd—you cannot feed capons so.

KING.   I have nothing with this answer, Hamlet, these
95   words are not mine.

HAMLET.   No, nor mine now. [*To* POLONIUS.] My lord, you play'd once i' th' university, you say?

POLONIUS.   That did I, my lord, and was accounted a good actor.

100 HAMLET.   What did you enact?

POLONIUS.   I did enact Julius Caesar. I was kill'd i' th' Capitol; Brutus kill'd me.[41]

HAMLET.   It was a brute part of him to kill so capital a calf[42] there. Be the players ready?

105 ROSENCRANTZ.   Ay, my lord, they stay upon your patience.

QUEEN.   Come hither, my dear Hamlet, sit by me.

HAMLET.   No, good mother, here's metal more attractive.[43]
                             Lying down at OPHELIA*'s feet.*

POLONIUS.   [*To the* KING.] O ho, do you mark that?

HAMLET.   Lady, shall I lie in your lap?

110 OPHELIA.   No, my lord.

HAMLET.   I mean, my head upon your lap?

OPHELIA.   Ay, my lord.

[handwritten margin note: Play → the Mouse trap]

44. **country matters.** Indecencies
45. **nothing.** No thing, the word *thing* being a slang term for the organs of reproduction
46. **your . . . jig-maker.** The best maker of amusements such as jigs
47. **sables.** Rich furs (Hamlet is saying two things at once. On the one hand, he is saying that he will forget mourning clothes and start wearing fancy furs. On the other hand, the word sable, in heraldry, meant the color black, and so he is also saying that he will persist in wearing mourning clothes.)
48. **'a must . . . thinking on.** If a man doesn't build churches (or undertake such lavish good deeds), he will be forgotten.
49. **hobby-horse.** Costume in the form of a horse worn by Morris dancers. The hobby-horse was associated with lewdness.
50. **For O . . . forgot.** Refrain from a popular ballad that is now lost, one that possibly dealt with hobby-horses being banned because of the lewdness associated with them.
51. **dumb show.** Pantomime
52. **protestation.** Solemn oath
53. **Anon.** Soon
54. **miching mallecho.** Stealthy misdeed
55. **Belike.** Most likely
56. **argument.** A word combining the meanings of plot, theme, and summary
57. **keep counsel.** Keep a secret

| **Words For Everyday Use** | **con • dole** (kən dōl´) *vi.,* express sympathy |

HAMLET. Do you think I meant country matters?[44]

OPHELIA. I think nothing, my lord.

115 HAMLET. That's a fair thought to lie between maids' legs.

OPHELIA. What is, my lord?

HAMLET. Nothing.[45]

OPHELIA. You are merry, my lord.

HAMLET. Who, I?

120 OPHELIA. Ay, my lord.

HAMLET O God, your only jig-maker.[46] What should a
man do but be merry, for look you how cheerfully my
mother looks, and my father died within 's two hours.

OPHELIA. Nay, 'tis twice two months, my lord.

125 HAMLET. So long? Nay then let the dev'l wear black,
for I'll have a suit of sables.[47] O heavens, die two
months ago, and not forgotten yet? Then there's hope a
great man's memory may outlive his life half a year,
but, by'r lady, 'a must build churches then, or else shall
130 'a suffer not thinking on,[48] with the hobby-horse,[49] whose
epitaph is, "For O, for O, the hobby-horse is forgot."[50]

The trumpets sounds. Dumb show[51] follows.

*Enter a King and a Queen very lovingly, the Queen embrac-
ing him and he her. She kneels and makes show of protestation[52] unto him. He takes her up and declines his head upon
her neck. He lies him down upon a bank of flowers. She,
seeing him asleep, leaves him. Anon[53] come in another
man, takes off his crown, kisses it, pours poison in the
sleeper's ears, and leaves him. The Queen returns, finds the
King dead, makes passionate action. The pois'ner with some
three or four mutes come in again, seem to <u>condole</u> with her.
The dead body is carried away. The pois'ner woos the Queen
with gifts; she seems harsh and unwilling awhile, but in the
end accepts love.*   *Exeunt.*

OPHELIA. What means this, my lord?

HAMLET. Marry, this' miching mallecho,[54] it means
mischief.

135 OPHELIA. Belike[55] this show imports the argument[56] of
the play.

Enter PROLOGUE.

HAMLET. We shall know by this fellow. The players
cannot keep counsel,[57] they'll tell all.

◄ What example
does Hamlet give to
back up his assertion
that people should
strive to be merry?

◄ According to
Hamlet, there is hope
that people might
remember a great
man for how long?

◄ What real event
does the pantomime
at the beginning of
the play recall?

58. **naught.** Of no consequence, unimportant (Hamlet is making indecent remarks and so is being irrelevant and frivolous.)

59. **mark.** Attend to, as one might attend to the mark, or target, of an arrow

60. **posy . . . ring.** Verse inscribed on a ring or a children's rhyme chanted while dancing in a circle

61. **Phoebus' cart.** The chariot of Phoebus Apollo, the sun god

62. **Neptune's salt wash.** The sea, ruled in classical mythology by the god Neptune

63. **Tellus' orbed ground.** The earth, after the earth goddess Tellus

64. **Hymen.** Goddess of marriage

65. **comutual.** Mutually

66. **distrust.** Fear

67. **Discomfort.** Distress, make uncomfortable

68. **For . . . extremity.** In women, fear and love are joined and are either entirely present or entirely absent.

69. **operant powers.** Vital energies

70. **leave to do.** Stop carrying out

71. **None . . . first.** The only women who marry a second husband are those who have killed their first husbands.

Words For Everyday Use

clem • en • cy (klem´ən sē) *n.*, forbearance; leniency; mercy

sheen (shēn) *n.*, brightness; luster

OPHELIA.   Will 'a tell us what this show meant?

140 HAMLET.   Ay, or any show that you will show him. Be
not you asham'd to show, he'll not shame to tell you
what it means.

OPHELIA.   You are naught,[58] you are naught. I'll mark[59]
the play.

145 PROLOGUE.   For us, and for our tragedy,
          Here stooping to your <u>clemency</u>,
          We beg your hearing patiently.   *Exit.*

HAMLET.   Is this a prologue, or the posy of a ring?[60]

OPHELIA.   'Tis brief, my lord.

150 HAMLET.   As woman's love.

Enter two PLAYERS, KING *and* QUEEN.

PLAYER KING.   Full thirty times hath Phoebus' cart[61]
          gone round
Neptune's salt wash[62] and Tellus' orbed ground,[63]
And thirty dozen moons with borrowed <u>sheen</u>
About the world have times twelve thirties been,
155 Since love our hearts and Hymen[64] did our hands
Unite comutual[65] in most sacred bands.

PLAYER QUEEN.   So many journeys may the sun and
          moon
Make us again count o'er ere love be done!
But woe is me, you are so sick of late,
160 So far from cheer and from your former state,
That I distrust you. Yet though I distrust,[66]
Discomfort[67] you, my lord, it nothing must,
For women's fear and love hold quantity,
In neither aught, or in extremity.[68]
165 Now what my love is, proof hath made you know,
And as my love is siz'd, my fear is so.
Where love is great, the littlest doubts are fear;
Where little fears grow great, great love grows there.

PLAYER KING.   Faith, I must leave thee, love, and shortly
          too
170 My operant powers[69] their functions leave to do,[70]
And thou shalt live in this fair world behind,
Honor'd, belov'd, and haply one as kind
For husband shalt thou—

PLAYER QUEEN.   O, confound the rest!
Such love must needs be treason in my breast.
175 In second husband let me be accurs'd!
None wed the second but who kill'd the first.[71]

◄ What, according
to Hamlet, is as brief
as this prologue?

◄ How long have
the king and queen
been married?

◄ What does the
queen indicate that
she would never do?

72. **wormwood.** Bitterness, from the name of a bitter herb
73. **base respects of thrift.** Low considerations of profit and advantage
74. **enactures.** Enacting, carrying out (The king is saying that strong emotions, once expressed, spend and thus destroy themselves.)
75. **slender accident.** A slight occurrence or minor change
76. **for aye.** Forever
77. **favorite.** Favored person, close companion
78. **hitherto.** Up until now
79. **who . . . friend.** A person who doesn't need friends will find that many people want to be his or her friend.
80. **Directly seasons.** At once makes
81. **devices still.** Strategies always
82. **anchor's cheer.** The meager food and drink of an anchorite, a religious person who lives a life of seclusion from the world
83. **opposite . . . joy.** Opposing force that wipes joy from the face

HAMLET.   [*Aside.*] That's wormwood![72]

PLAYER QUEEN.   The instances that second marriage move
Are base respects of thrift,[73] but none of love.
180 A second time I kill my husband dead,
When second husband kisses me in bed.

◄ To what does the queen compare remarriage after the death of a spouse?

PLAYER KING.   I do believe you think what now you speak
But what we do determine, oft we break.
Purpose is but the slave to memory,
185 Of violent birth, but poor validity,
Which now, the fruit unripe, sticks on the tree,
But fall unshaken when they mellow be.
Most necessary 'tis that we forget
To pay ourselves what to ourselves is debt.
190 What to ourselves in passion we propose,
The passion ending, doth the purpose lose.
The violence of either grief or joy
Their own enactures[74] with themselves destroy.
Where joy most revels, grief doth most lament;
195 Grief joys, joy grieves, on slender accident.[75]
This world is not for aye,[76] nor 'tis not strange
That even our loves should with our fortunes change:
For 'tis a question left us yet to prove,
Whether love lead fortune, or else fortune love.
200 The great man down, you mark his favorite[77] flies,
The poor advanc'd makes friends of enemies.
And hitherto[78] doth love on fortune tend,
For who not needs shall never lack a friend,[79]
And who in want a hollow friend doth try,
205 Directly seasons[80] him his enemy.
But orderly to end where I begun,
Our wills and fates do so contrary run
That our devices still[81] are overthrown,
Our thoughts are ours, their ends none of our own:
210 So think thou wilt no second husband wed
But die thy thoughts when thy first lord is dead.

◄ Why doesn't the king believe the queen when she says that she will not remarry?

PLAYER QUEEN.   Nor earth to me give food, nor heaven light,
Sport and repose lock from me day and night,
To desperation turn my trust and hope,
215 An anchor's cheer[82] in prison be my scope!
Each opposite that blanks the face of joy[83]
Meet what I would have well and it destroy!

84. **fain . . . beguile.** Eagerly would I pass
85. **mischance.** Misfortune
86. **twain.** Two
87. **methinks.** I think
88. **Mouse-trap.** Hamlet is using the play to trap Claudius
89. **tropically.** As a trope, or figure of speech, with a pun on trope/trap
90. **murther.** Murder
91. **anon.** Shortly
92. **free souls.** Untroubled consciences
93. **Let . . . unwrung.** Let the galled old horse wince; our withers (the top, back part of a horse, between the shoulder blades) are not pressed too tightly.
94. **chorus.** In ancient drama, the chorus danced and chanted summaries or commentaries on the action in the scenes of the body of the play.
95. **I could . . . dallying.** If your activity with your lover were a puppet show, I could act as a chorus to that show, explaining what is going on between you (with an indecent pun on the word *puppets,* a slang term referring to the genitals).
96. **keen.** Sharp
97. **mistake your husbands.** Cheat on, or take another in place of, your husbands
98. **the croaking . . . revenge.** Hamlet quotes a line from another play.
99. **Confederate season.** The occasion, or time, serving as a confederate, or accomplice
100. **else.** There being

Both here and hence pursue me lasting strife,
If once I be a widow, ever I be a wife!

220 HAMLET.   If she should break it now!

PLAYER KING.   'Tis deeply sworn. Sweet, leave me here a while,
My spirits grow dull, and fain I would beguile[84]
The tedious day with sleep.   *Sleeps.*

PLAYER QUEEN.   Sleep rock thy brain,
And never come mischance[85] between us twain![86] *Exit.*

225 HAMLET.   Madam, how like you this play?

QUEEN.   The lady doth protest too much, methinks.[87]

HAMLET.   O but she'll keep her word.

KING.   Have you heard the argument? is there no offense in't?

230 HAMLET.   No, no, they do but jest, poison in jest—no offense i' th' world.

KING.   What do you call the play?

HAMLET.   "The Mouse-trap."[88] Marry, how? tropically:[89] this play is the image of a murther[90] done in Vienna;
235 Gonzago is the duke's name, his wife, Baptista. You shall see anon.[91] 'Tis a knavish piece of work, but what of that? Your Majesty, and we that have free souls,[92] it touches us not. Let the gall'd jade winch, our withers are unwrung.[93]

Enter LUCIANUS.

240 This is one Lucianus, nephew to the king.

OPHELIA.   You are as good as a chorus,[94] my lord.

HAMLET.   I could interpret between you and your love, if I could see the puppets dallying.[95]

OPHELIA.   You are keen,[96] my lord, you are keen.

245 HAMLET.   It would cost you a groaning to take off mine edge.

OPHELIA.   Still better, and worse.

HAMLET.   So you mistake your husbands.[97] Begin, murtherer, leave thy damnable faces and begin. Come, the
250 croaking raven doth bellow for revenge.[98]

LUCIANUS.   Thoughts black, hands apt, drugs fit, and time agreeing,
Confederate season,[99] else[100] no creature seeing,

◄ What does Gertrude think about the queen in the play?

◄ What is Claudius worried about?

◄ Why does Hamlet call the play "The Mouse-Trap"?

◄ Does Hamlet actually believe that Claudius has a "free" or unburdened soul?

◄ Of what is Hamlet accusing Ophelia?

101. **midnight weeds collected.** Poisonous weeds gathered at midnight and therefore (or so the superstitious belief was in Shakespeare's day) more powerful
102. **Hecat's ban.** The curse of Hecate, goddess of witchcraft
103. **thrice.** Three times. The number three was considered a magical number.
104. **usurps.** Takes over, said of one who unlawfully takes the place of a king or of another person of high station
105. **false fire.** Blanks discharged by firearms
106. **Give o'er.** Stop
107. **strooken.** Stricken
108. **hart ungalled.** Deer untouched
109. **a forest of feathers.** Feathers were worn in the caps of actors playing the roles of young gallants.
110. **turn Turk.** Betray, like a Christian turning to the Turkish (Moslem) religion
111. **two . . . shoes.** Roses worn by actors to cover the ties of their shoes
112. **Fellowship.** Partnership
113. **a cry of players.** Humorous epithet for an acting troupe. A cry was a pack of hounds.
114. **Damon.** Friend, after the true
115. **dismantled.** Deprived
116. **Jove.** In Roman myth, the king of the gods.
117. **pajock.** Word of uncertain meaning, perhaps a nonsense word
118. **rhym'd.** In Shakespeare's day, the words *was* and *ass* rhymed
119. **for a thousand pound.** As though it were worth a thousand pounds (a pound is a unit of money).
120. **Didst perceive.** Did you see?
121. **comedy.** Technically, a comedy was any play with a happy outcome. The outcome of this one has been happy for Hamlet
122. **belike.** It is likely
123. **perdy.** An oath combining the Old French words *par*, or by and *dé*, or God.

Words For Everyday Use

dire (dīr) *adj.*, having dreadful consequences
prop • er • ty (dīr) *n.*, quality; characteristic
re • cord • er (ri kôrd´ər) *n.*, wind instrument with eight finger holes

Thou mixture rank, of midnight weeds collected,[101]
With Hecat's ban[102] thrice[103] blasted, thrice infected,
255 Thy natural magic and <u>dire property</u>
On wholesome life usurps[104] immediately.

Pours the poison in his ears.

HAMLET.   'A poisons him i' th' garden for his estate.
His name's Gonzago, the story is extant, and written in
very choice Italian. You shall see anon how the murtherer gets the love of Gonzago's wife.

260 OPHELIA.   The King rises.

HAMLET.   What, frighted with false fire?[105]

QUEEN.   How fares my lord?

POLONIUS.   Give o'er[106] the play.

265 KING.   Give me some light. Away!

POLONIUS.   Lights, lights, lights!

Exeunt all but HAMLET and HORATIO.

HAMLET.   "Why, let the strooken[107] deer go weep,
            The hart ungalled[108] play,
         For some must watch while some must sleep,
270   Thus runs the world away."
Would not this, sir, and a forest of feathers[109]—if the
rest of my fortunes turn Turk[110] with me—with two
Provincial roses on my raz'd shoes[111], get me a fellowship[112] in a cry of players?[113]

275 HORATIO.   Half a share.

HAMLET.   A whole one, I.
            "For thou dost know, O Damon[114] dear,
               This realm dismantled[115] was
            Of Jove[116] himself, and now reigns here
280   A very, very"—pajock.[117]

HORATIO.   You might have rhym'd.[118]

HAMLET.   O good Horatio, I'll take the ghost's word for
a thousand pound.[119] Didst perceive?[120]

HORATIO.   Very well, my lord.

285 HAMLET.   Upon the talk of the pois'ning?

HORATIO.   I did very well note him.

HAMLET.   Ah, ha! Come, some music! Come, the
<u>recorders</u>!
            For if the King like not the comedy,[121]
290   Why then belike[122] he likes it not, perdy.[123]
Come, some music!

◀ Why does the king rise?

◀ What did Horatio and Hamlet both perceive?

124. **voutsafe.** Vouchsafe; grant
125. **marvelous distemp'red.** Extremely out of sorts
126. **choler.** Anger
127. **more richer.** Richer
128. **signify.** Tell
129. **purgation.** Purging (of sickness or of sin). The word recalls Hamlet's dead father who is in purgatory.
130. **put . . . affair.** Make your speech more orderly, and do not run so wildly away from the topic I have raised with you.
131. **pardon.** Permission to go
132. **hath strook.** Has stricken
133. **admiration.** Bewilderment
134. **stonish.** Astonish
135. **ere.** Before
136. **were . . . mother.** Even if she were so foul as to be ten times worse than what our mother is.

Words
For
Everyday
Use

im • part (im pärt´) *vi.,* make known; tell

Enter ROSENCRANTZ *and* GUILDENSTERN.

King is upset.

GUILDENSTERN.   Good my lord, voutsafe[124] me a word with you.

HAMLET.   Sir, a whole history.

295   GUILDENSTERN.   The King, sir—

HAMLET.   Ay, sir, what of him?

GUILDENSTERN.   Is in his retirement marvelous distemp'red.[125]

HAMLET.   With drink, sir?

300   GUILDENSTERN.   No, my lord, with choler.[126]

◄ *What is King Claudius feeling?*

HAMLET.   Your wisdom should show itself more richer[127] to signify[128] this to the doctor, for, for me to put him to his purgation[129] would perhaps plunge him into more choler.

305   GUILDENSTERN.   Good my lord, put your discourse into some frame, and start not so wildly from my affair.[130]

HAMLET.   I am tame, sir. Pronounce.

GUILDENSTERN.   The Queen, your mother, in most great affliction of spirit, hath sent me to you.

◄ *Who has sent for Hamlet?*

310   HAMLET.   You are welcome.

GUILDENSTERN.   Nay, good my lord, this courtesy is not of the right breed. If it shall please you to make me a wholesome answer, I will do your mother's commandement; if not, your pardon[131] and my return shall be the
315   end of my business.

HAMLET.   Sir, I cannot.

ROSENCRANTZ.   What, my lord?

HAMLET.   Make you a wholesome answer—my wit's diseas'd. But, sir, such answer as I can make, you shall
320   command, or rather, as you say, my mother. Therefore no more, but to the matter: my mother, you say—

ROSENCRANTZ.   Then thus she says: your behavior hath strook[132] her into amazement and admiration.[133]

◄ *What is Gertrude's reaction to Hamlet's behavior?*

HAMLET.   O wonderful son, that can so stonish[134] a
325   mother! But is there no sequel at the heels of this mother's admiration? Impart.

ROSENCRANTZ.   She desires to speak with you in her closet ere[135] you go to bed.

HAMLET.   We shall obey, were she ten times our mother.[136]

137. **pickers and stealers.** Hands

138. **distemper.** Ill temper

139. **bar . . . liberty.** Do not allow yourself sufficient freedom (although there is also, perhaps, a hint of threat that Hamlet's action might land him in prison)

140. **While . . . grows.** "While the grass grows, the trees are green." A proverb

141. **musty.** Old

142. **go about . . . toil?** Why do you go around and try to get on my windward side as if you wished to drive me into a net? A hunting expression

143. **if my . . . unmannerly.** If my dutiful attentions to you seem too bold it is because I am driven to unmannerliness by my affection for you.

144. **I pray you.** Please, I request that you do so.

145. **know no touch of it.** Cannot play it

146. **Govern these ventages.** Cover these holes.

147. **discourse.** Speak

148. **stops.** Fingerholes

149. **compass.** Reach

150. **this little organ.** The recorder

151. **fret.** Pun playing on two senses of the word *fret:* 1. to press down the string of a lute, 2. to irritate

Words For Everyday Use

be • seech (bē sēch´) *vt.*, ask earnestly; implore

el • o • quent (el´ə kwənt) *adj.*, vividly expressive; persuasive

330 Have you any further trade with us?

ROSENCRANTZ.   My lord, you once did love me.

HAMLET.   And do still, by these pickers and stealers.[137]

ROSENCRANTZ.   Good my lord, what is your cause of
distemper?[138] You do surely bar the door upon your
335 own liberty[139] if you deny your griefs to your friend.

HAMLET.   Sir, I lack advancement.

ROSENCRANTZ.   How can that be, when you have the
voice of the King himself for your succession in
Denmark?

340 HAMLET.   Ay, sir, but "While the grass grows"[140]—the
proverb is something musty.[141]

Enter the PLAYERS *with recorders.*

O, the recorders! Let me see one.—To withdraw with
you—why do you go about to recover the wind of me,
as if you would drive me into a toil?[142]

345 GUILDENSTERN.   O my lord, if my duty be too bold, my
love is too unmannerly.[143]

HAMLET.   I do not well understand that. Will you play
upon this pipe?

GUILDENSTERN.   My lord, I cannot.

350 HAMLET.   I pray you.[144]

GUILDENSTERN.   Believe me, I cannot.

HAMLET.   I do beseech you.

GUILDENSTERN.   I know no touch of it,[145] my lord.

HAMLET.   It is as easy as lying. Govern these ventages[146]
355 with your fingers and thumbs, give it breath with your
mouth, and it will discourse[147] most eloquent music.
Look you, these are the stops.[148]

GUILDENSTERN.   But these cannot I command to any
utt'rance of harmony. I have not the skill.

360 HAMLET.   Why, look you now, how unworthy a thing
you make of me! You would play upon me, you would
seem to know my stops, you would pluck out the heart
of my mystery, you would sound me from my lowest
note to the top of my compass;[149] and there is much
365 music, excellent voice, in this little organ,[150] yet cannot
you make it speak. 'Sblood, do you think I am easier to
be play'd on than a pipe? Call me what instrument you
will, though you fret[151] me, yet you cannot play upon me.

◄ *What point is
Hamlet making to
Guildenstern? In
what sense has
Guildenstern
attempted to "play
upon" Hamlet?*

Handwritten margin notes:
Hamlet is tired of their meddling

the Queen wants to speak to Hamlet.

152. **presently.** At once
153. **By the mass.** An oath
154. **Methinks.** I think
155. **the top of my bent.** To the furthest extent that I can reach, as far as I can bend
156. **lose not thy nature.** Do not become unnatural or monstrous
157. **Nero.** Roman emperor who killed his mother
158. **my tongue . . . hypocrites.** May my tongue speak something different than what in my soul I believe, thus making them hypocritical. Hamlet's rage is so great that in his soul he desires to kill his mother. It is indeed unnatural, and thus he has reason for worrying that he might be losing his nature.
159. **somever she be shent.** In time she be punished
160. **To give them seals.** To give those words a legal stamp of approval

ACT III, SCENE iii
1. **commission.** Official orders
2. **dispatch.** Draw up
3. **terms of our estate.** Requirement placed upon me as king
4. **Out of his brows.** Reference to the lowering of eyebrows that occurs when someone looks upon another person with hatred
5. **We . . . provide.** We shall equip ourselves.

Words For Everyday Use   con • ta • gion (kən tā´jən) *n.*, spreading of disease

Enter POLONIUS.

God bless you, sir.

370 POLONIUS.   My lord, the Queen would speak with you,
and presently.[152]

HAMLET.   Do you see yonder cloud that's almost in
shape of a camel?

POLONIUS.   By th' mass[153] and 'tis, like a camel indeed.

375 HAMLET.   Methinks[154] it is like a weasel.

POLONIUS.   It is back'd like a weasel.

HAMLET.   Or like a whale.

POLONIUS.   Very like a whale.

HAMLET.   Then I will come to my mother by and by.
380 [*Aside.*] They fool me to the top of my bent.[155]—I will
come by and by.

POLONIUS.   I will say so.   *Exit.*

HAMLET.   "By and by" is easily said. Leave me, friends.
                                    Exeunt all but HAMLET.

'Tis now the very witching time of night,
385 When churchyards yawn and hell itself breathes out
Contagion to this world. Now could I drink hot blood
And do such bitter business as the day
Would quake to look on. Soft, now to my mother.
O heart, lose not thy nature![156] let not ever
390 The soul of Nero[157] enter this firm bosom,
Let me be cruel, not unnatural;
I will speak daggers to her, but use none.
My tongue and soul in this be hypocrites[158]—
How in my words somever she be shent,[159]
395 To give them seals[160] never my soul consent!   *Exit.*

◀ *In what way does
Hamlet play upon
Polonius here?*

◀ *What does
Hamlet say that he
could do at this
time?*

◀ *In what way does
Hamlet intend to
honor his dead
father's wishes?*

SCENE iii

Enter KING, ROSENCRANTZ, *and* GUILDENSTERN.

KING.   I like him not, nor stands it safe with us
To let his madness range. Therefore prepare you.
I your commission[1] will forthwith dispatch,[2]
And he to England shall along with you.
5 The terms of our estate[3] may not endure
Hazard so near 's as doth hourly grow
Out of his brows.[4]

GUILDENSTERN.   We will ourselves provide.[5]

◀ *What does
Claudius plan to do
about Hamlet? Why?*

6. **many bodies . . . Majesty.** It was common in Renaissance times to equate the king with the political body he served, and indeed the king was sometimes pictured as being made up of his subjects. Guildenstern takes this notion to ludicrous lengths, however, when he imagines the subjects of the realm feeding (like lice) on the body of the king. That, in a metaphorical sense, is what Rosencrantz and Guildenstern are doing.

7. **noyance.** Annoyance, danger

8. **weal.** Well-being, wealth

9. **cess.** Many editors give the meaning of this word as cessation, meaning an ending, but such a reading makes little sense. It also makes little sense that the word should be related to the Latin *cessio,* the past participle of *ceders,* to cede or give up. It is more likely that this obscure word shares with the Italian *cesso,* or privy, meaning a hole or pit into which other things are drawn.

10. **gulf.** Whirlpool

11. **massy.** Massive

12. **annexment.** Thing annexed, or joined to, something else

13. **a massy wheel . . . ruin.** The general idea is that Fortune's wheel, when the Fortune is that of a king, has many attachments. Other people's fortunes are also at stake.

14. **Arm you.** Prepare yourselves (as a warrior takes up arms)

15. **viage.** Voyage

16. **closet.** Room chamber

17. **arras.** Tapestry, wall hanging

18. **convey.** Place, carry

19. **process.** Proceedings

20. **tax him home.** Upbraid or censure him as a mother might scold an errant child on the way back home

21. **meet.** Appropriate

22. **of vantage.** As well, in addition (to the advantage)

23. **liege.** Lord

24. **the primal eldest curse.** The curse placed upon Cain in Genesis 4 for killing his brother

25. **Though . . . will.** Though my desire is as keen as my intent

26. **double business.** Two contradictory or incompatible goals or tasks

27. **Whereto.** To what end

Words For Everyday Use

mor • tise (môr´tis) *vt.,* join; fasten securely

bois • ter • ous (bois´tər əs) *adj.,* noisy; unruly

fet • ter (fet´ər) *n.,* restraint; anything that serves to restrict

Most holy and religious fear it is
To keep those many many bodies safe
10   That live and feed upon your Majesty.[6]

ROSENCRANTZ.   The single and peculiar life is bound
With all the strength and armor of the mind
To keep itself from noyance,[7] but much more
That spirit upon whose weal[8] depends and rests
15   The lives of many. The cess[9] of majesty
Dies not alone, but like a gulf[10] doth draw
What's near it with it. Or it is a massy[11] wheel
Fix'd on the summit of the highest mount,
To whose huge spokes ten thousand lesser things
20   Are mortis'd and adjoin'd, which when it falls,
Each small annexment,[12] petty consequence
Attends the boist'rous ruin.[13] Never alone
Did the King sigh, but with a general groan.

KING.   Arm you,[14] I pray you, to this speedy viage,[15]
25   For we will fetters put about this fear,
Which now goes too free-footed.

ROSENCRANTZ.   We will haste us.
            Exeunt Gentlemen ROSENCRANTZ *and* GUILDENSTERN.
Enter POLONIUS.

POLONIUS.   My lord, he's going to his mother's closet.[16]
Behind the arras[17] I'll convey[18] myself
To hear the process.[19] I'll warrant she'll tax him home,[20]
30   And as you said, and wisely was it said,
'Tis meet[21] that some more audience than a mother,
Since nature makes them partial, should o'erhear
The speech, of vantage.[22] Fare you well, my liege,[23]
I'll call upon you ere you go to bed,
35   And tell you what I know.

KING.   Thanks, dear my lord.
                        Exit POLONIUS.

O, my offense is rank, it smells to heaven,
It hath the primal eldest curse[24] upon't,
A brother's murther. Pray can I not,
Though inclination be as sharp as will.[25]
40   My stronger guilt defeats my strong intent,
And, like a man to double business[26] bound,
I stand in pause where I shall first begin,
And both neglect. What if this cursed hand
Were thicker than itself with brother's blood,
45   Is there not rain enough in the sweet heavens
To wash it white as snow? Whereto[27] serves mercy

◄ *Where does
Polonius hide?*

listen to
conversation
between
Queen +
Hamlet.

◄ *Why does
Claudius find it
impossible to pray?*

Soliloquy

28. **visage.** Face
29. **ere.** Before
30. **effects.** Consequences, objects gained
31. **retain th' offense.** Still engage in what was offensive
32. **corrupted currents.** Dirty or foul flowing waters, with a pun on currents in the sense of currencies, or valid media of exchange
33. **shuffling.** Evasion
34. **the action.** The legal case and the deed
35. **his.** Its
36. **we ourselves . . . evidence.** English law established the principle that a person should not be required to give witness against himself, but Claudius says that such is not the case in heaven.
37. **rests.** Remains
38. **limed.** Caught in lime, a substance used to capture birds
39. **assay.** Attempt
40. **strings of steel.** It was believed that the heart was held in place by tendons known as heart strings.
41. **pat.** Easily
42. **scann'd.** Thought about
43. **broad blown.** Fully blossomed out
44. **flush.** Filled out by growth
45. **save.** Except
46. **our circumstance . . . thought.** Our earthy circumstances and (limited) ability to reason about these matters
47. **take.** Overtake, kill
48. **season'd.** Prepared
49. **passage.** To the other world
50. **hent.** Occasion and group

Words For Everyday Use

fore • stall (fôr stôl´) *vt.*, prevent; hinder
gild • ed (gild´əd) *adj.*, coated with gold; made more attractive
sole (sōl) *adj.*, one and only
au • dit (ô´dit) *n.*, account; record

But to confront the visage[28] of offense?
And what's in prayer but this twofold force,
To be forestalled ere[29] we come to fall,
50 Or pardon'd being down? then I'll look up.
My fault is past, but, O, what form of prayer
Can serve my turn? "Forgive me my foul murther"?
That cannot be, since I am still possess'd
Of those effects[30] for which I did the murther:
55 My crown, mine own ambition, and my queen.
May one be pardon'd and retain th' offense?[31]
In the corrupted currents[32] of this world
Offense's gilded hand may shove by justice,
And oft 'tis seen the wicked prize itself
60 Buys out the law, but 'tis not so above:
There is no shuffling,[33] there the action[34] lies
In his[35] true nature, and we ourselves compell'd,
Even to the teeth and forehead of our faults,
To give in evidence.[36] What then? What rests?[37]
65 Try what repentance can. What can it not?
Yet what can it, when one can not repent?
O wretched state! O bosom black as death!
O limed[38] soul, that struggling to be free
Art more engag'd! Help, angels! Make assay,[39]
70 Bow, stubborn knees, and heart, with strings of steel,[40]
Be soft as sinews of the new-born babe!
All may be well. *He kneels.*

Enter HAMLET.

HAMLET.   Now might I do it pat,[41] now 'a is a-praying;
And now I'll do't—and so 'a goes to heaven,
75 And so am I reveng'd. That would be scann'd:[42]
A villain kills my father, and for that
I, his sole son, do this same villain send
To heaven.
Why, this is hire and salary, not revenge.
80 'A took my father grossly, full of bread,
With all his crimes broad blown,[43] as flush[44] as May,
And how his audit stands who knows save[45] heaven?
But in our circumstance and course of thought[46]
'Tis heavy with him. And am I then revenged,
85 To take[47] him in the purging of his soul,
When he is fit and season'd[48] for his passage?[49]
No!
Up, sword, and know thou a more horrid hent:[50]
When he is drunk asleep, or in his rage,
90 Or in th' incestious pleasure of his bed,

◄ Why can't
Claudius ask for
forgiveness?

◄ According to
Claudius, how does
heavenly justice differ
from earthly justice?

◄ Does Claudius feel
that all is hopeless?
How do you know?

◄ What might
Hamlet do at this
moment?

◄ Why does Hamlet
decide not to kill
Claudius at this
time?

Handwritten margin notes: Claudius has a speech + adm. to killing his brother. He prays to atone for his sins. Claudius is praying. Hamlet didn't have an opport. to kill the King praying.

51. **game.** Gambling
52. **relish.** Trace, hope
53. **stays.** Waits
54. **physic.** Medicine (Claudius's prayer)

ACT III, SCENE iv

1. **broad.** Unlicensed, outrageous
2. **silence me.** Shut up
3. **round.** Direct
4. **fear me not.** Don't doubt me
5. **how now?** What's this? (both a question and a rebuke)
6. **Have . . . me.** Have you forgotten to whom you are speaking?
7. **rood.** The holy cross
8. **would.** I wish, if only
9. **I'll set . . . can speak.** An understated threat
10. **glass.** Mirror

At game[51] a-swearing, or about some act
That has no relish[52] of salvation in't—
Then trip him, that his heels may kick at heaven,
And that his soul may be as damn'd and black
95 As hell, whereto it goes. My mother stays,[53]
This physic[54] but prolongs thy sickly days.   *Exit.*

KING.   [*Rising.*] My words fly up, my thoughts remain
       below:
Words without thoughts never to heaven go.   *Exit.*

◄ *Need Hamlet fear that Claudius, dying at this point, would be saved? Why, or why not?*

SCENE iv

Enter QUEEN GERTRUDE *and* POLONIUS.

POLONIUS.   'A will come straight. Look you lay home to
       him.
Tell him his pranks have been too broad[1] to bear with,
And that your Grace hath screen'd and stood between
Much heat and him. I'll silence me[2] even here;
5 Pray you be round[3] with him.

QUEEN.   I'll warr'nt you fear me not.[4] Withdraw,
I hear him coming.   POLONIUS *hides behind the arras.*

Enter HAMLET.

HAMLET.   Now, mother, what's the matter?

QUEEN.   Hamlet, thou hast thy father much offended.

10 HAMLET.   Mother, you have my father much offended.

QUEEN.   Come, come, you answer with an idle tongue.

HAMLET.   Go, go, you question with a wicked tongue.

QUEEN.   Why, how now,[5] Hamlet?

HAMLET.   What's the matter now?

QUEEN.   Have you forgot me?[6]

HAMLET.   No, by the rood,[7] not so:
15 You are the Queen, your husband's brother's wife,
And would[8] it were not so, you are my mother.

QUEEN.   Nay, then I'll set those to you that can speak.[9]

HAMLET.   Come, come, and sit you down, you shall
       not boudge;
You go not till I set you up a glass[10]
20 Where you may see the inmost part of you.

QUEEN.   What wilt thou do? Thou wilt not murther me?
Help ho!

◄ *To whom does Gertrude refer when she uses the phrase "thy father"? To whom does Hamlet refer when he uses the same phrase?*

◄ *What does Hamlet say that he wishes were not so?*

◄ *What does Hamlet intend to do?*

◄ *What does Gertrude fear?*

11. **for a ducat.** I'll wager a ducat that I can kill it (A ducat is a coin.)
12. **thy better.** Claudius
13. **damned custom.** Bad habits
14. **brass'd.** Made it so brazen; hardened it
15. **proof and bulwark.** Protection and fortification
16. **sets a blister there.** Prostitutes in Elizabethan England were sometimes punished by being branded on the forehead with a hot iron.
17. **dicers.** People who play at dice, gamblers
18. **body of contraction.** The one body (the joined husband and wife) created by the marriage contract
19. **rhapsody.** Medley or simple stringing together
20. **this . . . mass.** The earth, compound because it is made up of the four elements of earth, air, water, and fire
21. **visage.** Look
22. **index.** The table of contents, with a pun on *index* in the sense of a pointing, or judgment
23. **counterfeit presentment.** Presentation; depiction. Hamlet is likely showing his mother portraits of King Hamlet and Claudius.
24. **front.** Forehead

Words For Everyday Use

pen • e • tra • ble (pen´i trə bəl) *adj.,* that can be penetrated or affected

POLONIUS. [*Behind.*] What ho, help!

HAMLET. [*Drawing.*] How now? A rat? Dead, for a
 ducat,[11] dead!   *Kills* POLONIUS *through the arras.*

25 POLONIUS. [*Behind.*] O, I am slain.

QUEEN.   O me, what hast thou done?

HAMLET. Nay, I know not. Is it the King?

QUEEN. O, what a rash and bloody deed is this!

HAMLET. A bloody deed! almost as bad, good mother,
As kill a king, and marry with his brother.

30 QUEEN. As kill a king!

HAMLET.   Ay, lady, it was my word.
           Parts the arras and discovers POLONIUS.
Thou wretched, rash, intruding fool, farewell!
I took thee for thy better.[12] Take thy fortune;
Thou find'st to be too busy is some danger.—
Leave wringing of your hands. Peace, sit you down,
35 And let me wring your heart, for so I shall
If it be made of <u>penetrable</u> stuff,
If damned custom[13] have not brass'd[14] it so
That it be proof and bulwark[15] against sense.

QUEEN. What have I done, that thou dar'st wag thy
 tongue
40 In noise so rude against me?

HAMLET.   Such an act
That blurs the grace and blush of modesty,
Calls virtue hypocrite, takes off the rose
From the fair forehead of an innocent love
And sets a blister there,[16] makes marriage vows
45 As false as dicers'[17] oaths, O, such a deed
As from the body of contraction[18] plucks
The very soul, and sweet religion makes
A rhapsody[19] of words. Heaven's face does glow
O'er this solidity and compound mass[20]
50 With heated visage,[21] as against the doom;
Is thought-sick at the act.

QUEEN.   Ay me, what act,
That roars so loud and thunders in the index?[22]

HAMLET. Look here upon this picture, and on this,
The counterfeit presentment[23] of two brothers.
55 See what a grace was seated on this brow:
Hyperion's curls, the front[24] of Jove himself,
An eye like Mars, to threaten and command,

◄ *Whom does
Hamlet think might
be behind the
curtain?*

◄ *Does Gertrude
seem to know that
her husband was
murdered?*

◄ *On what does
Hamlet blame
Polonius's death?*

◄ *Does Hamlet
seem concerned
about having mur-
dered Polonius?
What does concern
him at this point?*

25. **station.** Stance
26. **seal.** Emblem
27. **mildewed . . . brother.** A mildewed ear (of corn) that blasted, or blighted, his healthy brother. The choice of metaphor is related, of course, to the manner of the poisoning. Claudius poured poison into his brother's ear.
28. **heyday in the blood.** Excitement in the blood (the passions)
29. **waits upon.** Serves
30. **apoplex'd.** Stricken
31. **err.** Make such a mistake
32. **ecstasy.** Madness
33. **thrall'd.** Enslaved
34. **to serve in.** To serve in helping one to see
35. **cozen'd . . . hoodman-blind.** Deceived you in a game of blind-man's-bluff
36. **sans.** Without
37. **mope.** Fail to respond
38. **mutine.** Rebel, mutiny
39. **If thou . . . fire.** If hell can so rebel in the body of a mature woman, then there is no hope for youth, in whom virtue would have to be no more long lasting than the wax of a lighted candle.
40. **compulsive ardure.** Compelling ardor, or passion
41. **frost.** Age (from frosty, white hair)
42. **reason panders will.** Reason, which should place limits on the will (desires) instead acts as its panderer, pushing one toward vices
43. **grained.** Ingrained
44. **leave their tinct.** Change color
45. **enseamed.** Greasy, with a pun on semen
46. **Stew'd.** Steeped, with a pun on stew, a brothel
47. **tithe.** A tenth part of one's income, given to the church. Claudius, as a king, is not a twentieth of a tenth of what the elder Hamlet was.
48. **precedent.** Preceding and accustomed
49. **Vice.** A stock figure from a morality play. Such a figure represented sin and was usually a low, common farcical character, or clown.

Words For Everyday Use

her • ald (her´əld) *n.,* person who makes official announcements

ma • tron (mā´trən) *n.,* married woman of mature appearance

sty (stī) *n.,* filthy enclosure, usually for pigs

A station[25] like the herald Mercury
New lighted on a heaven-kissing hill,
60 A combination and a form indeed,
Where every god did seem to set his seal[26]
To give the world assurance of a man.
This was your husband. Look you now what follows:
Here is your husband, like a mildewed ear,
65 Blasting his wholesome brother.[27] Have you eyes?
Could you on this fair mountain leave to feed,
And batten on this moor? ha, have you eyes?
You cannot call it love, for at your age
The heyday in the blood[28] is tame, it's humble,
70 And waits upon[29] the judgment, and what judgment
Would step from this to this? Sense sure you have,
Else could you not have motion, but sure that sense
Is apoplex'd,[30] for madness would not err,[31]
Nor sense to ecstasy[32] was ne'er so thrall'd[33]
75 But it reserv'd some quantity of choice
To serve in[34] such a difference. What devil was't
That thus hath cozen'd you at hoodman-blind?[35]
Eyes without feeling, feeling without sight,
Ears without hands or eyes, smelling sans[36] all
80 Or but a sickly part of one true sense
Could not so mope.[37] O shame, where is thy blush?
Rebellious hell,
If thou canst mutine[38] in a matron's bones,
To flaming youth let virtue be as wax
85 And melt in her own fire.[39] Proclaim no shame
When the compulsive ardure[40] gives the charge,
Since frost[41] itself as actively doth burn,
And reason panders will.[42]

QUEEN.   O Hamlet, speak no more!
Thou turn'st my eyes into my very soul,
90 And there I see such black and grained[43] spots
As will not leave their tinct.[44]

HAMLET.   Nay, but to live
In the rank sweat of an enseamed[45] bed,
Stew'd[46] in corruption, honeying and making love
Over the nasty sty!

QUEEN.   O, speak to me no more!
95 These words like daggers enter in my ears.
No more, sweet Hamlet!

HAMLET.   A murtherer and a villain!
A slave that is not twentieth part the tithe[47]
Of your precedent[48] lord, a Vice[49] of kings,

◄ What two pic-
tures does Hamlet
ask his mother to
compare?

◄ What choice
made by Gertrude
seems inconceivable
to Hamlet?

◄ How does
Gertrude react to
Hamlet's comments?

50. **cutpurse.** Thief
51. **diadem.** Crown
52. **shreds and patches.** Motley, the multi-colored bits and pieces that made up the clothing of a clown
53. **dread.** To be dreaded, or feared
54. **amazement.** Bewilderment
55. **Conceit.** Imagination
56. **bend.** Direct (from the bending of a bow to direct an arrow)
57. **vacancy.** Nothing, empty space
58. **incorporal.** Bodiless, insubstantial
59. **excrements.** Growth from the body, such as hair or nails, normally dead, but here alive because Hamlet's hair, which normally would be bedded down, is standing up like sleeping soldiers startled by an alarm.
60. **distemper.** Disturbance of mind or spirit
61. **conjoin'd.** Joined together
62. **effects.** Deeds, the results that I intend
63. **want true color.** Lack their proper hue and character
64. **perchance for.** Possibly instead of
65. **habit.** Garb, clothing

Words For Everyday Use	**whet** (wet) *vt.*, make keen; stimulate

A cutpurse[50] of the empire and the rule,
100 That from a shelf the precious diadem[51] stole,
And put it in his pocket—

QUEEN.   No more!

Enter GHOST *in his nightgown.*

HAMLET.   A king of shreds and patches[52]—
Save me, and hover o'er me with your wings,
105 You heavenly guards! What would your gracious figure?

QUEEN.   Alas, he's mad!

HAMLET.   Do you not come your tardy son to chide,
That, laps'd in time and passion, lets go by
Th' important acting of your dread[53] command? O, say!

110 GHOST.   Do not forget! This visitation
Is but to <u>whet</u> thy almost blunted purpose.
But look, amazement[54] on thy mother sits,
O, step between her and her fighting soul.
Conceit[55] in weakest bodies strongest works,
115 Speak to her, Hamlet.

HAMLET.   How is it with you, lady?

QUEEN.   Alas, how is't with you,
That you do bend[56] your eye on vacancy,[57]
And with th' incorporal[58] air do hold discourse?
Forth at your eyes your spirits wildly peep,
120 And as the sleeping soldiers in th' alarm,
Your bedded hair, like life in excrements,[59]
Start up and stand an end. O gentle son,
Upon the heat and flame of thy distemper[60]
Sprinkle cool patience. Whereon do you look?

125 HAMLET.   On him, on him! look you how pale he glares!
His form and cause conjoin'd,[61] preaching to stones,
Would make them capable.—Do not look upon me,
Lest with this piteous action you convert
My stern effects,[62] then what I have to do
130 Will want true color[63]—tears perchance for[64] blood.

QUEEN.   To whom do you speak this?

HAMLET.   Do you see nothing there?

QUEEN.   Nothing at all, yet all that is I see.

HAMLET.   Nor did you nothing hear?

QUEEN.   No, nothing but ourselves.

HAMLET.   Why, look you there, look how it steals away!
135 My father, in his habit[65] as he lived!

◄ What does Hamlet see that his mother does not?

◄ Why has the ghost come? What does he ask Hamlet to do concerning Gertrude?

◄ What does Hamlet say would be roused to action by seeing the ghost and hearing his appeal?

66. **coinage.** Creation, thing coined or minted
67. **ecstasy.** Madness
68. **cunning.** Skillful
69. **unction.** Soothing oil used to anoint the body for medical or religious purposes
70. **rank.** Overgrown
71. **mining.** Undermining
72. **pursy.** Luxurious, fat like a purse stuffed with coins
73. **curb.** Bow
74. **leave.** Permission
75. **cleft.** Past participle of *cleave,* to split or divide
76. **twain.** Two
77. **worser.** Worse
78. **Assume.** Put on, pretend to have
79. **custom . . . put on.** Custom is a monster. It makes people insensitive and therefore gives them devilish habits. Yet custom can also be angelic, making a habit of fair and good action like a servant's uniform that one readily puts on.
80. **use.** Habitual action
81. **the stamp of nature.** One's natural proclivities
82. **potency.** Strength
83. **when . . . of you.** When you have so reformed as to show that you desire to be blessed (saved), then I'll be willing to ask for your blessing before departing.
84. **this.** Polonius
85. **scourge.** One who scourges, or punishes
86. **bestow.** Dispose of
87. **will answer well.** Will give good reason for

Words For Everyday Use

por • tal (pôrt´ l) *n.,* doorway; entrance
tem • per • ate • ly (tem´pər it lē) *adv.,* moderately; with self-restraint
gam • bol (gam´bəl) *vi.,* frolic; skip about
ul • cer • ous (ul´sər əs) *adj.,* having an ulcer, an open sore
com • post (käm´pōst) *n.,* decomposing vegetables used for fertilizer
ab • sti • nence (ab´stə nəns) *n.,* act of doing without pleasure

Look where he goes, even now, out at the <u>portal</u>!

Exit G<small>HOST</small>.

Q<small>UEEN</small>.   This is the very coinage[66] of your brain,
This bodiless creation ecstasy[67]
Is very cunning[68] in.

H<small>AMLET</small>.   Ecstasy?
140 My pulse as yours doth <u>temperately</u> keep time,
And makes as healthful music. It is not madness
That I have utt'red. Bring me to the test,
And I the matter will reword, which madness
Would <u>gambol</u> from. Mother, for love of grace,
145 Lay not that flattering unction[69] to your soul,
That not your trespass but my madness speaks;
It will but skin and film the <u>ulcerous</u> place,
Whiles rank[70] corruption, mining[71] all within,
Infects unseen. Confess yourself to heaven,
150 Repent what's past, avoid what is to come,
And do not spread the <u>compost</u> on the weeds
To make them ranker. Forgive me this my virtue,
For in the fatness of these pursy[72] times
Virtue itself of vice must pardon beg,
155 Yea, curb[73] and woo for leave[74] to do him good.

Q<small>UEEN</small>.   O Hamlet, thou hast cleft[75] my heart in twain.[76]

H<small>AMLET</small>.   O, throw away the worser[77] part of it,
And live the purer with the other half.
Good night, but go not to my uncle's bed—
160 Assume[78] a virtue, if you have it not.
That monster custom, who all sense doth eat,
Of habits devil, is angel yet in this,
That to the use of actions fair and good
He likewise gives a frock or livery
165 That aptly is put on.[79] Refrain tonight,
And that shall lend a kind of easiness
To the next <u>abstinence</u>, the next more easy;
For use[80] almost can change the stamp of nature,[81]
And either master the devil or throw him out
170 With wondrous potency.[82] Once more good night,
And when you are desirous to be blest,
I'll blessing beg of you.[83] For this same lord,

Pointing to P<small>OLONIUS</small>.

I do repent; but heaven hath pleas'd it so
To punish me with this,[84] and this with me,
175 That I must be their scourge[85] and minister.
I will bestow[86] him, and will answer well[87]
The death I gave him. So again good night.

◄ What does Gertrude believe has happened?

◄ What proof can Hamlet offer that he is not crazy?

◄ What does Hamlet tell his mother that she should do?

◄ What advice does Hamlet give his mother about dealing with her desire to be with Claudius?

88. **bloat.** Bloated
89. **Pinch wanton.** Pinch you wantonly
90. **reechy.** Nasty
91. **paddling in.** Fingering
92. **ravel all this matter out.** Unravel all this (reveal to him my secret)
93. **in craft.** By design
94. **a paddock . . . gib.** A toad, a bat, and a cat, familiars of witches
95. **dear concernings.** Important matters
96. **No, in . . . down.** Hamlet explains that letting out his secret could be dangerous and gives as an analogy a familiar story about an ape that climbed to the roof of a house, opened a basket containing birds, watched them fly out, and then imitated the actions of the birds and so fell to his death.
97. **concluded on.** Decided
98. **sweep my way.** Clear the path before me
99. **knavery.** Ill-doing
100. **enginer . . . petar.** The military engineer who sets mines, blown up by his own bomb
101. **delve.** Dig
102. **prating.** Prattling, talkative
103. **knave.** Deceitful rascal or lowborn person

Words
For
Everyday
Use

ad • der (ad´ər) *n.*, poisonous snake
man • date (man´dāt) *n.*, written order or command from authority

I must be cruel only to be kind.
This bad begins and worse remains behind.

180 One word more, good lady.

QUEEN.   What shall I do?

HAMLET.   Not this, by no means, that I bid you do:
Let the bloat[88] king tempt you again to bed,
Pinch wanton[89] on your cheek, call you his mouse,
And let him, for a pair of reechy[90] kisses,
185 Or paddling in[91] your neck with his damn'd fingers,
Make you to ravel all this matter out,[92]
That I essentially am not in madness
But mad in craft.[93] 'Twere good you let him know
For who that's but a queen, fair, sober, wise,
190 Would from a paddock, from a bat, a gib,[94]
Such dear concernings[95] hide? Who would do so?
No, in despite of sense and secrecy,
Unpeg the basket on the house's top,
Let the birds fly, and like the famous ape,
195 To try conclusions in the basket creep,
And break your own neck down.[96]

QUEEN.   Be thou assur'd, if words be made of breath,
And breath of life, I have no life to breathe
What thou hast said to me.

200 HAMLET.   I must to England, you know that?

QUEEN.   Alack,
I had forgot. 'Tis so concluded on.[97]

HAMLET.   There's letters seal'd, and my two school-
      fellows,
Whom I will trust as I will adders fang'd,
They bear the mandate, they must sweep my way[98]
205 And marshal me to knavery.[99] Let it work,
For 'tis the sport to have the enginer
Hoist with his own petar,[100] an't shall go hard
But I will delve[101] one yard below their mines,
And blow them at the moon. O, 'tis most sweet
210 When in one line two crafts directly meet.
This man shall set me packing;
I'll lug the guts into the neighbor room.
Mother, good night indeed. This counselor
Is now most still, most secret, and most grave,
215 Who was in life a foolish prating[102] knave.[103]
Come, sir, to draw toward an end with you.
Good night, mother.

                    Exeunt severally, HAMLET *tugging in* POLONIUS.

◀ What does
Hamlet believe will
be the result of his
having killed
Polonius?

◀ What does
Hamlet want to
keep Claudius from
discovering?

◀ Of what does
Gertrude assure
her son?

◀ How does Hamlet
feel toward
Rosencrantz and
Guildenstern?

◀ According to
Hamlet, how is
Polonius different in
death than he was
in life?

Responding to the Selection

What do you think of Hamlet at this point in the play? Do you find him a sympathetic character? What are his virtues? What are his faults? What do you think might occur in the rest of the play, and why?

Reviewing the Selection

Recalling and Interpreting

1. **R:** What question is Hamlet considering when he first appears in this act? What, according to Hamlet, is "a consummation / Devoutly to be wish'd"?

2. **I:** What, according to Hamlet, keeps a person from escaping the troubles of this life? What, according to Hamlet, does thinking too much—"the pale cast of thought"—do to people?

3. **R:** What question does Hamlet pose to Ophelia, and what does he tell her that she should do?

4. **I:** How does Hamlet regard women, love, romance, and marriage? Why might he feel this way?

5. **R:** What does Claudius conclude about Hamlet after overhearing the conversation with Ophelia?

6. **I:** Why does Claudius decide to send Hamlet to England?

7. **R:** What, according to Hamlet, is "the purpose of playing," or acting?

8. **I:** What is Hamlet hoping will happen when the king sees the play?

9. **R:** What does Hamlet ask Horatio to do during the play?

10. **I:** What does Hamlet think of Horatio's judgment? of Horatio in general?

11. **R:** What kinds of comments does Hamlet make to Ophelia during the play within a play?

12. **I:** Why might Hamlet speak to Ophelia as he does?

13. **R:** What is the actual name of the play within the play? What other name does Hamlet give it?

14. **I:** Why does Hamlet give the play this name? What does the play reveal to be true?

15. **R:** What instrument does Hamlet command Guildenstern to play?

16. **I:** Why does Hamlet demand that Guildenstern play this instrument? What point does Hamlet want to make to Guildenstern?

17. R: What does Hamlet caution himself against doing before going to his mother's chamber?

18. I: What is Hamlet's mood just before going to his mother's chamber?

19. R: What is Claudius attempting to do when Hamlet discovers him, alone and unguarded? Why doesn't Hamlet kill Claudius at this point?

20. I: Considering Claudius's final lines in act III, scene iii, what is ironic about Hamlet's decision not to kill Claudius at this point?

21. R: Where does Polonius hide? Why does he do this? What happens to him?

22. I: Does Polonius deserve the fate that he receives? Why, or why not?

23. R: Of what does Hamlet accuse his mother? What two people does he ask her to compare? How does his mother react to her son's comments?

24. I: Why does Gertrude feel as she does? What troubles her about her own actions?

25. R: Who appears to Hamlet while the prince is speaking with his mother? What reason does this figure give for appearing at this time?

26. I: What conclusion does Gertrude draw from her son's conversation with this figure? At the end of the scene, do you think that Gertrude still believes this conclusion to be true? Why, or why not?

27. R: What does Hamlet say will be the consequence of his action in his mother's room?

28. I: How does Hamlet intend to deal with Rosencrantz and Guildenstern, given what he says at the end of the act?

Synthesizing

29. At one point in the play, Hamlet speaks of himself as a scourge, or whip, whose purpose is to bring about justice. How does Hamlet deal with Ophelia? with Polonius? with his mother? How are these dealings related to Hamlet's ideas about what is just? Why does Hamlet spare Claudius? What justice does he want to visit on the king? What justice does he have in mind for Rosencrantz and Guildenstern?

30. Are Hamlet's actions in act III just? Does he behave in a way that you believe to be morally correct? Why, or why not?

Understanding Literature (QUESTIONS FOR DISCUSSION)

1. **Aside.** An **aside** is a statement made by a character in a play, intended to be heard by the audience, but not by other characters on the stage. What is revealed about Claudius in an aside just before the "To be or not to be" soliloquy (act III, scene i, lines 48–54)?

2. **Irony and Cliché. Irony** is a difference between appearance and reality. A **cliché** is a tired or hackneyed expression. Polonius and Claudius often express moral platitudes, pious clichés that Hamlet refers to, disparagingly, as the "saws of old books." Find some examples in acts I–III of pious clichés mouthed by Claudius and Polonius. Do these two men live up to their own words? Explain.

3. **Soliloquy.** A **soliloquy** is a speech given by a character who is, or believes himself to be, alone and in which the character reveals his or her thoughts to the audience. Act III contains two soliloquies. The first of these, in scene i, lines 55–87, is perhaps the most famous (and most debated) soliloquy in all of dramatic literature. Read this "To be, or not to be" soliloquy closely and paraphrase it. What do you believe Hamlet to be saying here? What is Hamlet's opinion of this life? What option does he consider? What makes him pause? In what way does Hamlet relate reasons for not killing one's self to reasons for not taking action in general? What, according to Hamlet, keeps people from taking actions? Then think about the second soliloquy in this act, which appears just after the play within a play and just before Hamlet visits his mother, in act III, scene ii, lines 384–395. How has Hamlet's mood changed in this soliloquy? What kinds of actions does Hamlet say that he is now ready to undertake?

4. **Motivation. Motivation** is a force that moves a character to think, feel, or behave in a certain way. One problem that has troubled critics for centuries is why Hamlet should have chosen to treat Ophelia so cruelly. Review the interactions between Hamlet and Ophelia in act III, scene i. Ophelia tells Hamlet that "Rich gifts wax poor when givers prove unkind." In what way has Hamlet been unkind to Ophelia? In what way has Ophelia been unkind to Hamlet? Why does Hamlet respond so angrily to Ophelia? Of what does he accuse her? What does he suggest is true of all women? What does he say of all men, including himself? Why might Hamlet feel as he does about women and about marriage? Are his feelings justified?

5. Drama. A **drama** is a story told through characters played by actors. Hamlet is famous for containing a drama within a drama. Why does Hamlet ask to have the drama within this drama performed? What does Hamlet learn as a result?

6. Theme. A **theme** is a main idea in a literary work. One of the recurring themes in this play is how one might achieve salvation. Claudius says that one of the virtues of prayer is that it has the force to pardon those who have fallen. Why isn't Claudius able to ask for forgiveness and so be saved? Ironically, why does Hamlet spare the king's life when he finds Claudius at prayer? What does Hamlet want to do instead? Why might the seventeenth-century critic Samuel Johnson have thought Hamlet's intention here too horrible to contemplate?

7. Mimesis. Mimesis, as defined by the Greek philosopher Aristotle, is the imitation of life in art. Review Hamlet's instructions to the players in act III, scene ii. What theory of acting and of playwriting does Hamlet espouse? What value does drama have, in Hamlet's view? What makes a performance good or bad?

8. Freudian Criticism and the Oedipus Complex.
Freudian criticism is analysis and interpretation of literature based on theories of the father of psychoanalysis, Sigmund Freud. The **Oedipus complex** is the name that Freud gave to a conflict that he believed to be universal among male children, a repressed desire to kill their fathers and so supplant them and have their mothers to themselves. In a footnote in his book *The Interpretation of Dreams,* Freud argued that Hamlet suffered from an unresolved Oedipus complex. According to Freud,

Hamlet is able to do anything—except take vengeance on the man who did away with his father and took that father's place with his mother, the man who shows him the repressed wishes of his own childhood realized. Thus the loathing which should drive him on to revenge is replaced in him by self-reproaches, by scruples of conscience, which remind him that he himself is literally no better than the sinner whom he is to punish. Here I have translated into conscious terms what was bound to remain unconscious in Hamlet's mind; and if anyone is inclined to call him a hysteric, I can only accept the fact as one that is implied by my interpretation. The distaste for sexuality expressed by Hamlet in his conversation with Ophelia fits very well with this.

Assuming that Freud's theory is correct, how would it explain Hamlet's delay in taking revenge on Claudius, his behavior toward Ophelia, his suicidal tendencies, his general distaste for life, his obsession with his mother's relationship with Claudius, and his behavior in the "closet scene" when he confronts his mother?

9. Motivation and Irony of Situation. Motivation is a force that moves a character to think, feel, or behave in a certain way. **Irony of situation** is when an event occurs in a literary work that violates the expectations of the characters, the reader, or the audience. The force that sets in motion the action of this play is Hamlet's motivation to take revenge for the killing of his father. Given this fact, what is ironic about the deed that Hamlet performs when he stabs Polonius through the arras? What makes this an example of irony of situation, a violation of Hamlet's expectations of himself? In what way has he committed the very deed that he has set out to punish?

10. Crisis, or Turning Point. The **crisis,** or **turning point,** is the part of a plot in which something decisive happens to determine the future course of events and the eventual working out of the conflict. What crisis, or turning point, in Hamlet's fortunes occurs during the scene with his mother? What immediate consequence does Hamlet expect this event to have? What do you think might be the long-term consequences of Hamlet's action?

ACT IV, SCENE i

1. **Bestow . . . on us.** Leave this place to us
2. **rapier.** Sword
3. **brainish.** Brain-sick
4. **had been.** Would have been
5. **out of haunt.** Hidden away, not allowed to move about freely
6. **owner of.** Person who has
7. **divulging.** Being shown to others
8. **draw apart.** Take elsewhere
9. **like some ore . . . metals base.** Like a precious ore (such as gold) in a mine made up mostly of worthless metals
10. **hence.** From here

Words For Everyday Use

ap • pre • hen • sion (ap´rē hen´shən) *n.,* anxious feeling of foreboding

prov • i • dence (präv´ə dəns) *n.,* foresight; care or preparation in advance

pith (pith) *n.,* essential or central part; essence

coun • te • nance (koun´tə nəns) *vt.,* condone; give approval to

Act IV

Enter KING *and* QUEEN *with* ROSENCRANTZ *and* GUILDENSTERN.

KING.   There's matter in these sighs, these profound *(deep)*
    heaves—
You must translate, 'tis fit we understand them. *what is going on?*
Where is your son?

QUEEN.   Bestow this place on us[1] a little while. *Leave us for*
            Exeunt ROSENCRANTZ *and* GUILDENSTERN. *awhile*

5   Ah, mine own lord, what have I seen tonight!

KING.   What, Gertrude? How does Hamlet?

QUEEN.   Mad as the sea and wind when both contend   ◄ *Does Gertrude*
Which is the mightier. In his lawless fit,   *keep her son's*
Behind the arras hearing something stir, *rich Tapestry*   *secret?*
10   Whips out his rapier,[2] cries, "A rat, a rat!"
And in this brainish[3] apprehension kills *fear /sword*
The unseen good old man.

KING.   O heavy deed! *(act)*
It had been[4] so with us had we been there.
His liberty is full of threats to all, *freedom things*   ◄ *What does*
15   To you yourself, to us, to every one.   *happen*   *Claudius realize*
Alas, how shall this bloody deed be answer'd? *for a reason*   *about the killing of*
It will be laid to us, whose providence *state of mind*   *Polonius?*
Should have kept short, restrain'd, and out of haunt[5] *hid*   ◄ *What does*
This mad young man; but so much was our love   *Claudius think people*
20   We would not understand what was most fit,   *will believe about the*
But like the owner of[6] a foul disease *Person who has*   *killing of Polonius?*
To keep it from divulging,[7] let it feed *Show others*
Even on the pith of life. Where is he gone?
QUEEN.   *To be elsewhere* To draw apart[8] the body he hath kill'd
25   O'er whom his very madness, like some ore
Among a mineral of metals base,[9] *gold*
Shows itself pure: 'a weeps for what is done.

KING.   O Gertrude, come away!
The sun no sooner shall the mountains touch, *evil*
30   But we will ship him hence,[10] and this vile deed
We must with all our majesty and skill
Both countenance and excuse. Ho, Guildenstern! — *tolerate + excuse*

Enter ROSENCRANTZ *and* GUILDENSTERN.

Friends both, go join you with some further aid:
Hamlet in madness hath Polonius slain,

11. **closet.** Bedchamber, boudoir
12. **what's untimely done.** What's done before its natural time
13. **So, haply, slander.** There is a gap in the the Quarto 2 version here. This phrase has traditionally been inserted here to fill the gap.
14. **his blank.** Its target
15. **woundless.** Incapable of being wounded

ACT IV, SCENE ii
1. **Compounded.** Joined or mingled
2. **keep your counsel and not mine own.** Know your secrets but not be able to keep my own
3. **replication.** Reply
4. **countenance.** Looks
5. **like an ape an apple.** This is a traditional, reconstructed reading not found in any text. Quarto 1 gives "as an Ape doeth nuttes," Quarto 2 "like an apple," and the First Folio "like an ape."
6. **knavish.** Witty, sarcastic, roguish

ore – metal mineral o rock
– bronze coin of Norway

pith – essential or impt. part

slander – false or defanatory statement
– (a person's name)

arras – rich tapestry

| Words For Everyday Use | **stowed** (stōd) *adj.*, safely packed away |
| | **kin** (kin) *adj.*, related |

35 And from his mother's closet[11] hath he dragg'd him.
Go seek him out, speak fair, and bring the body
Into the chapel. I pray you haste in this. *hurry up*

bedchamber

Exeunt ROSENCRANTZ *and* GUILDENSTERN.

Come, Gertrude, we'll call up our wisest friends
And let them know both what we mean to do — *not*
40 And what's untimely done,[12] so, haply, slander,[13]
Whose whisper o'er the world's diameter,
As level as the cannon to his blank,[14]
Transports his pois'ned shot, may miss our name,
And hit the woundless[15] air. O, come away!
45 My soul is full of discord and dismay. *Exeunt.*

a natural death

◄ What is Claudius's chief concern with regard to the murder?

SCENE ii

Enter HAMLET.

HAMLET. Safely stow'd.

GENTLEMEN. [*Within.*] Hamlet! Lord Hamlet!

HAMLET. But soft, what noise? Who calls on Hamlet?
O, here they come.

Enter ROSENCRANTZ *and* GUILDENSTERN.

5 ROSENCRANTZ. What have you done, my lord, with the
dead body?

HAMLET. Compounded[1] it with dust, whereto 'tis kin.

ROSENCRANTZ. Tell us where 'tis, that we may take it
thence
And bear it to the chapel.

HAMLET. Do not believe it.

10 ROSENCRANTZ. Believe what?

HAMLET. That I can keep your counsel and not mine
own.[2] Besides, to be demanded of a sponge, what replication[3] should be made by the son of a king?

ROSENCRANTZ. Take you me for a sponge, my lord?

◄ In what sense, according to Hamlet, is Rosencrantz like a sponge?

15 HAMLET. Ay, sir, that soaks up the King's countenance,[4]
his rewards, his authorities. But such officers do the King
best service in the end: he keeps them, like an ape an
apple,[5] in the corner of his jaw, first mouth'd, to be last
swallow'd. When he needs what you have glean'd, it is
20 but squeezing you, and, sponge, you shall be dry again.

ROSENCRANTZ. I understand you not, my lord.

HAMLET. I am glad of it, a knavish[6] speech sleeps in a
foolish ear.

7. **body . . . body.** Elizabethan political theory saw the king as the head of a body that was the state (which was in turn made up of the common people). Hamlet is making some jest based on this notion, but the exact meaning of his comment is unclear. Perhaps he is simply making fun of scholarly quibbling about political abstractions.

8. **Of nothing.** This phrase sheds some light on Hamlet's possible meaning: Claudius is not even a man. If a king is viewed abstractly as a thing, as the state, made up of a head (the sovereign) and a body (the people, or the body politic), then this king is nothing, for he is not the rightful sovereign.

9. **Hide fox . . . after.** A phrase from a children's game similar to hide-and-go-seek

ACT IV, SCENE iii

1. **to find the body.** This line is humorous, given what immediately preceded it. It can be interpreted as meaning that Claudius (who hasn't a body) is looking for it.

2. **distracted.** Dim-witted, undiscerning

3. **scourge.** Punishment

4. **Deliberate pause.** The result of deliberation

5. **appliance.** Application, remedy

6. **Without.** Outside

7. **politic.** Shrewd, capable of determining policy (an apt if callous statement to be made about the worms who are eating the body of the former Lord Chamberlain)

8. **emperor for diet.** A pun on the Diet of Worms, a convocation held by the leader of the Holy Roman empire in 1521 so that Martin Luther might explain his new protestant doctrine. Hamlet, of course, had been a student at the university of Wittenberg, where Luther first put forth his beliefs (see "The Intellectual Climate of the Play" on page xi).

9. **fat.** Fatten

10. **is but variable service.** Are but different dishes

ROSENCRANTZ.   My lord, you must tell us where the
25   body is, and go with us to the King.

HAMLET.   The body is with the King, but the King is
not with the body.[7] The King is a thing—

GUILDENSTERN.   A thing, my lord?

HAMLET.   Of nothing,[8] bring me to him. Hide fox, and
30   all after.[9]   *Exeunt.*

SCENE iii

Enter KING *and two or three.*

KING.   I have sent to seek him, and to find the body.[1]
How dangerous is it that this man goes loose!
Yet must not we put the strong law on him.
He's lov'd of the distracted[2] multitude,
5   Who like not in their judgment, but their eyes,
And where 'tis so, th' offender's scourge[3] is weigh'd,
But never the offense. To bear all smooth and even,
This sudden sending him away must seem
Deliberate pause.[4] Diseases desperate grown
10   By desperate appliance[5] are reliev'd,
Or not at all.

Enter ROSENCRANTZ.

How now, what hath befall'n?

ROSENCRANTZ.   Where the dead body is bestow'd, my lord,
We cannot get from him.

KING.   But where is he?

ROSENCRANTZ.   Without,[6] my lord, guarded, to know
     your pleasure.

15   **KING.**   Bring him before us.

ROSENCRANTZ.   Ho, bring in the lord.

They HAMLET *and* GUILDENSTERN *enter.*

KING.   Now, Hamlet, where's Polonius?

HAMLET.   At supper.

KING.   At supper? where?

HAMLET.   Not where he eats, but where 'a is eaten; a
20   certain convocation of politic[7] worms are e'en at him.
Your worm is your only emperor for diet:[8] we fat[9] all
creatures else to fat us, and we fat ourselves for maggots; your fat king and your lean beggar is but variable
service,[10] two dishes, but to one table— that's the end.

◄ Why can't
Claudius simply have
Hamlet arrested for
this murder?

◄ What will eventu-
ally happen both to
a "fat king" and to a
"lean beggar"?

11. **a progress.** An official journey undertaken by a king or queen, usually in the company of many courtiers and servants, for the purpose of seeing and being seen by the common people

12. **nose him.** Smell him

13. **tender.** Feel tenderly about

14. **bark.** Ship

15. **I see . . . that sees them.** Cherubim are an order of winged angels, ranked second to the seraphim. Hamlet reminds Claudius that heaven (and perhaps Hamlet) knows what the king's intentions are.

16. **My mother.** Compare this to Hamlet's previous description of his father as one upon whom "every god did seem to set his seal / To give the world assurance of a man."

17. **at foot.** On foot

18. **at aught.** Worth anything

19. **cicatrice.** Wound

20. **free awe.** Unconstrained fear

25   KING.   Alas, alas!

HAMLET.   A man may fish with the worm that hath eat of a king, and eat of the fish that hath fed of that worm.

KING.   What dost thou mean by this?

HAMLET.   Nothing but to show you how a king may go
30   a progress[11] through the guts of a beggar.

KING.   Where is Polonius?

HAMLET.   In heaven, send thither to see; if your messenger find him not there, seek him i' th' other place yourself. But if indeed you find him not within this
35   month, you shall nose him[12] as you go up the stairs into the lobby.

KING.   [To ATTENDANTS.] Go seek him there.

HAMLET.   'A will stay till you come.   *Exeunt* ATTENDANTS.

KING.   Hamlet, this deed, for thine especial safety—
Which we do tender,[13] as we dearly grieve
40   For that which thou hast done—must send thee hence
With fiery quickness; therefore prepare thyself,
The bark[14] is ready, and the wind at help,
Th' associates tend, and every thing is bent
For England.

HAMLET.   For England.

KING.   Ay, Hamlet.

HAMLET.   Good.

45   KING.   So is it, if thou knew'st our purposes.

HAMLET.   I see a cherub that sees them.[15] But come, for England! Farewell, dear mother.

KING.   Thy loving father, Hamlet.

HAMLET.   My mother:[16] father and mother is man and
50   wife, man and wife is one flesh—so, my mother. Come, for England!   *Exit.*

KING.   Follow him at foot,[17] tempt him with speed aboard.
Delay it not, I'll have him hence tonight.
Away, for every thing is seal'd and done
55   That else leans on th' affair. Pray you make haste.
            Exeunt ROSENCRANTZ *and* GUILDENSTERN.
And, England, if my love thou hold'st at aught[18]—
As my great power thereof may give thee sense,
Since yet thy cicatrice[19] looks raw and red
After the Danish sword, and thy free awe[20]

◄ In what way does Hamlet disparage the kingship which Claudius committed murder to acquire?

◄ Where has Hamlet hidden the body? Does he feel remorse for what he has done? How do you know?

◄ What reason does Claudius give for sending Hamlet away?

◄ What does Hamlet suggest that he knows?

21. **coldly set.** Consider with cool disregard
22. **sovereign process.** Royal design or intent
23. **hectic.** Fever, such as that brought on by tuberculosis
24. **How e'er my haps.** Whatever my fortunes

ACT IV, SCENE iv
1. **conveyance.** Escorted passage
2. **If . . . with us.** If Claudius wishes to see me about any matter
3. **in his eye.** In his presence
4. **softly.** Carefully (This is the reading of Quarto 2. The Folio gives "safely.")
5. **the main.** Whole country
6. **That hath . . . the name.** That has value in it except the honor (or name) to be received by reclaiming it
7. **To pay . . . farm it.** I would not pay five ducats (a small amount) for the privilege of farming it.
8. **ranker.** Greater
9. **Polack.** The Pole (that is, the Polish king)
10. **debate.** Settle
11. **straw.** Minor matter
12. **imposthume.** Festering wound, abscess

Words For Everyday Use

hom • age (häm´ij) *n.*, anything given to show allegiance
ren • dez • vous (rän´dā vōō´) *n.*, agreed meeting place
gar • ri • soned (gar´ə sənd) *adj.*, fortified with military troops

60 Pays <u>homage</u> to us—thou mayst not coldly set[21]
Our sovereign process,[22] which imports at full,
By letters congruing to that effect,
The present death of Hamlet. Do it, England,
For like the hectic[23] in my blood he rages,
65 And thou must cure me. Till I know 'tis done,
How e'er my haps,[24] my joys were ne'er begun.   *Exit.*

◄ What message is in the letters that Claudius has sent to England with Hamlet?

SCENE iv

Enter FORTINBRAS *with his army over the stage.*

FORTINBRAS.   Go, captain, from me greet the Danish king.
Tell him that by his license Fortinbras
Craves the conveyance[1] of a promis'd march
Over his kingdom. You know the <u>rendezvous.</u>
5 If that his Majesty would aught with us,[2]
We shall express our duty in his eye,[3]
And let him know so.

◄ Why has Fortinbras arrived? What previous promise does he want Claudius to keep?

CAPTAIN.   I will do't, my lord.

FORTINBRAS.   Go softly[4] on.   *Exeunt all but the* CAPTAIN.

Enter HAMLET, ROSENCRANTZ, GUILDENSTERN, *etc.*

HAMLET.   Good sir, whose powers are these?

10 CAPTAIN.   They are of Norway, sir.

HAMLET.   How purpos'd, sir, I pray you?

CAPTAIN.   Against some part of Poland.

HAMLET.   Who commands them, sir?

CAPTAIN.   The nephew to old Norway, Fortinbras.

◄ What do Fortinbras and Hamlet have in common?

15 HAMLET.   Goes it against the main[5] of Poland, sir,
Or for some frontier?

CAPTAIN.   Truly to speak, and with no addition,
We go to gain a little patch of ground
That hath in it no profit but the name.[6]
20 To pay five ducats, five, I would not farm it;[7]
Nor will it yield to Norway or the Pole
A ranker[8] rate, should it be sold in fee.

◄ How valuable is the land that the Poles and Norwegians will be fighting over?

HAMLET.   Why then the Polack[9] never will defend it.

CAPTAIN.   Yes, it is already <u>garrison'd.</u>

25 HAMLET.   Two thousand souls and twenty thousand ducats
Will not debate[10] the question of this straw.[11]
This is th' imposthume[12] of much wealth and peace,

13. **This is th' . . . that inward breaks.** This is like an abscess that breaks within the apparently healthy body (of the nation). Hamlet seems to be saying that in times of wealth and peace, people invent squabbles over minor matters and that these squabbles can bring about ruin. Hamlet soon, however, changes his own assessment of the matter.

14. **buy.** Be with

15. **discourse.** Faculty of reasoning

16. **fust.** Mold

17. **craven.** Cowardly

18. **Sith.** Since

19. **gross.** As large and therefore obvious

20. **mass and charge.** Size and expense

21. **Makes mouths . . . event.** Mocks the unseen consequences

22. **an eggshell.** Something worthless

23. **trick.** Illusion

24. **try.** Justify

25. **continent.** Container

That inward breaks,[13] and shows no cause without
Why the man dies. I humbly thank you, sir.

30   CAPTAIN.   God buy[14] you, sir.   *Exit.*

    ROSENCRANTZ.   Will't please you go, my lord?

    HAMLET.   I'll be with you straight—go a little before.
                     Exeunt all but HAMLET.
How all occasions do inform against me,
And spur my dull revenge! What is a man,
If his chief good and market of his time
35   Be but to sleep and feed? a beast, no more.
Sure He that made us with such large discourse,[15]
Looking before and after, gave us not
That capability and godlike reason
To fust[16] in us unus'd. Now whether it be
40   Bestial oblivion, or some craven[17] scruple
Of thinking too precisely on th' event—
A thought which quarter'd hath but one part wisdom
And ever three parts coward—I do not know
Why yet I live to say, "This thing's to do,"
45   Sith[18] I have cause and will, and strength, and means
To do't. Examples gross[19] as earth exhort me:
Witness this army of such mass and charge,[20]
Led by a delicate and tender prince,
Whose spirit with divine ambition puff'd
50   Makes mouths at the invisible event,[21]
Exposing what is mortal and unsure
To all that fortune, death, and danger dare,
Even for an eggshell.[22] Rightly to be great
Is not to stir without great argument,
55   But greatly to find quarrel in a straw
When honor's at the stake. How stand I then,
That have a father kill'd, a mother stain'd,
Excitements of my reason and my blood,
And let all sleep, while to my shame I see
60   The imminent death of twenty thousand men,
That for a fantasy and trick[23] of fame
Go to their graves like beds, fight for a plot
Whereon the numbers cannot try[24] the cause,
Which is not tomb enough and continent[25]
65   To hide the slain? O, from this time forth,
My thoughts be bloody, or be nothing worth!   *Exit.*

(handwritten annotations: "alone", "soliloquy", "man has reason", "mold", "scruple — coward", "revenge", "criticizes himself for the", "worthless", "things he has left unaccomplished")

◀ What sort of person is, in Hamlet's estimation, no more than a beast?

◀ What gifts have people been given?

◀ What has Hamlet had the "cause and will and strength and means" to do?

◀ According to Hamlet, what will a great person do when his or her honor is at stake? What does he feel when he compares himself to Fortinbras? Why?

◀ What does Hamlet say about his thoughts from this point on?

ACT IV, SCENE V

1. **distract.** Extremely moved emotionally
2. **hems.** Utters meaningless sounds
3. **Spurns enviously at straws.** Becomes extremely upset over minor matters
4. **in doubt.** Of questionable meaning
5. **collection.** Suppositions
6. **yawn.** Gape in surprise
7. **strew.** Spread, like seed
8. **ill-breeding minds.** Minds that perpetuate evil
9. **toy.** Trifle
10. **amiss.** Calamity
11. **jealousy.** Suspicion
12. **beauteous.** Beautiful
13. **How now.** How are you
14. *She sings.* Ophelia's songs are fragments of ballads, presumably ones known to Shakespeare's audience, though few have survived. Ophelia does not sing one ballad through but rather, in her madness, moves from part of one ballad to part of another.
15. **cockle hat.** A cockle, or scallop shell, worn on a hat was a sign that the wearer had been on pilgrimage to a holy shrine in Spain
16. **shoon.** Shoes. The cockle hat and the sandals are the uniform of the pilgrim. Lovers were commonly described in song and in poetry as pilgrims (as in John Donne's "Such a pilgrimage were sweet").

sings ballads about death.

| Words For Everyday Use | **im • por • tu • nate** (im pôr´cho͞o nit) *adj.*, urgent; persistent |

Enter HORATIO, QUEEN GERTRUDE, *and a* GENTLEMAN.

QUEEN.   I will not speak with her.

GENTLEMAN.   She is <u>importunate</u>, indeed distract.[1]
Her mood will needs be pitied.

QUEEN.   What would she have?

GENTLEMAN.   She speaks much of her father, says she
     hears
5   There's tricks i' th' world, and hems,[2] and beats her heart,
Spurns enviously at straws,[3] speaks things in doubt[4]
That carry but half sense. Her speech is nothing,
Yet the unshaped use of it doth move
The hearers to collection;[5] they yawn[6] at it,
10   And botch the words up fit to their own thoughts,
Which as her winks and nods and gestures yield them,
Indeed would make one think there might be thought,
Though nothing sure, yet much unhappily.

HORATIO.   'Twere good she were spoken with, for she
     may strew[7]
15   Dangerous conjectures in ill-breeding minds.[8]

QUEEN.   Let her come in.   *In the*   *Exit* GENTLEMAN.
[*Aside.*] To my sick soul, as sin's true nature is,
Each toy[9] seems prologue to some great amiss,[10]
So full of artless jealousy[11] is guilt,
20   It spills itself in fearing to be spilt.

Enter OPHELIA *distracted, with her hair down, playing on a
lute.*

OPHELIA.   Where is the beauteous[12] majesty of Denmark?

QUEEN.   How now,[13] Ophelia?

OPHELIA.   "How should I your true-love   *She sings.*[14]
          know
          From another one?
          By his cockle hat[15] and staff,
25   And his sandal shoon."[16]

QUEEN.   Alas, sweet lady, what imports this song?

OPHELIA.   Say you? Nay, pray you mark.
          "He is dead and gone, lady,   *Song.*
30   He is dead and gone,
          At his head a grass-green turf,
          At his heels a stone."
O ho!

Side notes:

◄ Of whom are Gertrude and the gentleman speaking? How is this person behaving?

◄ What reason does Horatio give for speaking with Ophelia?

◄ What emotion is Gertrude feeling? What does this emotion cause her to think?

Ophelia is mad.

◄ What two losses has Ophelia suffered? How are these two losses reflected in the two verses of this song?

insane

She sings about death + behave erratically

17. **Larded.** Strewn

18. **God dild you.** God yield (or reward) you, an expression of thanks

19. **the owl . . . daughter.** In a familiar folk tale, Jesus appears at a bake shop in the guise of a beggar. The baker's daughter scolds her mother for being generous with him, and so Jesus turns her into an owl.

20. **we know . . . we may be.** Ophelia, like the owl, has gone through a transformation.

21. **God . . . table.** A common expression of blessing

22. **Conceit.** Figure of speech

23. **clo'es.** Clothes

24. **dupp'd.** Did up (latched)

25. **Tomorrow . . . more.** According to a tradition traceable to Chaucer's *The Parliament of Fowls,* on St. Valentine's Day, birds chose their mates. Another tradition held that the first person whom one saw on St. Valentine's Day would be one's beloved.

26. **Indeed, la!** The last thing Ophelia wants to hear at this point, one might imagine, is some man commenting on how pretty she is. Claudius's bungling attempt to soothe her reveals his shallowness and incomprehension.

27. **without an oath.** In the stanza that follows, Ophelia substitutes the words Gis and Cock for Jesus and God, respectively, thus singing the stanza "without an oath."

28. **So would . . . my bed.** Some critics take these last two lines of the ballad to be Ophelia's bitter commentary on Hamlet's behavior toward her.

29. **all will be well.** Not likely, given Ophelia's state of mind. Compare Claudius's "All may be well," act III, scene iii, line 72, also spoken in utter distress.

30. **your good counsel.** Of course, Ophelia has received no counsel at all. In her madness, she may think that she has received counsel on the subject of her brother's learning that her beloved Hamlet has killed their father. If so, the previous line about laying "him i' th' cold ground" could refer both to Polonius and to Hamlet.

QUEEN.   Nay, but, Ophelia—

35   **OPHELIA.**   Pray you mark.
[*Sings.*] "White his shroud as the mountain snow"—

Enter KING.

QUEEN.   Alas, look here, my lord.

OPHELIA.   "Larded[17] all with sweet flowers,   *Song.*
             Which bewept to the ground did not go
40   With true-love showers."

KING.   How do you, pretty lady?

OPHELIA.   Well, God dild you![18] They say the owl was a
baker's daughter.[19] Lord, we know what we are, but
know not what we may be.[20] God be at your table![21]

45   **KING.**   Conceit[22] upon her father.

OPHELIA.   Pray let's have no words of this, but when
they ask you what it means, say you this:
             "Tomorrow is Saint Valentine's day,   *Song.*
             All in the morning betime,
50   And I a maid at your window,
                To be your Valentine.

             "Then up he rose and donn'd his clo'es,[23]
             And dupp'd[24] the chamber-door,
             Let in the maid, that out a maid
55   Never departed more."[25]

KING.   Pretty Ophelia!

OPHELIA.   Indeed, la![26] Without an oath[27] I'll make an
end on't.
Sings.   "By Gis, and by Saint Charity,
                Alack, and fie for shame!
60   Young men will do't if they come to't,
                By Cock, they are to blame.

             "Quoth she, 'Before you tumbled me,
                You promis'd me to wed.'"
(He answers.)
65   " 'So would I 'a' done, by yonder sun,
                And thou hadst not come to my bed.'"[28]

KING.   How long hath she been thus?

OPHELIA.   I hope all will be well.[29] We must be patient,
but I cannot choose but weep to think they would lay
70   him i' th' cold ground. My brother shall know of it,
and so I thank you for your good counsel.[30] Come, my
coach! Good night, ladies, good night. Sweet ladies,
good night, good night.   *Exit.*

◄ *What might hap-
pen when Laertes
hears of Polonius's
death? Who might
be laid in the cold
ground? To what
two people might
Ophelia's word
"him" refer?*

31. **All.** While Claudius says that *all* of Ophelia's grief stems from her father's death, she is grieving over all of the recent tragedies she has experienced.

32. **muddied.** Their thoughts made dark and incoherent, like muddy water stirred up

33. **greenly.** Inexpertly, like a young, or green, person and not like a king

34. **hugger-mugger.** Secrecy

35. **to inter him.** To bury him. Claudius is speaking of burying Polonius secretly, but he might also be secretly intending to bury Hamlet.

36. **buzzers.** Gossipers

37. **necessity, of matter beggar'd.** People's need to spread rumors, having no real matter, or evidence

38. **Will . . . to arraign.** Will not stop at blaming me

39. **murd'ring-piece.** A cannon that shot pelts for the purpose of killing a number of infantrymen at a time

40. **superfluous death.** Superfluous, or unnecessary, because they have already killed him with their words many times over

41. **Swissers.** Swiss guards

42. **overpeering of his list.** Looking over its boundary, overflowing

43. **impiteous.** Lacking in pity

44. **in a riotous head.** At the head of a riotous crowd

45. **rabble.** Contemptuous term for the common people

46. **Antiquity.** The past

47. **The ratifiers . . . word.** Time-honored customs are what approves and supports every word.

48. **false trail.** Like dogs heading down a false trail, the mob seeks revenge on Claudius for the murder of Polonius.

Words
For
Everyday
Use

bat • tal • ion (bə tal´yən) *n.*, large group joined together

pes • ti • lent (pes´tə lənt) *adj.*, contagious; dangerous

ar • raign (ə rān´) *vt.*, call to account; accuse

su • per • flu • ous (sə per´floo əs) *adj.*, surplus; excess

KING. Follow her close, give her good watch, I pray you.

Exit HORATIO.

75 O, this is the poison of deep grief, it springs
All[31] from her father's death—and now behold!
O Gertrude, Gertrude,
When sorrows come, they come not single spies,
But in battalions: first, her father slain;
80 Next, your son gone, and he most violent author
Of his own just remove; the people muddied,[32]
Thick and unwholesome in their thoughts and whispers
For good Polonius' death; and we have done but greenly[33]
In hugger-mugger[34] to inter him;[35] poor Ophelia
85 Divided from herself and her fair judgment,
Without the which we are pictures, or mere beasts;
Last, and as much containing as all these,
Her brother is in secret come from France,
Feeds on this wonder, keeps himself in clouds,
90 And wants not buzzers[36] to infect his ear
With pestilent speeches of his father's death,
Wherein necessity, of matter beggar'd,[37]
Will nothing stick our person to arraign[38]
In ear and ear. O my dear Gertrude, this,
95 Like to a murd'ring-piece,[39] in many places
Gives me superfluous death.[40]   *A noise within.*

QUEEN.   Alack, what noise is this?

KING.   Attend!
Where is my Swissers?[41] Let them guard the door.

Enter a MESSENGER.

What is the matter?

MESSENGER.   Save yourself, my lord!
100 The ocean, overpeering of his list,[42]
Eats not the flats with more impiteous[43] haste
Than young Laertes, in a riotous head,[44]
O'erbears your officers. The rabble[45] call him lord,
And as the world were now but to begin,
105 Antiquity[46] forgot, custom not known,
The ratifiers and props of every word,[47]
They cry, "Choose we, Laertes shall be king!"
Caps, hands, and tongues applaud it to the clouds,
"Laertes shall be king, Laertes king!"   *A noise within.*

110 QUEEN.   How cheerfully on the false trail[48] they cry!
O, this is counter, you false Danish dogs!

Enter LAERTES *with others.*

◄ Why does Claudius order that Ophelia be watched?

◄ Is Ophelia's grief "All from her father's death"? Explain.

◄ According to Claudius, what are people without judgment, or the ability to reason?

◄ Why is Claudius worried about what the people are saying to Laertes?

◄ What danger does Claudius face?

[Handwritten margin notes: "King talks about Ophelias", "Laertes enters & believes", "that claudius poisoned his father...", "some plot to kill his brs death"]

49. **give me leave.** Let me go, permit me to pass through

50. **brands . . . mother.** Laertes is saying that if any part of his blood (the seat of the passions) is calm at this moment, then his mother must have been a harlot and he must be the son of a different father. In Shakespeare's day, prostitutes were sometimes branded in the center of their foreheads with a hot iron.

51. **hedge.** Surround and protect like a hedge

52. **can but peep.** Because the king is hedged about by God's protection, treason can only peep, as through a hedge, at what it wishes to do.

53. **Acts little of its will.** Treason cannot often carry out its will (because of the divinity that protects kings). This notion that God protects the divinely appointed king and punishes treason, despite what people might try to do, was standard belief in Shakespeare's day. It is a masterful piece of irony that Shakespeare should put this speech in the mouth of the treasonous Claudius.

54. **both the worlds.** Heaven and hell. Notice the difference between Laertes's reaction to his father's murder and Hamlet's.

55. **give to negligence.** Care little about, set at naught

56. **Who shall . . . My will.** Claudius's question (Who can hold you back?) and Laertes's answer (Only my will.) provide an interesting commentary on Hamlet's delay. Laertes says that the only thing that could hold him back from his revenge is his own will. Perhaps the same thing is true of Hamlet, with this difference: something in Hamlet does not want revenge. Everything in Laertes does.

57. **my means.** My resources (with which to carry out my revenge)

58. **husband them so well.** Use them so economically

59. **writ.** Written

[handwritten margin notes: "thinks his mother 'harlot' — prostitute"]

[handwritten margin notes: "Laerter wants revenge against claudius for his fathers death"]

Words For Everyday Use	**al • le • giance** (ə lē′jəns) *n.*, loyalty to a person or cause

KING. The doors are broke.

LAERTES. Where is this king? Sirs, stand you all without.

ALL. No, let's come in.

LAERTES. I pray you give me leave.[49]

115 **ALL.** We will, we will.

LAERTES. I thank you, keep the door. [*Exeunt* LAERTES'
followers.] O thou vile king,
Give me my father! *where is my fr.?*

QUEEN. Calmly, good Laertes.

LAERTES. That drop of blood that's calm proclaims me
bastard,

120 Cries cuckold to my father, brands the harlot
Even here between the chaste unsmirched brow
Of my true mother.[50]

KING. What is the cause, Laertes,
That thy rebellion looks so giant-like?
Let him go, Gertrude, do not fear our person:

125 There's such divinity doth hedge[51] a king
That treason can but peep[52] to what it would,
Acts little of his will.[53] Tell me, Laertes,
Why thou art thus incens'd. Let him go, Gertrude.
Speak, man.

LAERTES. Where is my father?

KING. Dead.

QUEEN. But not by him.

130 **KING.** Let him demand his fill.

LAERTES. How came he dead? I'll not be juggled with.
To hell, allegiance! vows, to the blackest devil!
Conscience and grace, to the profoundest pit!
I dare damnation. To this point I stand,

135 That both the worlds[54] I give to negligence,[55]
Let come what comes, only I'll be reveng'd
Most throughly for my father.

KING. Who shall stay you?

LAERTES. My will,[56] not all the world's:
And for my means,[57] I'll husband[58] them so well,

140 They shall go far with little.

KING. Good Laertes,
If you desire to know the certainty
Of your dear father, is't writ[59] in your revenge

[margin handwritten notes:]
let me go

[printed margin notes:]
◀ Why is Laertes
upset?
Thinks Claudius killed Polonius.

◀ According to
Claudius, what pro-
tects a king? Did the
same force protect
the previous king?
God protected the K-8

Laertes wants to harm himself—Claudius.

◀ How do Hamlet
and Laertes differ in
their reactions to the
killing of their
fathers?
manages to talk himself out of warning to harm him.

◀ Claudius points
out that Laertes, in
his impulsiveness, is
on the verge of doing
something wrong.
What is that?

60. **swoopstake.** Like a gambler who takes all the stakes at once, betting on all the possibilities

61. **ope.** Open

62. **life-rend'ring pelican.** The pelican was believed to pierce its own chest and so feed its young.

63. **Repast.** Feed

64. **sensibly.** Emotionally

65. **level.** Truly (from a carpenter's level, used to test whether something is straight, or true)

66. **'pear.** Appear

67. **sense and virtue.** Sensitivity and capability

68. **thy madness . . . the beam.** We shall have recompense or payment equal in weight to the calamity of your madness

69. **Nature . . . loves.** Love is like a chemical process in which a substance is refined, or made pure. The substance refined by love is human nature. Just as a refined substance is more reactive, so human nature, refined by love, is also reactive and seeks out, or bonds strongly with, the thing that it loves.

70. **Hey non . . . nonny.** A nonsense refrain common in light-hearted ballads. The use of such light-hearted phrases in the context of grief is a sign of Ophelia's madness.

71. **persuade.** Argue for

72. **It could not move thus.** Laertes says that he is more moved to take action by Ophelia's madness than he would be if she were sane and attempting to persuade him to take revenge.

73. **You must . . . a-down-a.** Ophelia asks those listening to her to join in the song, singing a nonsense refrain.

74. **the wheel.** 1. the wheel of fortune; 2. a refrain

75. **It is . . . daughter.** Hamlet accused Ophelia of being unchaste. Ophelia here remembers a folk tale or ballad in which a deceitful servant compromised the daughter of his master. Unfortunately, no precise identification has been given to the source to which Ophelia refers, which would most likely have been familiar to Shakespeare's audience.

76. **This nothing's . . . matter.** These mad words make more sense than sane ones would. Laertes seems to feel that Ophelia's previous remark is revealing. Unfortunately, because the work to which Ophelia refers is unknown, it is impossible to say what interpretation Laertes has placed on Ophelia's comment about the false steward.

77. **rosemary.** In the passage that follows, Ophelia hands out flowers. In Shakespeare's day, as in our own, certain plants and flowers had symbolic significance. The significance of the plants mentioned by Ophelia may be as follows: rosemary = remembrance; pansies = thoughts; fennel = flatterers; columbines = infidelity; rue = regret; daisy = unfaithfulness (or dissembling); violets = faithfulness. These were all traditional associations. Ophelia offers fennel and columbines, for flattery and infidelity, to Claudius. She offers rue, for regret, to herself and to Gertrude. She says that violets, or faithfulness, all withered when her father died, for in her madness she associates the loss of Hamlet's faithfulness to her with the death of her father. Indeed, by killing Polonius, Hamlet has proved unfaithful. As a result of killing the old man, Hamlet has had to leave and has thus proved unfaithful.

Words For Everyday Use   **bier** (bir) *n.,* platform for a corpse

That, swoopstake,[60] you will draw both friend and foe,
Winner and loser?

145 LAERTES.   None but his enemies.

KING.   Will you know them then?

LAERTES.   To his good friends thus wide I'll ope[61] my
arms
And like the kind life-rend'ring pelican,[62]
Repast[63] them with my blood.

KING.   Why, now you speak
Like a good child and a true gentleman.
150 That I am guiltless of your father's death,
And am most sensibly[64] in grief for it,
It shall as level[65] to your judgment 'pear[66]
As day does to your eye.

                    A noise within: "Let her come in!"

LAERTES.   How now, what noise is that?

Enter OPHELIA.

155 O heat, dry up my brains! tears seven times salt
Burn out the sense and virtue[67] of mine eye!
By heaven, thy madness shall be paid with weight
Till our scale turn the beam.[68] O rose of May!
Dear maid, kind sister, sweet Ophelia!
160 O heavens, is't possible a young maid's wits
Should be as mortal as an old man's life?
Nature is fine in love, and where 'tis fine,
It sends some precious instance of itself
After the thing it loves.[69]

165 OPHELIA.   "They bore him barefac'd on the bier,   *Song.*
                    Hey non nonny, nonny, hey nonny,[70]
                    And in his grave rain'd many a tear"—
Fare you well, my dove!

LAERTES.   Hadst thou thy wits and didst persuade[71]
revenge,
170 It could not move thus.[72]

OPHELIA.   You must sing, "A-down, a-down," and you
call him a-down-a.[73] O how the wheel[74] becomes it! It
is the false steward, that stole his master's daughter.[75]

LAERTES.   This nothing's more than matter.[76]

175 OPHELIA.   There's rosemary,[77] that's for remembrance;
pray you, love, remember. And there is pansies, that's
for thoughts.

LAERTES.   A document in madness, thoughts and
remembrance fitted.

◄ According to
Claudius, who is not
quilty for Polonius's
death?

*Laertes
misfortunes
are caused
by
Hamlet.*

◄ What two things
have proved to be
mortal?

*Oph. thinks
by killing
pol that
he is
unfaithful*

flowers

78. **You may wear . . . difference.** Gertrude has different reasons than Ophelia for feeling regret.

79. **For bonny . . . joy.** This line from a song is, perhaps, a remembrance of Hamlet.

80. **"And will . . . again?"** Throughout her mad scenes, Ophelia confuses her sorrow over the loss of Hamlet and her sorrow over the loss of her father. This line is an example. It comes from a ballad about someone who has died, but the line could apply equally well to a lost love.

81. **flaxen . . . poll.** Pale yellow was his hair. Flax is a pale yellow plant whose fibers are spun into linen. In many traditional ballads, young people are spoken of as being "flaxen-haired." It is an odd line to appear in the middle of a ballad about a dead man with a white beard. Again, Ophelia is mixing up her lost love and father.

82. **cast away moan.** The line is ambiguous. It may mean to project or express our sorrows. Alternately, it may mean to cast away our sorrows as one might cast or throw a fishing net.

83. **God buy you.** God be with you

84. **commune with.** Share in

85. **collateral.** Collaborative

86. **touch'd.** Involved, guilty

87. **trophy.** Monument

88. **hatchment.** Tablet bearing a coat of arms

89. **ostentation.** Ceremony

90. **the great axe.** The executioner's ax

Words For Everyday Use

flax • en (flak´sən) *adj.*, pale yellow; straw-colored

180 OPHELIA. [*To* CLAUDIUS.] There's fennel for you, and
  columbines. [*To* GERTRUDE.] There's rue for you, and
  here's some for me, we may call it herb of grace a'
  Sundays. You may wear your rue with a difference.[78]
  There's a daisy. I would give you some violets, but they
185 wither'd all when my father died. They say 'a made a
  good end—
  [*Sings.*] "For bonny sweet Robin is all my joy."[79]

◄ What withered when Ophelia's father died?

(remberance 2 Hamlet)

LAERTES. Thought and afflictions, passion, hell itself,
  She turns to favor and to prettiness.

190 OPHELIA. "And will 'a not come again?[80]   *Song.*
        And will 'a not come again?
          No, no, he is dead,
          Go to thy death-bed,
        He never will come again.

195   His beard was as white as snow,
        All flaxen was his poll,[81]
          He is gone, he is gone,
          And we cast away moan,[82]
        God 'a' mercy on his soul!"
200 And of all Christians' souls, I pray God. God buy you.[83]
                              Exit.

she's confused &
her br. hamlet
yellow
God be w' you

LAERTES. Do you see this, O God?
KING. Laertes, I must commune with[84] your grief,
  Or you deny me right. Go but apart,
  Make choice of whom your wisest friends you will,
205 And they shall hear and judge 'twixt you and me.
  If by direct or by collateral[85] hand
  They find us touch'd, we will our kingdom give,
  Our crown, our life, and all that we call ours
  To you in satisfaction; but if not,
210 Be you content to lend your patience to us,
  And we shall jointly labor with your soul
  To give it due content.

I share your grief

guilty

◄ Claudius says that he would be willing to give up his kingdom to Laertes if Laertes found what to be true?

LAERTES.   Let this be so.
  His means of death, his obscure funeral—
  No trophy,[87] sword, nor hatchment[88] o'er his bones,
215 No noble rite nor formal ostentation[89]—
  Cry to be heard, as 'twere from heaven to earth,
  That I must call't in question.

No ceremony

KING.   So you shall,
  And where th' offense is, let the great axe[90] fall.
  I pray you go with me.   *Exeunt.*

executioners

◄ Where does Claudius say that the "great axe" should fall?

ACT IV, SCENE vi

1. **overlook'd.** Looked over
2. **means.** Access
3. **two days . . . sea.** At sea two days
4. **appointment.** Furnishings
5. **thieves of mercy.** Merciful thieves
6. **repair.** Come
7. **fly.** Flee
8. **dumb.** Speechless
9. **too light . . . matter.** The words are too light, like a cannonball too small for the bore (the interior of the barrel) of the cannon.

Words For Everyday Use

val • or (val´ər) *n.*, marked courage; bravery

Enter HORATIO *and others.*

HORATIO.   What are they that would speak with me?

GENTLEMAN.   Sea-faring men, sir. They say they have
letters for you.

Horatio meets with sailors

◄ Who wishes to
speak with Horatio?

HORATIO.   Let them come in.   *Exit* GENTLEMAN.
5 I do not know from what part of the world
I should be greeted, if not from Lord Hamlet.

and gives him a letter from Hamlet's adventures on sea

Enter SAILORS.

FIRST SAILOR.   God bless you, sir.

HORATIO.   Let him bless thee too.

FIRST SAILOR.   'A shall, sir, and 't please him. There's a
10 letter for you, sir—it came from th' embassador that
was bound for England—if your name be Horatio, as I
am let to know it is.

HORATIO.   [*Reads.*] "Horatio, when thou shalt have
overlook'd[1] this, give these fellows some means[2] to the
15 King, they have letters for him. Ere we were two days
old at sea,[3] a pirate of very warlike appointment[4] gave
us chase. Finding ourselves too slow of sail, we put on a
compell'd <u>valor</u>, and in the grapple I boarded them. On
the instant they got clear of our ship, so I alone became
20 their prisoner. They have dealt with me like thieves of
mercy,[5] but they knew what they did: I am to do a
good turn for them. Let the King have the letters I have
sent, and repair[6] thou to me with as much speed as
thou wouldest fly[7] death. I have words to speak in
25 thine ear will make thee dumb,[8] yet are they much too
light for the bore of the matter.[9] These good fellows
will bring thee where I am. Rosencrantz and
Guildenstern hold their course for England, of them I
have much to tell thee. Farewell.
30   He that thou knowest thine,
                                    Hamlet."
Come, I will give you way for these your letters,
And do 't the speedier that you may direct me
To him from whom you brought them.   *Exeunt.*

pirates

◄ From whom does
this letter come?
Who was captured
by pirates?

attacked the ship

Hamlet has been captured + taken prisoner

Letter—tells Horatio that Hamlet has an incredible story to tell him when he arrives back Tomorrow.

ACT IV, SCENE vii

1. **my acquittance seal.** Certify that I am not guilty
2. **Sith.** Since
3. **knowing.** Understanding
4. **It well appears.** So it appears
5. **unsinow'd.** Unsinewed, weak
6. **Lives . . . looks.** Lives for signs of approval from him
7. **conjunctive.** Conjoined
8. **as the star . . . by her.** It was believed that the stars were embedded within hollow glass spheres that encircled the earth
9. **a public count.** A public accounting or trial
10. **the general gender.** Common people
11. **spring . . . stone.** Reference to a folk belief that certain waters had the ability to turn wood into stone (perhaps by impregnating the wood with minerals)
12. **gyves.** Shackles, fetters
13. **too slightly timber'd.** Made of wood that is too light
14. **loud.** Strong, fierce
15. **reverted.** Returned

Words
For
Everyday
Use

cap • i • tal (kap´ət l) *adj.*, extremely serious; calling for the death penalty

The King tells Laertes that Hamlet

Enter KING *and* LAERTES.

KING. Now must your conscience my acquittance seal,[1]
And you must put me in your heart for friend,
Sith[2] you have heard, and with a knowing[3] ear,
That he which hath your noble father slain
5 Pursued my life.

◄ According to Claudius, why should Laertes consider him a friend?

is responsible for

LAERTES.   It well appears.[4] But tell me
Why you proceeded not against these feats
So criminal and so <u>capital</u> in nature,
As by your safety, greatness, wisdom, all things else
You mainly were stirr'd up.

◄ What does *his* Laertes want to know?

to his death.

KING.   O, for two special reasons,
10 Which may to you perhaps seem much unsinow'd,[5] lo
But yet to me th' are strong. The Queen his mother
Lives almost by his looks,[6] and for myself—
My virtue or my plague, be it either which—
She is so conjunctive[7] to my life and soul,
15 That, as the star moves not but in his sphere,
I could not but by her.[8] The other motive,
Why to a public count[9] I might not go,
Is the great love the general gender[10] bear him
Who, dipping all his faults in their affection,
20 Work like the spring that turneth wood to stone,[11]
Convert his gyves[12] to graces, so that my arrows,
Too slightly timber'd[13] for so loud[14] a wind,
Would have reverted[15] to my bow again,
But not where I have aim'd them.

◄ What two reasons did Claudius have for not bringing Hamlet to trial for the murder?

LAERTES.   And so have I a noble father lost,
26 A sister driven into desp'rate terms,
Whose worth, if praises may go back again,
Stood challenger on mount of all the age
For her perfections—but my revenge will come.

◄ What does Laertes say will come?

30 KING.   Break not your sleeps for that. You must not
think
That we are made of stuff so flat and dull
That we can let our beard be shook with danger
And think it pastime. You shortly shall hear more.
I lov'd your father, and we love ourself,
35 And that, I hope, will teach you to imagine—

Enter a MESSENGER *with letters.*   *Messenger arrives*

How now? What news?   *with Hamlets letter +*

Tells king that Hamlet is alive.

16. **naked.** With nothing, destitute
17. **abuse.** Misuse, trickery
18. **character.** Handwriting
19. **devise.** Hazard a guess for
20. **Thus . . . thou.** This statement is often accompanied in the theater by the gesture of a sword thrust.
21. **as checking at.** Having diverted himself from
22. **ripe . . . device.** Well thought out, fully planned
23. **uncharge the practice.** Not bring accusations about the action
24. **organ.** Instrument (by which Hamlet is killed)

MESSENGER.   Letters, my lord, from Hamlet:
These to your Majesty, this to the Queen.

KING.   From Hamlet? Who brought them?

MESSENGER.   Sailors, my lord, they say, I saw them not.
40 They were given me by Claudio. He receiv'd them
Of him that brought them.

KING.   Laertes, you shall hear them.
—Leave us.   *Exit* MESSENGER.
[*Reads.*] "High and mighty, You shall know I am set
naked[16] on your kingdom. Tomorrow shall I beg leave
45 to see your kingly eyes, when I shall, first asking you
pardon thereunto, recount the occasion of my sudden
and more strange return.

                              Hamlet."

What should this mean? Are all the rest come back?
50 Or is it some abuse,[17] and no such thing?

LAERTES.   Know you the hand?

KING.   'Tis Hamlet's character.[18] "Naked"!
And in a postscript here he says "alone."
Can you devise[19] me?

LAERTES.   I am lost in it, my lord. But let him come,
55 It warms the very sickness in my heart
That I shall live and tell him to his teeth,
"Thus didst thou."[20]

KING.   If it be so, Laertes—
As how should it be so? how otherwise?—
Will you be rul'd by me?

LAERTES.   Ay, my lord,
60 So you will not o'errule me to a peace.

KING.   To thine own peace. If he be now returned
As checking at[21] his voyage, and that he means
No more to undertake it, I will work him
To an exploit, now ripe in my device,[22]
65 Under the which he shall not choose but fall;
And for his death no wind of blame shall breathe,
But even his mother shall uncharge the practice,[23]
And call it accident.

LAERTES.   My lord, I will be rul'd,
The rather if you could devise it so
70 That I might be the organ.[24]

KING.   It falls right.
You have been talk'd of since your travel much,

25. **sum of parts.** Qualities, taken as a whole
26. **Of . . . siege.** Of least importance (in comparison to your other qualities). Claudius is often referred to in the play as a flatterer.
27. **very riband.** Mere ribbon
28. **becomes.** Suits
29. **since.** Ago
30. **can well.** Can do or perform well
31. **incorps'd . . . beast.** Placed in the same body as the horse and made part man and part horse
32. **So far . . . did.** His abilities so far exceeded what I could image that I could not imagine displays of horsemanship as good as those that he actually performed.
33. **made confession of you.** Spoke about you
34. **for . . . especial.** For your swordsmanship especially
35. **scrimers.** Master fencers
36. **play.** Fence

| Words For Everyday Use | **liv • er • y** (liv´ər ē) *n.*, identifying dress of a particular group |
| | **grave • ness** (grāv´nis) *n.*, seriousness |

And that in Hamlet's hearing, for a quality
Wherein they say you shine. Your sum of parts[25]
Did not together pluck such envy from him
75 As did that one, and that, in my regard,
Of the unworthiest siege.[26]

LAERTES.   What part is that, my lord?

KING.   A very riband[27] in the cap of youth,
Yet needful too, for youth no less becomes[28]
The light and careless <u>livery</u> that it wears
80 Than settled age his sables and his weeds,
Importing health and <u>graveness</u>. Two months since[29]
Here was a gentleman of Normandy:
I have seen myself, and serv'd against, the French,
And they can well[30] on horseback, but this gallant
85 Had witchcraft in't, he grew unto his seat,
And to such wondrous doing brought his horse,
As had he been incorps'd and demi-natur'd
With the brave beast.[31] So far he topp'd my thought,
That I in forgery of shapes and tricks
90 Come short of what he did.[32]

LAERTES.   A Norman was't?

KING.   A Norman.

LAERTES.   Upon my life, Lamord.

KING.   The very same.

LAERTES.   I know him well. He is the brooch indeed
And gem of all the nation.

95 KING.   He made confession of you,[33]
And gave you such a masterly report
For art and exercise in your defense,
And for your rapier most especial[34]
That he cried out 'twould be a sight indeed
100 If one could match you. The scrimers[35] of their nation
He swore had neither motion, guard, nor eye,
If you oppos'd them. Sir, this report of his
Did Hamlet so envenom with his envy
That he could nothing do but wish and beg
105 Your sudden coming o'er to play[36] with you.
Now, out of this—

LAERTES.   What out of this, my lord?

KING.   Laertes, was your father dear to you?
Or are you like the painting of a sorrow,
A face without a heart?

LAERTES.   Why ask you this?

Plan to cover Laert sword with poison.

Claudius

◄ What did Claudius hear about Laertes?

will be present

◄ How did Hamlet react to the report of Laertes's skill with a sword?

will pursue Ss less wise.

37. **in passages of proof.** Proved by what happens
38. **qualifies.** Weakens
39. **week.** Wick. The burned portion of the wick that must be removed for the candle to flame properly
40. **still.** Always
41. **plurisy.** Excess, as in lungs inflamed by illness
42. **his . . . too much.** Its own excess
43. **like . . . easing.** It was believed in Shakespeare's day that every sigh cost a person a drop of blood. Claudius compares the act of speaking about what one should do to the sighing that would sap one's blood.
44. **quick . . . ulcer.** To the center of the wound, to the point
45. **To cut . . . church.** Churches were by law and by custom held to be places of sanctuary, or safety from prosecution or harm.
46. **murther sanctuarize.** Provide protection against murder
47. **close.** Closed
48. **put on.** Encourage
49. **in fine.** In short
50. **remiss.** Not cautious, negligent
51. **foils.** Swords
52. **unbated.** Unblunted, not covered with a protective tip as is done when the swordplay is merely for sport
53. **a pass of practice.** An interchange meant merely for exercise
54. **unction.** Ointment
55. **mountebank.** Traveling salesperson
56. **mortal.** Deadly
57. **cataplasm so rare.** Poultice or dressing so effective
58. **simples.** Medicinal herbs, medicines
59. **virtue.** Power, efficacy
60. **touch my point.** Place on my sword
61. **gall.** Rub
62. **fit us to our shape.** Accomplish our designs
63. **drift.** Plan
64. **look through.** Be revealed by
65. **assay'd.** Tried

Words For Everyday Use

a • bate (ə bāt´) *vt.*, make less
a • bate • ment (ə bāt´mənt) *n.*, amount deducted
re • quite (ri kwīt´) *vt.*, retaliate against
con • ta • gion (kən tā´jən) *n.*, agent causing disease

110 KING.   Not that I think you did not love your father,
But that I know love is begun by time,
And that I see, in passages of proof[37]
Time qualifies[38] the spark and fire of it.

There lives within the very flame of love
115 A kind of week[39] or snuff that will <u>abate</u> it,
And nothing is at a like goodness still,[40]
For goodness, growing to a plurisy,[41]
Dies in his own too much.[42] That we would do,
We should do when we would; for this "would" changes,
120 And hath <u>abatements</u> and delays as many
As there are tongues, are hands, are accidents,
And then this "should" is like a spendthrift sigh,
That hurts by easing.[43] But to the quick of th' ulcer:[44]

Hamlet comes back. What would you undertake
125 To show yourself indeed your father's son
More than in words?

LAERTES.   To cut his throat i' th' church.[45]

KING.   No place indeed should murther sanctuarize,[46]
Revenge should have no bounds. But, good Laertes,
Will you do this, keep close[47] within your chamber.
130 Hamlet return'd shall know you are come home.
We'll put on[48] those shall praise your excellence,
And set a double varnish on the fame
The Frenchman gave you, bring you in fine[49] together,
And wager o'er your heads. He, being remiss,[50]
135 Most generous, and free from all contriving,
Will not peruse the foils,[51] so that with ease,
Or with a little shuffling, you may choose
A sword unbated,[52] and in a pass of practice[53]
<u>Requite</u> him for your father.

LAERTES.   I will do't,
140 And for that purpose I'll anoint my sword.
I bought an unction[54] of a mountebank,[55]
So mortal[56] that, but dip a knife in it,
Where it draws blood, no cataplasm so rare,[57]
Collected from all simples[58] that have virtue[59]
145 Under the moon, can save the thing from death
That is but scratch'd withal. I'll touch my point[60]
With this <u>contagion</u>, that if I gall[61] him slightly,
It may be death.

KING.   Let's further think of this,
Weigh what convenience both of time and means
150 May fit us to our shape.[62] If this should fail,
And that our drift[63] look through[64] our bad performance,
'Twere better not assay'd;[65] therefore this project

◄ What would have happened already if Hamlet had followed the advice that Claudius now gives to Laertes?

◄ What would Laertes be willing to do? In what way does he differ from Hamlet?

◄ Is Hamlet indeed "free from all contriving"? Explain.

◄ What is the plan for killing Hamlet?

66. **back or second.** Backup plan
67. **blast in proof.** Blow up in our faces when we try it out
68. **Soft.** An expression like our modern-day "Well, now" that directs cautious attention to something
69. **cunnings.** Abilities
70. **ha't.** Have it
71. **preferr'd.** Procured for
72. **for the nonce.** For the occasion
73. **stuck.** Sticking, sword thrust
74. **askaunt.** Alongside
75. **hoary.** Gray, as with age
76. **glassy.** Mirrorlike
77. **Therewith.** With which (Ophelia made garlands by intertwining willow branches and flowers.)
78. **liberal.** Unchecked, free-talking
79. **cold.** Chaste
80. **pendant.** Overhanging
81. **crownet weeds.** Crowning garlands
82. **Clamb'ring.** Climbing
83. **envious sliver.** Spiteful small branch
84. **chaunted.** Chanted, sang
85. **lauds.** Hymns, tunes
86. **incapable of her own distress.** Not understanding her own danger
87. **indued.** Accustomed
88. **that element.** The water
89. **their drink.** The water that they had soaked up
90. **It is our trick.** It is normal for us
91. **these.** Laertes's tears
92. **woman . . . out.** The woman in me will be gone
93. **fain would.** Desires to

Words For Everyday Use

chal • ice (chal´is) *n.*, cup for holy wine
ven • om'd (ven´əmd) *adj.*, poisoned
tread (tred) *vi.*, walk; step

gar • land (gar´lənd) *n.*, wreath or chain of flowers
bough (bou) *n.*, branch of a tree

Should have a back or second,[66] that might hold
If this did blast in proof.[67] Soft,[68] let me see.
155 We'll make a solemn wager on your cunnings[69]—
I ha't![70]
When in your motion you are hot and dry—
As make your bouts more violent to that end—
And that he calls for drink, I'll have preferr'd[71] him
160 A <u>chalice</u> for the nonce,[72] whereon but sipping,
If he by chance escape your <u>venom'd</u> stuck,[73]
Our purpose may hold there. But stay, what noise?

Enter QUEEN.

QUEEN.   One woe doth <u>tread</u> upon another's heel,
So fast they follow. Your sister's drown'd, Laertes.

165 LAERTES.   Drown'd! O, where?

QUEEN.   There is a willow grows askaunt[74] the brook,
That shows his hoary[75] leaves in the glassy[76] stream,
Therewith[77] fantastic <u>garlands</u> did she make
Of crow-flowers, nettles, daisies, and long purples
170 That liberal[78] shepherds give a grosser name,
But our cold[79] maids do dead men's fingers call them.
There on the pendant[80] <u>boughs</u> her crownet weeds[81]
Clamb'ring[82] to hang, an envious sliver[83] broke,
When down her weedy trophies and herself
175 Fell in the weeping brook. Her clothes spread wide,
And mermaid-like awhile they bore her up,
Which time she chaunted[84] snatches of old lauds,[85]
As one incapable of her own distress,[86]
Or like a creature native and indued[87]
180 Unto that element.[88] But long it could not be
Till that her garments, heavy with their drink,[89]
Pull'd the poor wretch from her melodious lay
To muddy death.

LAERTES.   Alas, then she is drown'd?

QUEEN.   Drown'd, drown'd.

185 LAERTES.   Too much of water hast thou, poor Ophelia,
And therefore I forbid my tears; but yet
It is our trick,[90] Nature her custom holds,
Let shame say what it will; when these[91] are gone,
The woman will be out.[92] Adieu, my lord,
190 I have a speech a' fire that fain would[93] blaze,
But that this folly drowns it.   *Exit.*

KING.   Let's follow, Gertrude.
How much I had to do to calm his rage!
Now fear I this will give it start again,
Therefore let's follow.   *Exeunt.*

◄ What backup
plan does Claudius
devise?

◄ What has hap-
pened to Ophelia?

◄ How did Ophelia
die?

◄ What does
Laertes try not to do?
Is he successful?

◄ What does
Claudius tell
Gertrude that he has
been doing?

Responding to the Selection

With what character in act IV do you most sympathize, and why?

Reviewing the Selection

Recalling and Interpreting

1. **R:** Where does Hamlet tell Claudius that Polonius is?

2. **I:** Does Hamlet show remorse for killing Polonius? How can you explain Hamlet's reaction?

3. **R:** After telling Hamlet that he is to go to England, and after the exit of Rosencrantz and Guildenstern, what does Claudius reveal when he is left alone on stage?

4. **I:** Are Rosencrantz and Guildenstern aware of Claudius's intentions? Why does Claudius feel certain that his request will be carried out?

5. **R:** With whom does Hamlet speak in act IV, scene iv? What does Hamlet learn from this person?

6. **I:** How does Hamlet respond to the news?

7. **R:** In what condition is Ophelia when she comes before Gertrude and Claudius? What are the two subjects of Ophelia's songs?

8. **I:** What might be the causes of Ophelia's madness?

9. **R:** Who has returned from France, and what are the people saying to this person?

10. **I:** Why is Claudius so worried about what is being said to Laertes?

11. **R:** What does Laertes seek when he bursts into the presence of the king?

12. **I:** How does Laertes's reaction to the killing of his father differ from Hamlet's reaction to the killing of his father?

13. **R:** What does Claudius tell Laertes to calm him down? What does Claudius say to Laertes at the end of scene v?

14. **I:** Why might Claudius want to win Laertes over?

15. **R:** How does Hamlet come to be back in Denmark?

16. **I:** How does Claudius feel about Hamlet's return to Denmark? How do you know?

17. **R:** What happens to Ophelia?

18. **I:** Is Ophelia's death a suicide? Why, or why not?

Synthesizing

19. What are the consequences of the killing of Polonius?

20. Is Hamlet responsible for the death of Ophelia? Why, or why not?

Understanding Literature (QUESTIONS FOR DISCUSSION)

1. Symbol. A **symbol** is something that stands both for itself and for something beyond itself. Of what are the following things symbols in this play?

> The rue that Ophelia offers both to Gertrude and to herself.
> The willow tree on which Ophelia hangs garlands.
> The brook on which Ophelia floats.

2. Foil. A **foil** is a character whose attributes, or characteristics, contrast with, and therefore throw into relief, the attributes of another character. In this act, both Fortinbras and Laertes serve as foils for Hamlet. In what significant ways does Hamlet differ from these other two young men?

3. Character. A **character** is a figure in a literary work. The term *character* is also used to denote the personality of such a figure. How has Ophelia changed since her first appearance in the play? What do you think was the exact nature of her former relationship with Hamlet? What about Ophelia's character leads you to this conclusion?

4. Theme. A **theme** is a main idea in a literary work. One of the recurring themes in *Hamlet* is the consequences of deception and dishonesty. What are the consequences of deception for Polonius? for Ophelia? for Gertrude? for Claudius? What sort of deception is being planned in the last scene of act IV?

5. Theme. A **theme** is a main idea in a literary work. One of the themes of *Hamlet* is the relationship between thought and action. In the "To be, or not to be" soliloquy in act III, how does Hamlet describe this relationship? How does he describe it in the "How all occasions do inform against me" soliloquy in act IV?

ACT V, SCENE i

1. **she . . . salvation?** She committed suicide. The First Clown questions the idea that Ophelia is to be buried in hallowed ground, with a full Christian ceremony, given that she killed herself.

2. **straight.** Right away, with a pun on straight in the sense of not crooked, implying that the job should be well done

3. **crowner . . . her.** The coroner has held a hearing regarding her.

4. *se offendendo.* The First Clown is pretending to a knowledge of Latin, the language of learned discourse. *Se offendendo* is a malapropism for *se defendendo*, Latin for "in self defense."

5. **an act . . . to perform.** Again, the Clown is pretending to knowledge that he does not have, in this case knowledge of legal precedent. The law in Britain had long recognized that in order to be held responsible for an action, one had to be in one's right mind and thus capable of understanding what one was doing. An action performed in such a "witting" state involved three parts, a prior imagining of the act, a resolution to commit the act, and the act itself. The Clown's confusion is much to the point because Ophelia was not in a state of mind that would allow for premeditation. The Clown completely misses this point when he substitutes for the first two conditions what are merely synonyms for the third.

6. **argal.** A corruption of the Latin *ergo*, meaning "therefore"

7. **delver.** One who digs

8. **will he, nill he.** Willy nilly, whether he wishes to or not

9. **Here lies . . . his own life.** The Clown argues that if a man goes to the water intending to drown himself, he is guilty of committing suicide. If the water overtakes him and he drowns, he has not committed suicide.

10. **crowner's quest.** Coroner's inquest

11. **If this had . . . burial.** The Second Clown says that the truth is that this woman would not have been given a Christian burial if she had not been of the noble class.

12. **even-Christen.** Fellow Christians who are not nobles

13. **ancient gentlemen.** People with real ancestral claims to being gentlemen (A rallying cry among common people revolting against their masters during the fourteenth century was "When Adam delv'd and Eve span (spun),/Who was then the gentleman?"

14. **ditchers.** Ditch diggers

15. **hold up.** Continue, carry on

16. **bore arms.** A pun expressing the idea that Adam both had arms in the sense of limbs and arms in the sense of a coat of arms belonging to a noble family

Act V

Enter two CLOWNS *with spades and mattocks.*

FIRST CLOWN.   Is she to be buried in Christian burial when she willfully seeks her own salvation?[1]

SECOND CLOWN.   I tell thee she is, therefore make her grave straight.[2] The crowner hath sate on her,[3] and
5 finds it Christian burial.

FIRST CLOWN.   How can that be, unless she drown'd herself in her own defense?

SECOND CLOWN.   Why, 'tis found so.

FIRST CLOWN.   It must be *se offendendo,*[4] it cannot be
10 else. For here lies the point: if I drown myself wittingly, it argues an act, and an act hath three branches—it is to act, to do, to perform;[5] argal,[6] she drown'd herself wittingly.

SECOND CLOWN.   Nay, but hear you, goodman delver[7]—

15 FIRST CLOWN.   Give me leave. Here lies the water; good. Here stands the man, good. If the man go to this water and drown himself, it is, will he, nill he,[8] he goes, mark you that. But if the water come to him and drown him, he drowns not himself; argal, he that is not guilty
20 of his own death shortens not his own life.[9]

SECOND CLOWN.   But is this law?

FIRST CLOWN.   Ay marry, is't—crowner's quest[10] law.

SECOND CLOWN.   Will you ha' the truth an't? If this had not been a gentlewoman, she should have been
25 buried out a' Christian burial.[11]

FIRST CLOWN.   Why, there thou say'st, and the more pity that great folk should have count'nance in this world to drown or hang themselves, more than their even-Christen.[12] Come, my spade. There is no ancient
30 gentlemen[13] but gard'ners, ditchers,[14] and grave-makers; they hold up[15] Adam's profession.

SECOND CLOWN.   Was he a gentleman?

FIRST CLOWN.   'A was the first that ever bore arms.[16]

SECOND CLOWN.   Why, he had none.

35 FIRST CLOWN.   What, art a heathen? How dost thou understand the Scripture? The Scripture says Adam digg'd;

◄ Why is the first gravedigger surprised that Ophelia is going to be given a Christian burial?

Preparing Ophelia's grave.

◄ According to the gravedigger, what is a pity?

◄ What two senses of "arms" are being confused by the gravedigger?

17. **confess thyself.** From the saying "Confess thyself and be hanged"
18. **unyoke.** Finish (with this job or with your thinking), from the unyoking of cattle at the end of a day's plowing
19. **Marry.** By Mary, an oath
20. **Mass.** By the Mass, an oath
21. **Cudgel.** Beat
22. **your dull . . . beating.** Your jackass will not move faster because you beat him
23. **sup.** Drink
24. **contract . . . behove.** Shorten the time, for my desire
25. **meet.** Proper. The Clown sings a mixed up version of a popular song called "The Aged Lover Renounceth Love."
26. **Custom.** Habit
27. **a property of easiness.** Something that he feels comfortable about doing
28. **shipped me into the land.** Sent me into the earth
29. **As . . . such.** As if I had never been such a thing as a young man in love

Words
For
Everyday
Use

ma • son (mā´sən) *n.*, person who builds with stone
ten • ant (ten´ənt) *n.*, person who pays rent on a house or land

could he dig without arms? I'll put another question to thee. If thou answerest me not to the purpose, confess thyself—[17]

40 SECOND CLOWN.   Go to.

FIRST CLOWN.   What is he that builds stronger than either the <u>mason</u>, the shipwright, or the carpenter?

SECOND CLOWN.   The gallows-maker, for that outlives a thousand <u>tenants</u>.

◀ What answer does the second gravedigger give to the first's riddle?

45 FIRST CLOWN.   I like thy wit well, in good faith. The gallows does well; but how does it well? It does well to those that do ill. Now thou dost ill to say the gallows is built stronger than the church; argal, the gallows may do well to thee. To't again, come.

50 SECOND CLOWN.   Who builds stronger than a mason, a shipwright, or a carpenter?

FIRST CLOWN.   Ay, tell me that, and unyoke.[18]

SECOND CLOWN.   Marry,[19] now I can tell.

FIRST CLOWN.   To't.

55 SECOND CLOWN.   Mass,[20] I cannot tell.

Enter HAMLET *and* HORATIO *afar off.*

Hamlets surprised

◀ What answer to the riddle did the gravedigger have in mind?

FIRST CLOWN.   Cudgel[21] thy brains no more about it, for your dull ass will not mend his pace with beating,[22] and when you are ask'd this question next, say "a gravemaker": the houses he makes lasts till doomsday.
60 Go get thee in, and fetch me a sup[23] of liquor.

by the gravedigger's joke

Exit SECOND CLOWN. FIRST CLOWN *digs.*
"In youth when I did love, did love,   *Song.*
   Methought it was very sweet,
To contract—O—the time for—a—my behove,[24]
   O, methought there—a—was nothing—a—meet."[25]

65 HAMLET.   Has this fellow no feeling of his business? 'a sings in grave-making.

HORATIO.   Custom[26] hath made it in him a property of easiness.[27]

◀ Why isn't the gravedigger more solemn, given the nature of his work?

HAMLET.   'Tis e'en so, the hand of little employment
70 hath the daintier sense.

◀ According to Hamlet, who has daintier senses?

FIRST CLOWN.   "But age with his stealing steps   *Song.*
   Hath clawed me in his clutch,
   And hath shipped me into the land,[28]
   As if I had never been such."[29]
Throws up a shovelful of earth with a skull in it.

30. **jowls.** Slams, with a pun on jowls in the sense of the flesh that hangs on the jawbone

31. **Cain's jawbone.** This statement represents a popular belief that the Biblical Cain killed his brother with the jawbone of an ass. The actual weapon is not mentioned in the Biblical story, although Samson is said to have used the jawbone of an ass as a weapon.

32. **pate.** Head

33. **o'erreaches.** Overrules

34. **to beg it.** To beg for it (In other words, the courtier might hope by praising the horse to receive it as a gift from his master.)

35. **Ay.** Aye, yes

36. **my Lady Worm's.** Now the courtier has as his beloved My Lady the worm

37. **chopless.** Without chops, or cheeks

38. **sexton.** Person responsible for the maintenance of church property, including the property on which people used to be buried

39. **revolution.** Change (brought about by the revolving wheel of fortune)

40. **bones . . . breeding.** Were these bones worth no more than the cost involved in breeding them

41. **loggats.** A country game

42. **meet.** Proper

43. **quiddities . . . quillities.** His subtle arguments, or quibbles

44. **tenures.** Rights in property

45. **sconce.** Head

46. **statutes . . . recoveries.** Various legal devices

47. **fine pate.** Subtle, discriminating head

48. **vouch.** Assure

49. **indentures.** Legal document consisting of two copies written on the same piece of paper and cut in two by means of an uneven line. This was done as a precaution against forgery.

50. **conveyances of his lands.** Deeds conveying purchased lands to him

51. **They are . . . in that.** Legal documents, written on parchment, in the end offer no assurance, and people who think that they do are but sheep and calves, who follow the common way of thinking.

Words For Everyday Use

cour • ti • er (kôrt´ē ər) *n.*, royal attendant

bat • ter • y (bat´ər ē) *n.*, act of beating; pounding

parch • ment (pärch´mənt) *n.*, paper-thin animal skins used instead of paper from wood

75   HAMLET.   That skull had a tongue in it, and could sing
     once. How the knave jowls[30] it to the ground, as if 'twere
     Cain's jawbone,[31] that did the first murder! This might
     be the pate[32] of a politician, which this ass now o'er-
     reaches,[33] one that would circumvent God, might it not?

80   HORATIO.   It might, my lord.

     HAMLET.   Or of a courtier, which could say, "Good mor-
     row, sweet lord! How dost thou, sweet lord?" This might
     be my Lord Such-a-one, that prais'd my Lord Such-a-
     one's horse when 'a meant to beg it,[34] might it not?

85   HORATIO.   Ay,[35] my lord.

     HAMLET.   Why, e'en so, and now my Lady Worm's,[36]
     chopless,[37] and knock'd about the mazzard with a sex-
     ton's[38] spade. Here's fine revolution,[39] and we had so the
     trick to see't. Did these bones cost no more the breed-
90   ing,[40] but to play at loggats[41] with them? Mine ache to
     think on't.

     FIRST CLOWN.   "A pickaxe and a spade, a spade,   Song.
                         For and a shrouding sheet:
                         O, a pit of clay for to be made
95   For such a guest is meet."[42]

                                          Throws up another skull.

     HAMLET.   There's another. Why may not that be the
     skull of a lawyer? Where be his quiddities now, his quil-
     lities,[43] his cases, his tenures,[44] and his tricks? Why does
     he suffer this mad knave now to knock him about the
100 sconce[45] with a dirty shovel, and will not tell him of
     his action of battery? Hum! This fellow might be in 's
     time a great buyer of land, with his statutes, his recog-
     nizances, his fines, his double vouchers, his recover-
     ies.[46] Is this the fine of his fines, and the recovery of his
105 recoveries, to have his fine pate[47] full of fine dirt? Will
     his vouchers vouch[48] him no more of his purchases, and
     double ones too, than the length and breadth of a pair of
     indentures?[49] The very conveyances of his lands[50] will
     scarcely lie in this box, and must th' inheritor himself
110 have no more, ha?

     HORATIO.   Not a jot more, my lord.

     HAMLET.   Is not parchment made of sheepskins?

     HORATIO.   Ay, my lord, and of calves' skins too.

     HAMLET.   They are sheep and calves which seek out
115 assurance in that.[51] I will speak to this fellow. Whose
     grave's this, sirrah?

◀ What shocks
Hamlet?

[handwritten margin note: Hamlet finds a skull & is Totally disgusted by the fact that he knows someone who is buried in this grave.]

◀ In what, says
Hamlet, should a
person not seek
assurance?

52. **quick.** Living
53. **absolute.** Absolutist, requiring extreme accuracy of statement
54. **by the card.** By the book, with precision
55. **equivocation.** Double meaning, ambiguity
56. **pick'd.** Overly refined
57. **kibe.** Sore place on the heel

First Clown. Mine, sir.

[*Sings.*]   "O, a pit of clay for to be made
              For such a guest is meet."

120 **Hamlet.** I think it be thine indeed, for thou liest in't.

First Clown. You lie out on't, sir, and therefore 'tis not yours; for my part, I do not lie in't, yet it is mine.

Hamlet. Thou dost lie in't, to be in't and say it is thine. 'Tis for the dead, not for the quick;[52] therefore
125 thou liest.

First Clown. 'Tis a quick lie, sir, 'twill away again from me to you.

Hamlet. What man dost thou dig it for?

First Clown. For no man, sir.

130 **Hamlet.** What woman then?

First Clown. For none neither.

Hamlet. Who is to be buried in't?

First Clown. One that was a woman, sir, but, rest her soul, she's dead.

[margin note: Ophelia going to buried in]

135 **Hamlet.** How absolute[53] the knave is! we must speak by the card,[54] or equivocation[55] will undo us. By the Lord, Horatio, this three years I have took note of it: the age is grown so pick'd[56] that the toe of the peasant comes so near the heel of the courtier, he galls his
140 kibe.[57] How long hast thou been gravemaker?

◄ How are the peasants changing, according to Hamlet?

[margin note: this grave.]

First Clown. Of all the days i' th' year, I came to't that day that our last king Hamlet overcame Fortinbras.

Hamlet. How long is that since?

First Clown. Cannot you tell that? Every fool can tell
145 that. It was that very day that young Hamlet was born —he that is mad, and sent into England.

◄ Is the gravedigger aware that he is speaking to Hamlet?

Hamlet. Ay, marry, why was he sent into England?

First Clown. Why, because 'a was mad. 'A shall recover his wits there, or if 'a do not, 'tis no great mat-
150 ter there.

◄ What is the gravedigger's opinion of people in England?

Hamlet. Why?

First Clown. 'Twill not be seen in him there, there the men are as mad as he.

Hamlet. How came he mad?

155 **First Clown.** Very strangely, they say.

58. **with.** Because of
59. **ground.** Cause
60. **pocky corses.** Sore-covered corpses
61. **hold the laying in.** Last long enough to be buried
62. **tanner.** One who tans hides for a living
63. **hath lien.** Has lain
64. **Rhenish.** Rhine wine
65. **fancy.** Fanciful thinking
66. **gorge.** Throat or gullet
67. **mock.** Copy
68. **chop-fall'n.** Chapfallen, dejected, with the lower jaw hanging down or fallen away
69. **favor.** Appearance
70. **Prithee.** I pray thee
71. **Alexander.** Alexander the Great, the conqueror

Words For Everyday Use

pes • ti • lence (pes´tə ləns) *n.*, dangerous infectious disease
fla • gon (flag´ən) *n.*, container for liquids
gibe (jīb) *n.*, jeer; taunt
gam • bol (gam´bəl) *n.*, skipping or frolicking about

HAMLET.   How strangely?

FIRST CLOWN.   Faith, e'en with[58] losing his wits.

HAMLET.   Upon what ground?[59]

FIRST CLOWN.   Why, here in Denmark. I have been
160   sexton here, man and boy, thirty years.

HAMLET.   How long will a man lie i' th' earth ere he rot?

FIRST CLOWN.   Faith, if 'a be not rotten before 'a die—
as we have many pocky corses,[60] that will scarce hold
the laying in[61]—'a will last you some eight year or nine
165   year. A tanner[62] will last you nine year.

HAMLET.   Why he more than another?

FIRST CLOWN.   Why, sir, his hide is so tann'd with his
trade that 'a will keep out water a great while, and your
water is a sore decayer of your whoreson dead body.
170   Here's a skull now hath lien[63] you i' th' earth three and
twenty years.

◄ How long has the
skull been in the
earth?

HAMLET.   Whose was it?

FIRST CLOWN.   A whoreson mad fellow's it was. Whose
do you think it was?

175   HAMLET.   Nay, I know not.

FIRST CLOWN.   A <u>pestilence</u> on him for a mad rogue! 'a
pour'd a <u>flagon</u> of Rhenish[64] on my head once. This
same skull, sir, was, sir, Yorick's skull, the King's jester.

◄ To whom did the
skull belong?

HAMLET.   This?   *Takes the skull.*

180   FIRST CLOWN.   E'en that.

HAMLET.   Alas, poor Yorick! I knew him, Horatio, a fellow of infinite jest, of most excellent fancy.[65] He hath
bore me on his back a thousand times, and now how
abhorr'd in my imagination it is! my gorge[66] rises at it.
185   Here hung those lips that I have kiss'd I know not how
oft. Where be your <u>gibes</u> now, your <u>gambols</u>, your songs,
your flashes of merriment, that were wont to set the
table on a roar? Not one now to mock[67] your own grinning— quite chop-fall'n.[68] Now get you to my lady's
190   chamber, and tell her, let her paint an inch thick, to
this favor[69] she must come; make her laugh at that.
Prithee,[70] Horatio, tell me one thing.

◄ How close were
Hamlet and Yorick?

◄ In what sense
is Yorick now
"grinning"?

◄ To what end
must all people
come?

HORATIO.   What's that, my lord?

HAMLET.   Dost thou think Alexander[71] look'd a' this
195   fashion i' th' earth?

HORATIO.   E'en so.

72. **bunghole.** A hole in a keg of liquor
73. **too curiously.** With two much ingenuity
74. **loam.** Plaster made of clay
75. **flaw.** Fierce wind
76. **Foredo.** Do before, destroy before its time
77. **of some estate.** Of some importance
78. **couch we.** Crouch, lie down
79. **mark.** Watch
80. **ceremony else.** Additional ceremony (Laertes asks what additional rites will be performed at his sister's grave.)
81. **obsequies.** Religious rites, ceremonies
82. **warranty.** Authorization
83. **doubtful.** Questionable (because she may have committed suicide)
84. **that great command.** Claudius's command
85. **in ground . . . lodg'd.** Been buried in unsanctified ground (that which is reserved for sinners who died without blessing)
86. **for.** Instead of
87. **virgin crants.** Garlands made for dead maidens
88. **strewments.** Flowers strewn on a coffin
89. **the bringing . . . burial.** The bringing of her to her final home with ringing of funeral bells and proper burial rites

---

Words For Everyday Use

base (bās) *adj.*, inferior; valueless
loam (lōm) *n.*, rich, fertile soil
maimed (māmd) *adj.*, imperfect; defective
rite (rīt) *n.*, formal, ceremonial act

pro • fane (prō fān´) *vt.*, treat with irreverence or contempt
re • qui • em (rek´wē əm) *n.*, hymn for the dead

HAMLET. And smelt so? pah!   *Puts down the skull.*

HORATIO. E'en so, my lord.

HAMLET. To what base uses we may return, Horatio!
200 Why may not imagination trace the noble dust of
Alexander, till 'a find it stopping a bunghole?[72]

HORATIO. 'Twere to consider too curiously,[73] to consider
so.

HAMLET. No, faith, not a jot, but to follow him thither
with modesty enough and likelihood to lead it:
205 Alexander died, Alexander was buried, Alexander retur-
neth to dust, the dust is earth, of earth we make
loam,[74] and why of that loam whereto he was con-
verted might they not stop a beer-barrel?
Imperious Caesar, dead and turn'd to clay,
210 Might stop a hole to keep the wind away.
O that that earth which kept the world in awe
Should patch a wall t' expel the winter's flaw![75]
But soft, but soft awhile, here comes the King,

Enter KING, QUEEN, LAERTES, *and a* DOCTOR OF DIVINITY, *following the corse, with* LORDS *attendant.*

The Queen, the courtiers. Who is this they follow?
215 And with such maimed rites? This doth betoken
The corse they follow did with desp'rate hand
Foredo[76] it own life. 'Twas of some estate.[77]
Couch we[78] a while and mark.[79]   *Retiring with* HORATIO.

LAERTES. What ceremony else?[80]

220 **HAMLET.** That is Laertes, a very noble youth. Mark.

LAERTES. What ceremony else?

DOCTOR. Her obsequies[81] have been as far enlarg'd
As we have warranty.[82] Her death was doubtful,[83]
And but that great command[84] o'ersways the order,
225 She should in ground unsanctified been lodg'd[85]
Till the last trumpet, for[86] charitable prayers,
Shards, flints, and pebbles should be thrown on her.
Yet here she is allow'd her virgin crants,[87]
Her maiden strewments,[88] and the bringing home
230 Of bell and burial.[89]

LAERTES. Must there no more be done?

DOCTOR.   No more be done:
We should profane the service of the dead
To sing a requiem and such rest to her
As to peace-parted souls.

◄ What happens
to the greatest of
people?

◄ What does
Hamlet surmise from
the nature of the
rites that he
observes?

◄ What does
Hamlet think of
Laertes?

◄ Who is the per-
son who is being
buried? Why does
the priest say that no
more can be done for
this person?

[handwritten margin notes: "Laertes jumps into the grave", "crying", "with grief", "Hamlet upset —", "he's the only one"]

90. **thou liest howling.** I.e., in hell
91. **to have deck'd.** To have covered with flowers
92. **ingenious.** Discerning, capable
93. **quick.** Living
94. **Pelion.** A Greek mountain. In Greek myth, the Titans attempted to scale Mount Olympus, home of the Olympic gods, by piling Mount Pelion on top of Mount Ossa.
95. **Conjures the wandering stars.** Puts a spell on the planets, called "wandering stars" because of the seemingly erratic nature of their movements
96. **wonder-wounded.** Wonder struck
97. **Hamlet the Dane.** Rightly said only by one who considers himself the rightful king
98. **splenitive.** Full of spleen, or spitefulness
99. **wag.** Move (i.e., until the last motion of his dying body)

Words
For
Everyday
Use

churl • ish (churl´ish) *adj.*, stingy; mean

a • sun • der (ə sun´dər) *adv.*, into parts or pieces

LAERTES.   Lay her i' th' earth,
235 And from her fair and unpolluted flesh
May violets spring! I tell thee, <u>churlish</u> priest,
A minist'ring angel shall my sister be
When thou liest howling.[90]

HAMLET.   What, the fair Ophelia!

QUEEN.   [*Scattering flowers.*] Sweets to the sweet, farewell!
240 I hop'd thou shouldst have been my Hamlet's wife.
I thought thy bride-bed to have deck'd,[91] sweet maid,
And not have strew'd thy grave.

LAERTES.   O, treble woe
Fall ten times treble on that cursed head
Whose wicked deed thy most ingenious[92] sense
245 Depriv'd thee of! Hold off the earth a while,
Till I have caught her once more in mine arms.
                        Leaps in the grave.
Now pile your dust upon the quick[93] and dead,
Till of this flat a mountain you have made
T' o'ertop old Pelion,[94] or the skyish head
250 Of blue Olympus.

HAMLET.   [*Coming forward.*] What is he whose grief
Bears such an emphasis, whose phrase of sorrow
Conjures the wand'ring stars[95] and makes them stand
Like wonder-wounded[96] hearers? This is I,
Hamlet the Dane![97]   *Hamlet leaps in after Laertes.*

255 **LAERTES.**   The devil take thy soul!   *Grappling with him.*

HAMLET.   Thou pray'st not well.
I prithee take thy fingers from my throat.
For though I am not splenitive[98] and rash,
Yet have I in me something dangerous,
Which let thy wisdom fear. Hold off thy hand!

260 **KING.** Pluck them <u>asunder</u>.

QUEEN.   Hamlet, Hamlet!

ALL.   Gentlemen!

HORATIO.   Good my lord, be quiet.

The ATTENDANTS *part them, and they come out of the grave.*

HAMLET.   Why, I will fight with him upon this theme
Until my eyelids will no longer wag.[99]

QUEEN.   O my son, what theme?

265 **HAMLET.**   I lov'd Ophelia. Forty thousand brothers
Could not with all their quantity of love

◀ What does Laertes say to the priest?

◀ What had Gertrude hoped?

◀ How does Laertes feel toward Hamlet? Why?

◀ How does Laertes show his grief?

[handwritten: Hamlett Leartes fight in the grave]

◀ In what way, according to Hamlet, do he and Laertes differ?

[handwritten: Both leave the grave]

◀ What drives Hamlet to fight with Laertes?

[handwritten top margin: that loved Laertes]

100. **forbear him.** Bear with him (put up with him because he is obviously mad)
101. **'Swounds.** By God's wounds
102. **eisel.** Vinegar (i.e., bitterness)
103. **eat a crocadile.** Consume a crocodile (a beast celebrated in folklore for crying false tears)
104. **outface.** Outdo
105. **quick.** Alive
106. **pate.** Head
107. **burning zone.** The zone of the sun
108. **Ossa.** A mountain in Greece
109. **fit.** Seizure
110. **Anon.** Soon
111. **golden couplets.** Her two eggs containing young covered with gold-colored down
112. **disclosed.** Hatched
113. **Hercules.** Legendary strongman of Greek mythology
114. **wait upon.** Attend to
115. **present push.** Immediate undertaking
116. **living.** Lasting. Claudius's exact intention here is uncertain. It is likely that Gertrude has just exited, after the line "set some watch over your son," and that the "living monument" will be the death of Hamlet.
117. **Till then . . . be.** Until then, we shall be patient about carrying out our plan.

ACT V, SCENE ii

1. **so much for this.** Hamlet and Horatio are in mid-conversation as the scene opens.

Words For Everyday Use

prate (prāt) *vi.,* talk idly; chatter

Make up my sum. What wilt thou do for her?

KING.   O, he is mad, Laertes.

QUEEN.   For love of God, forbear him.[100]

270 HAMLET.   'Swounds,[101] show me what thou't do.
Woo't weep, woo't fight, woo't fast, woo't tear thyself?
Woo't drink up eisel,[102] eat a crocodile?[103]
I'll do't. Dost thou come here to whine?
To outface[104] me with leaping in her grave?
275 Be buried quick[105] with her, and so will I.
And if thou prate of mountains, let them throw
Millions of acres on us, till our ground,
Singeing his pate[106] against the burning zone,[107]
Make Ossa[108] like a wart! Nay, and thou'lt mouth,
280 I'll rant as well as thou.

QUEEN.   This is mere madness,
And thus a while the fit[109] will work on him;
Anon,[110] as patient as the female dove,
When that her golden couplets[111] are disclosed,[112]
His silence will sit drooping.

◄ What does Gertrude make of her son's behavior?

HAMLET.   Hear you, sir,
285 What is the reason that you use me thus?
I lov'd you ever. But it is no matter.
Let Hercules[113] himself do what he may,
The cat will mew, and dog will have his day.

                              Exit HAMLET.

KING.   I pray thee, good Horatio, wait upon[114] him.

                              Exit HORATIO.

290 [To LAERTES.] Strengthen your patience in our last night's
     speech,
We'll put the matter to the present push.—[115]
Good Gertrude, set some watch over your son.
This grave shall have a living[116] monument.
An hour of quiet shortly shall we see,
295 Till then in patience our proceeding be.[117]   Exeunt.

◄ What reason does Claudius give Laertes for being patient?

SCENE ii

Enter HAMLET and HORATIO.

HAMLET.   So much for this,[1] sir, now shall you see the
     other—
You do remember all the circumstance?

HORATIO.   Remember it, my lord!

HAMLET.   Sir, in my heart there was a kind of fighting

Hamlet talk about his Trip to Horatio.

2. **Methought.** I thought
3. **mutines in the bilboes.** Mutineers in their shackles
4. **Rashly.** Impetuously
5. **pall.** Grow pale, fail
6. **learn.** Teach
7. **sea-gown.** Sleeping garment worn by sailors
8. **them.** Rosencrantz and Guildenstern
9. **Finger'd.** Stole
10. **in fine.** In short
11. **withdrew.** Returned
12. **Larded.** Fattened
13. **Importing.** Arguing
14. **bugs.** Bug-a-boos, terrors
15. **in my life.** That would result from my continued life
16. **on the supervise.** On looking these over
17. **no leisure bated.** No time wasted
18. **to stay.** To wait for
19. **strook.** Struck
20. **make . . . brains.** Conceive of a way to start thinking about what to do
21. **fair.** In an elegant hand
22. **statists.** Politicians, statesmen
23. **yeman's service.** The office of a capable servant
24. **conjuration.** Request
25. **tributary.** Country that pays tribute
26. **wheaten garland.** A garland of wheat signified peace and prosperity.
27. **And . . . amities.** And that there might be but a small space, or comma, between their friendship, or amities
28. **of great charge.** Of great burden or import
29. **view.** Viewing

Words For Everyday Use

in • dis • cre • tion (in´di skresh´ ən) *n.,* lack of good judgment

5   That would not let me sleep. Methought[2] I lay
      Worse than the mutines in the bilboes.[3] Rashly—[4]
      And prais'd be rashness for it—let us know
      Our <u>indiscretion</u> sometime serves us well
      When our deep plots do pall,[5] and that should learn[6] us
10   There's a divinity that shapes our ends,
      Rough-hew them how we will—

HORATIO.   That is most certain.

HAMLET.   Up from my cabin,
      My sea-gown[7] scarf'd about me, in the dark
      Grop'd I to find out them,[8] had my desire,
15   Finger'd[9] their packet, and in fine[10] withdrew[11]
      To mine own room again, making so bold,
      My fears forgetting manners, to unseal
      Their grand commission; where I found, Horatio—
      Ah, royal knavery!—an exact command,
20   Larded[12] with many several sorts of reasons,
      Importing[13] Denmark's health and England's too,
      With, ho, such bugs[14] and goblins in my life,[15]
      That, on the supervise,[16] no leisure bated,[17]
      No, not to stay[18] the grinding of the axe,
25   My head should be strook[19] off.

HORATIO.   Is't possible?

HAMLET.   Here's the commission, read it at more leisure.
      But wilt thou hear now how I did proceed?

HORATIO.   I beseech you.

HAMLET.   Being thus benetted round with villainies,
30   Or I could make a prologue to my brains,[20]
      They had begun the play. I sat me down,
      Devis'd a new commission, wrote it fair.[21]
      I once did hold it, as our statists[22] do,
      A baseness to write fair, and labor'd much
35   How to forget that learning, but, sir, now
      It did me yeman's service.[23] Wilt thou know
      Th' effect of what I wrote?

HORATIO.   Ay, good my lord.

HAMLET.   An earnest conjuration[24] from the King,
      As England was his faithful tributary,[25]
40   As love between them like the palm might flourish,
      As peace should still her wheaten garland[26] wear
      And stand a comma 'tween their amities,[27]
      And many such-like as's of great charge,[28]
      That on the view[29] and knowing of these contents,

He couldn't sleep, t read a note

◄ What does Hamlet believe about God's role in human life at this point in the play?

◄ How did Hamlet discover what Claudius intended to do to him?

That the king of Engl. to kill Hamlet when he arrived in court,

30. **debatement further.** Further debate
31. **shriving time.** Time for confession and absolution, or forgiveness of sins
32. **was heaven ordinant.** Did heaven ordain, or decree, what would happen
33. **Subscrib'd it.** Signed it
34. **th' impression.** Impressed the wax with which the document was sealed with the seal of the royal throne of Denmark
35. **changeling.** Substitute. A changeling was literally one child substituted for another, especially as was done by fairies in folk tales
36. **to this was sequent.** Followed this
37. **did make love to.** Enjoyed
38. **insinuation.** Winding, crooked movement, like that of a snake
39. **the baser nature.** The person of lower rank and breeding
40. **pass.** Sword thrust
41. **fell.** Deadly
42. **mighty opposites.** I.e., Claudius and Hamlet
43. **stand me now upon.** Stand now upon me (Is it not now required of me)
44. **th' election.** The election to the kingship
45. **angle.** Fishing line
46. **proper.** Own
47. **coz'nage.** Cheating
48. **perfect conscience.** What is demanded by one's conscience, or sense of right and wrong
49. **quit him.** Kill him
50. **to be damn'd.** Hamlet has long worried that perhaps the ghost that he saw was a thing of the devil, and he has questioned the morality of revenge. Here he answers his own questions, saying that allowing such evil to flourish is to be damned.
51. **canker.** Cancerous growth
52. **of our nature.** To the Elizabethans, the word nature had a grand meaning encompassing not only what we would now refer to as human nature but also the divine order of things, including the divinely ordained place of a king as the head of a state.
53. **issue.** Outcome
54. **a man's . . . "one."** In the scheme of things, a man's life lasts no longer than it takes to say the word "one."
55. **portraiture.** Depiction
56. **sure.** Certainly
57. **bravery.** Effrontery, extravagant show

Words
For
Everyday
Use

sig • net (sig´nit) *n.*, official seal; stamp
in • ter • im (in´tər im) *n.*, period of time between

45 Without debatement further,[30] more or less,
    He should those bearers put to sudden death,
    Not shriving time[31] allow'd.

◄ With what message did Hamlet replace Claudius's letter?

HORATIO.   How was this seal'd?

HAMLET. Why, even in that was heaven ordinant.[32]
    I had my father's <u>signet</u> in my purse,
50 Which was the model of that Danish seal;
    Folded the writ up in the form of th' other,
    Subscrib'd[33] it, gave't th' impression,[34] plac'd it safely,
    The changeling[35] never known. Now the next day
    Was our sea-fight, and what to this was sequent[36]
55 Thou knowest already.

◄ How, according to Hamlet, did heaven help him to achieve his purpose?

HORATIO.   So Guildenstern and Rosencrantz go to't.

HAMLET. Why, man, they did make love to[37] this
    employment,
    They are not near my conscience. Their defeat
    Does by their own insinuation[38] grow.
60 'Tis dangerous when the baser nature[39] comes
    Between the pass[40] and fell[41] incensed points
    Of mighty opposites.[42]

◄ Why does Hamlet not have any remorse over having brought about the deaths of Rosencrantz and Guildenstern?

HORATIO.   Why, what a king is this!

HAMLET. Does it not, think thee, stand me now upon—[43]
    He that hath kill'd my king and whor'd my mother,
65 Popp'd in between th' election[44] and my hopes,
    Thrown out his angle[45] for my proper[46] life,
    And with such coz'nage[47]—is't not perfect conscience[48]
    To quit him[49] with this arm? And is't not to be damn'd,[50]
    To let this canker[51] of our nature[52] come
70 In further evil?

◄ What reasons does Hamlet give for wanting to kill Claudius?

HORATIO. It must be shortly known to him from
    England
    What is the issue[53] of the business there.

HAMLET. It will be short; the <u>interim's</u> mine,
    And a man's life's no more than to say "one."[54]
75 But I am very sorry, good Horatio,
    That to Laertes I forgot myself,
    For by the image of my cause I see
    The portraiture[55] of his. I'll court his favors.
    But sure[56] the bravery[57] of his grief did put me
80 Into a tow'ring passion.

◄ How much time does Hamlet believe that he has before he can take his revenge?

◄ Why does Hamlet regret his actions toward Laertes?

HORATIO.   Peace, who comes here?

Enter young OSRIC, *a courtier.*

58. **water-fly.** Creature that flits about, a derogatory term

59. **let . . . mess.** If a man who is no more than a beast is the lord of beasts (has a lot of property), then his manger, or crib, will be at the king's table, or mess.

60. **chough.** A rustic fellow or a jackdaw, a kind of bird known for its imitative abilities. This is a jibe at courtiers who are always willing to imitate and so ingratiate themselves to those who have power.

61. **spacious . . . dirt.** Hamlet here shows his contempt for worldly goods, such as the land, or dirt, owned by this common fellow who has become a prosperous landowner and so gained admittance to court.

62. **bonnet.** Cap

63. **indifferent.** Moderately, somewhat

64. **complexion.** Temperament

65. **most excellent differences.** Many superb qualities or accomplishments

66. **of very soft society.** Capable of mingling with ease in social circles

67. **great showing.** Superb appearance or presentation of himself

68. **card or calendar.** Map or guide

69. **continent . . . see.** Container of whatever parts, or refined qualities, a gentleman might wish to find (in another gentleman)

70. **his definement.** The defining of him

71. **perdition.** Loss

72. **dozy.** Make dizzy

73. **but yaw . . . of.** But go off course, at any rate, in comparison with

74. **in the verity of extolment.** To praise him truthfully

75. **of great article.** Of great worth

76. **infusion.** What he is infused, or filled, with

77. **dearth.** Dearness, value

78. **to make true diction.** To speak truly

79. **semblable.** Likeness

80. **trace him.** Follow him

81. **umbrage.** Shadow

Words For Everyday Use

sul • try (sul´trē) *adj.*, oppressively hot

gen • try (jen´trē) *adj.*, rank resulting from birth

in • fal • li • bly (in fal´ə blē) *adv.*, without error *a courtier*

OSRIC. Your lordship is right welcome back to Denmark.

HAMLET. I humbly thank you, sir.—Dost know this water-fly?[58]

HORATIO. No, my good lord.

85 HAMLET. Thy state is the more gracious, for 'tis a vice to know him. He hath much land, and fertile; let a beast be lord of beasts, and his crib shall stand at the King's mess.[59] 'Tis a chough,[60] but, as I say, spacious in the possession of dirt.[61]

◄ What does Hamlet think of property ownership?

90 OSRIC. Sweet lord, if your lordship were at leisure, I should impart a thing to you from his Majesty.

HAMLET. I will receive it, sir, with all diligence of spirit. Put your bonnet[62] to his right use, 'tis for the head.

OSRIC. I thank your lordship, it is very hot.

95 HAMLET. No, believe me, 'tis very cold, the wind is northerly.

OSRIC. It is indifferent[63] cold, my lord, indeed.

HAMLET. But yet methinks it is very sultry and hot for my complexion.[64]

100 OSRIC. Exceedingly, my lord, it is very sultry—as 'twere—I cannot tell how. My lord, his Majesty bade me signify to you that 'a has laid a great wager on your head. Sir, this is the matter—

HAMLET. I beseech you remember.

HAMLET moves him to put on his hat.

OSRIC. Nay, good my lord, for my ease, in good faith.

105 Sir, here is newly come to court Laertes, believe me, an absolute gentleman, full of most excellent differences,[65] of very soft society,[66] and great showing;[67] indeed, to speak sellingly of him, he is the card or calendar[68] of gentry; for you shall find in him the continent of what
110 part a gentleman would see.[69]

HAMLET. Sir, his definement[70] suffers no perdition[71] in you, though I know to divide him inventorially would dozy[72] th' arithmetic of memory, and yet but yaw neither in respect of[73] his quick sail; but in the verity of
115 extolment,[74] I take him to be a soul of great article,[75] and his infusion[76] of such dearth[77] and rareness as, to make true diction[78] of him, his semblable[79] is his mirror, and who else would trace him,[80] his umbrage,[81] nothing more.

OSRIC. Your lordship speaks most infallibly of him.

Match to take place —

queen wants hamlet to apologize to laertes

82. **concernancy.** Concern, matter at hand
83. **in . . . breath.** In our breath, which is so much more coarse than the refined Laertes
84. **Is't . . . tongue?** Might we not be able to understand what is being said if it were in some other language? Horatio is implying that what is being spoken is not English.
85. **imports the nomination of.** Is the purpose of naming
86. **it would . . . me.** If you held a high opinion of me, that would not be saying much for me.
87. **I dare . . . himself.** Again, Hamlet continues his exaggerated speech, imitating and mocking that of Osric. The meaning of Hamlet's statement, which is intended to be ludicrous but nonetheless has some sense to it, is that he dares not say that he knows how excellent Laertes is, for that would be to compare himself with the great Laertes, and such a comparison would be impossible because to understand another, one would have to be able, first, to understand oneself.
88. **in the imputation laid on him.** In the description given of him by others
89. **meed.** Merit
90. **unfellow'd.** Unmatched
91. **he has impawn'd.** Laertes has wagered
92. **poniards.** Daggers
93. **assigns.** Accouterments
94. **girdles, hangers.** Belts and hangers with which to attach the sheaths to the belts
95. **dear to fancy.** Pleasing to one's tastes
96. **responsive to.** Well adjusted to
97. **liberal conceit.** Creative, fanciful design
98. **edified by the margent.** Taught by an annotation in the margin

Words
For
Everyday
Use

ger • mane (jər mān´) *adj.,* truly relevant

HAMLET.   The concernancy,[82] sir? Why do we wrap the gentleman in our more rawer breath?[83]

120

OSRIC.   Sir?

HORATIO.   Is't not possible to understand in another tongue?[84] You will to't, sir, really.

◀ Of what has Hamlet been making fun, and why is Horatio impatient?

125 HAMLET.   What imports the nomination of[85] this gentleman?

OSRIC.   Of Laertes?

HORATIO.   His purse is empty already: all 's golden words are spent.

130 HAMLET.   Of him, sir.

OSRIC.   I know you are not ignorant—

HAMLET.   I would you did, sir, yet, in faith, if you did, it would not much approve me.[86] Well, sir?

OSRIC.   You are not ignorant of what excellence Laertes
135 is—

HAMLET.   I dare not confess that, lest I should compare with him in excellence, but to know a man well were to know himself.[87]

OSRIC.   I mean, sir, for his weapon, but in the
140 imputation laid on him[88] by them, in his meed[89] he's unfellow'd.[90]

◀ In what skill does Laertes show excellence?

HAMLET.   What's his weapon?

OSRIC.   Rapier and dagger.

HAMLET.   That's two of his weapons—but well.

OSRIC.   The King, sir, hath wager'd with him six Barbary
145 horses, against the which he has impawn'd,[91] as I take it, six French rapiers and poniards,[92] with their assigns,[93] as girdle, hangers,[94] and so. Three of the carriages, in faith, are very dear to fancy,[95] very responsive to[96] the hilts, most delicate carriages, and of very liberal conceit.[97]

◀ What is being wagered by Claudius and Laertes?

150 HAMLET.   What call you the carriages?

HORATIO.   I knew you must be edified by the margent[98] ere you had done.

OSRIC.   The carriages, sir, are the hangers.

HAMLET.   The phrase would be more germane to the
155 matter if we could carry a cannon by our sides; I would it might be hangers till then. But on: six Barb'ry horses against six French swords, their assigns, and three liberal-

99. **impawn'd.** Wagered

100. **The King . . . nine.** The terms of this wager are unclear. What is clear is that because Laertes is presumed to be the better fencer, Claudius has received some odds. Hamlet does not have to better Laertes overall in order for Claudius to win. He has only to better Laertes as many times as this unclear wager requires.

101. **come to immediate trial.** The contest will be carried out immediately

102. **vouchsafe the answer.** Condescend to grant an answer (to the challenge)

103. **How.** What

104. **the breathing . . . with me.** The time of day when I take my exercise

105. **and.** If

106. **'A . . . for 's turn.** Hamlet humorously and intentionally misconstrues the word commend as recommend and says that Osric would have to recommend himself because no one else would.

107. **lapwing . . . head.** This newly hatched bug runs about with the shell still on his head.

108. **dug.** Nipple

109. **drossy.** Shabby

110. **the tune of the time.** The argot, or speech, of the day

111. **yesty collection.** A frothy collection of fancy words (from the use of yeast to ferment beer)

112. **winnow'd.** Well sifted or thought out

113. **and do but . . . are out.** If you test them by blowing on them, their bubbles burst.

[handwritten notes: purpose of match — kill Hamlet — sword — (poison) + Claudius plan to have Hamlet drink a Toast out of a poisoned goblet.]

| Words For Everyday Use | **foil** (foil) *n.*, long, thin fencing sword |

conceited carriages; that's the French bet against the Danish. Why is this all impawn'd,[99] as you call it?

160 OSRIC.   The King, sir, hath laid, sir, that in a dozen passes between yourself and him, he shall not exceed you three hits; he hath laid on twelve for nine;[100] and it would come to immediate trial,[101] if your lordship would vouchsafe the answer.[102]

165 HAMLET.   How[103] if I answer no?

OSRIC.   I mean, my lord, the opposition of your person in trial.

HAMLET.   Sir, I will walk here in the hall. If it please his Majesty, it is the breathing time of day with me.[104] Let
170 the foils be brought, the gentleman willing, and the King hold his purpose, I will win for him and[105] I can; if not, I will gain nothing but my shame and the odd hits.

◄ What does Hamlet agree to do?

OSRIC.   Shall I deliver you so?

HAMLET.   To this effect, sir—after what flourish your
175 nature will.

OSRIC.   I commend my duty to your lordship.

HAMLET.   Yours. [Exit OSRIC.] 'A does well to commend it himself, there are no tongues else for 's turn.[106]

HORATIO.   This lapwing runs away with the shell on
180 his head.[107]

HAMLET.   'A did comply, sir, with his dug[108] before 'a suck'd it. Thus has he, and many more of the same breed that I know the drossy[109] age dotes on, only got the tune of the time,[110] and out of an habit of encounter,
185 a kind of yesty collection,[111] which carries them through and through the most profound and winnow'd[112] opinions, and do but blow them to their trial, the bubbles are out.[113]

Enter a LORD.

LORD.   My lord, his Majesty commended him to you
190 by young Osric, who brings back to him that you attend him in the hall. He sends to know if your pleasure hold to play with Laertes, or that you will take longer time.

HAMLET.   I am constant to my purposes, they follow
195 the King's pleasure. If his fitness speaks, mine is ready; now or whensoever, provided I be so able as now.

LORD.   The King and Queen and all are coming down.

114. **In happy time.** Just in time
115. **use some gentle entertainment.** Speak some kind words
116. **gain-giving.** Gainsaying, questioning, foreboding
117. **forestall their repair hither.** Put off their coming here
118. **defy augury.** Reject prediction, divination, or prophecy
119. **providence . . . sparrow.** This is a reference to Matthew 10:29: "Are not two sparrows sold for a farthing? and one of them shall not fall on the ground without your father," the import of which is that nothing happens that is not of God's design.
120. **it.** Hamlet is thinking, perhaps, of his own death, but he intentionally phrases this more generally. This *it* refers to all things that happen.
121. **Since no man . . . betimes.** Since no man knows anything about the life that he leaves behind him or what it means to leave that life early
122. **let be.** An ambiguous phrase meaning both "let what ever will be be" and "say no more"
123. **This presence.** Those present
124. **needs.** Necessarily
125. **a sore distraction.** A terrible madness
126. **exception.** Disapproval
127. **in this audience.** Before this audience
128. **disclaiming from a purpos'd evil.** Disavowal of an intention to do this evil deed

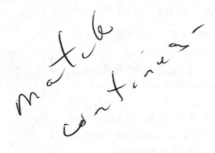

HAMLET.   In happy time.[114]

LORD.   The Queen desires you to use some gentle
200 entertainment[115] to Laertes before you fall to play.

HAMLET.   She well instructs me.   *Exit* LORD.

HORATIO.   You will lose, my lord.

HAMLET.   I do not think so; since he went into France I
have been in continual practice. I shall win at the odds.
205 Thou wouldst not think how ill all's here about my
heart—but it is no matter.

HORATIO.   Nay, good my lord—

HAMLET.   It is but foolery, but it is such a kind of
gain-giving,[116] as would perhaps trouble a woman.

210 HORATIO.   If your mind dislike any thing, obey it. I will
forestall their repair hither,[117] and say you are not fit.

HAMLET.   Not a whit, we defy augury.[118] There is special
providence in the fall of a sparrow.[119] If it[120] be now, 'tis
not to come; if it be not to come, it will be now; if it be
215 not now, yet it will come—the readiness is all. Since no
man, of aught he leaves, knows what is't to leave
betimes,[121] let be.[122]

*A table prepar'd, and flagons of wine on it. Enter Trumpets,
Drums, and Officers with cushions, foils, daggers;* KING,
QUEEN, LAERTES, OSRIC, *and all the State.*

KING.   Come, Hamlet, come, and take this hand from
me.   *The* KING *puts* LAERTES' *hand into* HAMLET's.

HAMLET.   Give me your pardon, sir. I have done you
wrong,
220 But pardon't as you are a gentleman.
This presence[123] knows,
And you must needs[124] have heard, how I am punish'd
With a sore distraction.[125] What I have done
That might your nature, honor, and exception[126]
225 Roughly awake, I here proclaim was madness.
Was't Hamlet wrong'd Laertes? Never Hamlet!
If Hamlet from himself be ta'en away,
And when he's not himself does wrong Laertes,
Then Hamlet does it not, Hamlet denies it.
230 Who does it then? His madness. If't be so
Hamlet is of the faction that is wronged,
His madness is poor Hamlet's enemy.
Sir, in this audience,[127]
Let my disclaiming from a purpos'd evil[128]

◄ What does the Queen want Hamlet to do before beginning the fencing match?

◄ Does Hamlet think that he has a chance of winning? Why? How is Hamlet feeling at this moment?

◄ What council does Horatio give to Hamlet? Do you think that Hamlet should take Horatio's advice?

◄ Why does Hamlet decide to go to the match even though he has a bad feeling about it?

◄ What, according to Hamlet, is the most important consideration with regard to death? Does Hamlet fear death?

◄ What excuse does Hamlet give to Laertes?

129. **in nature.** In respect to my natural feelings (for my dead father)
130. **in my . . . aloof.** With regard to my honor I am not yet satisfied
131. **and will no reconcilement.** And will not be reconciled with you
132. **Till by . . . ungor'd.** Until some honorable elders have, based on precedents, instructed me that I should keep the peace and that in so doing my reputation for honor will not be wounded.
133. **frankly.** Honestly, without blame
134. **foil.** Material used to set off a jewel or other ornament, a pun on the word foil meaning "sword"
135. **Stick fiery off.** Stand out like sparks of fire
136. **he is better'd.** He has improved
137. **This . . . well.** I like this one.
138. **have all a length?** Are all of the same length?
139. **stoups.** Flagons, containers
140. **Or quit . . . exchange.** Or requite himself in the third exchange for having lost the first two
141. **union.** A priceless pearl, which would dissolve in the wine
142. **kettle.** Kettle drum

235   Free me so far in your most generous thoughts
      That I have shot my arrow o'er the house
      And hurt my brother.

◄ With what name does Hamlet call Laertes?

      LAERTES.   I am satisfied in nature,[129]
      Whose motive in this case should stir me most
      To my revenge, but in my terms of honor
240   I stand aloof,[130] and will no reconcilement[131]
      Till by some elder masters of known honor
      I have a voice and president of peace
      To keep my name ungor'd.[132] But till that time
      I do receive your offer'd love like love,
245   And will not wrong it.

◄ What pretense does Laertes make to Hamlet? What is Laertes actually planning to do?

      HAMLET.   I embrace it freely,
      And will this brothers' wager frankly[133] play.
      Give us the foils. Come on.

      LAERTES.   Come, one for me.

      HAMLET.   I'll be your foil,[134] Laertes, in mine ignorance
      Your skill shall like a star i' th' darkest night
250   Stick fiery off[135] indeed.

      LAERTES.   You mock me, sir.

      HAMLET.   No, by this hand.

      KING.   Give them the foils, young Osric. Cousin Hamlet,
      You know the wager?

      HAMLET.   Very well, my lord.
      Your Grace has laid the odds a' th' weaker side.

255   KING.   I do not fear it, I have seen you both;
      But since he is better'd,[136] we have therefore odds.

      LAERTES.   This is too heavy; let me see another.

      HAMLET.   This likes me well.[137] These foils have all a
        length?[138]   *Prepare to play.*

      OSRIC.   Ay, my good lord.

260   KING.   Set me the stoups[139] of wine upon that table.
      If Hamlet give the first or second hit,
      Or quit in answer of the third exchange,[140]
      Let all the battlements their ord'nance fire.
      The King shall drink to Hamlet's better breath,
265   And in the cup an union[141] shall he throw,
      Richer than that which four successive kings
      In Denmark's crown have worn. Give me the cups,
      And let the kettle[142] to the trumpet speak,
      The trumpet to the cannoneer without,

143. **pass.** Thrust
144. **make . . . of me.** Play with me as though I were a mischievous child

[handwritten notes:] Queen grass the the goblet + drink, the poisoned wine. Hamlet won the match with poisoned Laertes sword.

Words For Everyday Use

pal • pa • ble (pal´pə bəl) *adj.*, that can be felt; solid

ca • rouse (kə rouz´) *vi.*, engage in boisterous drinking and merrymaking

dal • ly (dal´ē) *vi.*, waste time; loiter

270 The cannons to the heavens, the heaven to earth,
"Now the King drinks to Hamlet." Come begin;

Trumpets the while.

And you, the judges, bear a wary eye.

HAMLET.   Come on, sir.

LAERTES.   Come, my lord.

They play and HAMLET scores a hit.

HAMLET.   One.

LAERTES.   No.

HAMLET.   Judgment.

OSRIC.   A hit, a very <u>palpable</u> hit.

LAERTES.   Well, again.

275 KING.   Stay, give me drink. Hamlet, this pearl is thine.
Here's to thy health! Give him the cup.

Drum, trumpets sound flourish. A piece goes off within.

HAMLET.   I'll play this bout first, set it by a while.
Come. [*They play again.*] Another hit; what say you?

LAERTES.   A touch, a touch, I do confess't.

280 KING.   Our son shall win.

QUEEN.   He's fat, and scant of breath.
Here, Hamlet, take my napkin, rub thy brows.
The Queen <u>carouses</u> to thy fortune, Hamlet.

HAMLET.   Good madam!

KING.   Gertrude, <u>do not drink.</u>

QUEEN.   I will, my lord, I pray you pardon me.

285 KING.   [*Aside.*] It is the pois'ned cup, it is too late.

HAMLET.   I dare not drink yet, madam; by and by.

QUEEN.   Come, let me <u>wipe thy face.</u>

LAERTES.   My lord, I'll hit him now.

KING.   I do not think't.

LAERTES.   [*Aside.*] And yet it is almost against my
conscience.

290 HAMLET.   Come, for the third, Laertes, you do but <u>dally</u>.
I pray you pass[143] with your best violence;
I am sure you make a wanton of me.[144]

LAERTES.   Say you so? Come on.   *They play.*

OSRIC.   Nothing, neither way.

295 LAERTES.   Have at you now!

◄ After taking a drink himself, what does Claudius put into the cup? Why does Claudius tell the attendant to give Hamlet the cup?

◄ Why doesn't Claudius want Gertrude to drink?

◄ What has Claudius come to think that Laertes cannot do?

145. **woodcock . . . springe.** A bird to my own trap
146. **sounds.** Swoons
147. **Unbated and envenom'd.** Uncovered and poisoned
148. **temper'd.** Concocted
149. **Wretched.** Extremely unhappy, sorrowful
150. **chance.** Fateful occurrence

LAERTES *wounds* HAMLET; *then, in scuffling, they change rapiers.*

KING.   Part them, they are incens'd.

HAMLET.   Nay, come again.
          HAMLET *wounds* LAERTES. *The* QUEEN *falls.*

OSRIC.   Look to the Queen there ho!

HORATIO.   They bleed on both sides. How is it, my lord?

OSRIC.   How is't, Laertes?

LAERTES.   Why, as a woodcock to mine own springe,[145]
     Osric.
300 I am justly kill'd with mine own treachery.

HAMLET.   How does the Queen?

KING.   She sounds[146] to see them bleed.

QUEEN.   No, no, the drink, the drink—O my dear
     Hamlet—
The drink, the drink! I am pois'ned.   *Dies.*

HAMLET.   O villainy! Ho, let the door be lock'd!
305 Treachery! Seek it out.

LAERTES.   It is here, Hamlet. Hamlet, thou art slain. No
med'cine in the world can do thee good;
In thee there is not half an hour's life.
The treacherous instrument is in thy hand,
310 Unbated and envenom'd.[147] The foul practice
Hath turn'd itself on me. Lo here I lie,
Never to rise again. Thy mother's pois'ned.
I can no more—the King, the King's to blame.

HAMLET.   The point envenom'd too!
315 Then, venom, to thy work.   *Hurts the* KING.

ALL.   Treason! treason!

KING.   O, yet defend me, friends, I am but hurt.

HAMLET.   Here, thou incestious, murd'rous, damned
     Dane,
Drink off this potion! Is thy union here?
320 Follow my mother!   KING *dies.*

LAERTES.   He is justly served,
It is a poison temper'd[148] by himself.
Exchange forgiveness with me, noble Hamlet.
Mine and my father's death come not upon thee,
Nor thine on me!   *Dies.*

325 HAMLET.   Heaven make thee free of it! I follow thee.
I am dead, Horatio. Wretched[149] queen, adieu!
You that look pale, and tremble at this chance,[150]

◄ What happens to both Hamlet and Laertes?

[handwritten margin note:] Queen falls

[handwritten margin note:] King explains that Q. fell because of too much blood.

◄ What does Laertes reveal?

[handwritten margin note:] Gert. dies

◄ Whom does Laertes blame?

◄ How does Hamlet make sure that Claudius will die?

[handwritten margin note:] Laertes dies

◄ What does Laertes ask for before he dies?

151. **fell.** Terrible
152. **aright.** Correctly
153. **I am . . . Dane.** I am more like an ancient Roman than like a Dane. Horatio refers, here, to the preference of some ancient Romans of suicide to a dishonorable life.
154. **embassadors.** Ambassadors
155. **o'er-crows.** Crows over, like a cock that has won a cock fight
156. **th' election.** To the kingship
157. **has my dying voice.** Has my vote for his election
158. **occurrents.** Occurrences
159. **solicited.** Brought about, urged on (Here Hamlet breaks off his comment because he is dying.)
160. **aught.** Anything
161. **quarry cries on havoc.** Game (at the end of the hunt) speaks of riotous slaughter
162. **toward.** Being prepared

Hamlet stabs the King with the sword & the pours wine down the King's throat.

Claudius dies

Hamlet dies

Words For Everyday Use	**fe • lic • i • ty** (fə lis´i tē) *n.*, happiness; bliss

That are but mutes or audience to this act,
Had I but time—as this fell[151] sergeant, Death,
330 Is strict in his arrest—O, I could tell you—
But let it be. Horatio, I am dead,
Thou livest. Report me and my cause aright[152]
To the unsatisfied.

HORATIO.   Never believe it;
I am more an antique Roman than a Dane.[153]
335 Here's yet some liquor left.

HAMLET.   As th' art a man,
Give me the cup. Let go! By heaven, I'll ha't!
O God, Horatio, what a wounded name,
Things standing thus unknown, shall I leave behind me!
If thou didst ever hold me in thy heart,
340 Absent thee from <u>felicity</u> a while,
And in this harsh world draw thy breath in pain
To tell my story.   *A march afar off and a shot within.*
                    What warlike noise is this?
                        OSRIC *goes to the door and returns.*

OSRIC.   Young Fortinbras, with conquest come from
    Poland,
To th' embassadors[154] of England gives
345 This warlike volley.

HAMLET.   O, I die, Horatio,
The potent poison quite o'er-crows[155] my spirit.
I cannot live to hear the news from England,
But I do prophesy th' election[156] lights
On Fortinbras, he has my dying voice.[157]
350 So tell him, with th' occurrents[158] more and less
Which have solicited[159]—the rest is silence.   *Dies.*

HORATIO.   Now cracks a noble heart. Good night, sweet
    prince
And flights of angels sing thee to thy rest!
                                    March within.
Why does the drum come hither?
Enter FORTINBRAS *with the English* EMBASSADORS, *with Drum,
Colors, and Attendants.*

355 FORTINBRAS.   Where is this sight?

HORATIO.   What is it you would see?
If aught[160] of woe or wonder, cease your search.

FORTINBRAS.   This quarry cries on havoc.[161] O proud
    death,
What feast is toward[162] in thine eternal cell,

◄ What does
Hamlet ask Horatio
to do?

◄ What does
Horatio threaten to
do?

◄ What does
Hamlet ask Horatio
to do?

◄ Who has arrived?

Hamlet
approves
of
fortibras
K. → is ?
Dennach

163. **strook.** Stricken
164. **so jump upon this bloody question.** So immediately after this bloody contest
165. **put on.** Caused, arranged
166. **forc'd cause.** Forced (but not natural or true) cause
167. **of memory.** Ancient rights
168. **my vantage.** My advantageous situation
169. **whose voice . . . more.** Whose voice (expressed in Hamlet's dying support for Fortinbras's election) will carry weight with others
170. **presently.** In the present, immediately
171. **mischance/On plots and errors.** Folly, brought about by plots and erroneous suppositions
172. **been put on.** Become king
173. **Becomes.** Is appropriate for
174. **the field.** The battlefield
175. **ordinance.** Guns

Ros & Guildenster been Killed in England.

Horatio tells Fortinbras the about all going on misdeeds in Denmark

That thou so many princes at a shot
360 So bloodily hast strook?[163]

FIRST EMBASSADOR.   The sight is dismal,
And our affairs from England come too late.
The ears are senseless that should give us hearing,
To tell him his commandment is fulfill'd,
That Rosencrantz and Guildenstern are dead.
365 Where should we have our thanks?

HORATIO.   Not from his mouth,
Had it th' ability of life to thank you.
He never gave commandement for their death.
But since so jump upon this bloody question,[164]
You from the Polack wars, and you from England,
370 Are here arrived, give order that these bodies
High on a stage be placed to the view,
And let me speak to th' yet unknowing world
How these things came about. So shall you hear
Of carnal, bloody, and unnatural acts,
375 Of accidental judgments, casual slaughters,
Of deaths put on[165] by cunning and forc'd cause,[166]
And in this upshot, purposes mistook
Fall'n on th' inventors' heads: all this can I
Truly deliver.

FORTINBRAS.   Let us haste to hear it,
380 And call the noblest to the audience.
For me, with sorrow I embrace my fortune.
I have some rights, of memory[167] in this kingdom,
Which now to claim my vantage[168] doth invite me.

HORATIO.   Of that I shall have also cause to speak,
385 And from his mouth whose voice will draw on more.[169]
But let this same be presently[170] perform'd
Even while men's minds are wild, lest more mischance
On plots and errors[171] happen.

FORTINBRAS.   Let four captains
Bear Hamlet like a soldier to the stage,
390 For he was likely, had he been put on,[172]
To have prov'd most royal; and for his passage,
The soldiers' music and the rite of war
Speak loudly for him.
Take up the bodies. Such a sight as this
395 Becomes[173] the field,[174] but here shows much amiss.
Go bid the soldiers shoot.
    Exeunt marching; after the which a peal of ordinance[175] *are*
      shot off.

◄ What news do
the ambassadors
from England bring
with them?

◄ About what does
Horatio intend to
speak?

◄ What does
Fortinbras intend
to do?

◄ Why does
Horatio think that he
must speak right
away?

◄ What does
Fortinbras think of
Hamlet?

Responding to the Selection

In act V, scene ii, Hamlet says, "There's a divinity that shapes our ends, / Rough-hew them how we will," and Horatio answers, "That is most certain." If you were Horatio at the end of act V, would you still believe that people's ends are shaped by divine will? Explain your answer.

Reviewing the Selection

Recalling and Interpreting

1. **R:** What question about Ophelia does the First Clown pose at the beginning of act V?

2. **I:** Are these Clowns correct in what they assume about her?

3. **R:** Whose skull does Hamlet pick up and speak about?

4. **I:** What do the observations that Hamlet makes about the skulls have in common?

5. **R:** Who is buried, what is unusual about her rites, and how does Laertes respond to this?

6. **I:** Do you agree with the priest or with Laertes?

7. **R:** How does Hamlet respond when Laertes jumps into the grave? What does Hamlet say about his own feelings toward Ophelia?

8. **I:** What motivates Hamlet to jump into the grave? Does his statement about his feelings for Ophelia make sense, given his previous actions?

9. **R:** What does Hamlet tell Horatio that he thought as he lay aboard the ship on his way to England?

10. **I:** What evidence does Hamlet give Horatio of the action of divine providence?

11. **R:** What happens to Rosencrantz and Guildenstern, and why?

12. **I:** Do Rosencrantz and Guildenstern deserve their fates? Why, or why not?

13. **R:** What character is ridiculed by Hamlet for his excessive use of the popular jargon of the court?

14. **I:** Why does Hamlet say that Osric is "spacious in the possession of dirt," and why does he explain at length that Osric is a low, common fellow made good?

15. **R:** Shortly before the fencing match, Hamlet expresses a sense of foreboding to Horatio, and Horatio says that if Hamlet has any misgivings, he will go tell the people not to come and say that Hamlet is not well. What is Hamlet's response?

16. **I:** Does Hamlet believe that people are able to make things happen as they wish them to happen? Does Hamlet believe that people are capable of understanding life?

17. **R:** How do Gertrude, Claudius, Laertes, and Hamlet die?

18. **I:** What role does mischance, or accident, play in these deaths, and in the deaths of Rosencrantz and Guildenstern? In which cases do "purposes mistook" fall "on th' inventors' heads"?

Synthesizing

19. Does justice triumph at the end of this play? Why, or why not?

20. Fortinbras says of Hamlet that "he was likely, had he been put on, / To have proved most royal." Do you agree with this assessment? Why, or why not?

Understanding Literature (QUESTIONS FOR DISCUSSION)

1. **Resolution.** The **resolution** is that part of a plot in which the central conflict is resolved. What is the resolution of *Hamlet*?

2. **Foil.** A **foil** is a character whose attributes, or characteristics, contrast with and therefore throw into relief the attributes of another character. Throughout this play, Fortinbras and Laertes are presented as foils for Hamlet. Hamlet himself jokingly refers to Laertes as his foil during the fencing match. In what ways, despite their differences in character, is Hamlet reconciled with Laertes and Fortinbras in the final scene?

3. **Theme.** A **theme** is a main idea in a literary work. One theme that recurs throughout *Hamlet* is that of salvation and the means by which it is either achieved or lost. What indications are there in the final act that Hamlet has grown spiritually and will be saved?

4. **Theme.** A **theme** is a main idea in a literary work. Another theme that recurs throughout *Hamlet* is the relative value of thought and action. Ultimately, what do you think that the play is saying in regard to this question?

5. **Tragedy.** A **tragedy** is a drama that relates the fall of a person of high status. Tragedy tends to be serious. It celebrates the courage and dignity of a tragic hero in the face of doom. Sometimes that doom is made inevitable by a tragic flaw in the hero. In what ways does *Hamlet, Prince of Denmark* fit this definition of tragedy? What is Hamlet's tragic flaw?

Plot Analysis of *Hamlet, Prince of Denmark*

A **plot** is a series of events related to a **central conflict**, or struggle. The following diagram, known as Freytag's Pyramid, illustrates the main plot of *Hamlet*.

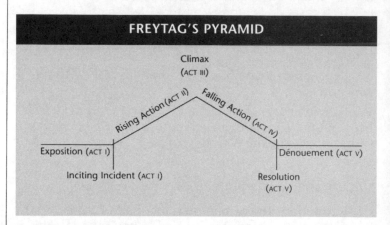

FREYTAG'S PYRAMID

Climax (ACT III)

Rising Action (ACT II)

Falling Action (ACT IV)

Exposition (ACT I)

Inciting Incident (ACT I)

Dénouement (ACT V)

Resolution (ACT V)

The parts of a plot are as follows:

The **exposition** is the part of a plot that provides background information about the characters, setting, or conflict.

The **inciting incident** is the event that introduces the central conflict.

The **rising action**, or complication, develops the conflict to a high point of intensity.

The **climax** is the high point of interest or suspense in the plot.

The **falling action** is all the events that follow the climax.

The **resolution** is the point at which the central conflict is ended, or resolved.

The **dénouement** is any material that follows the resolution and that ties up loose ends.

Exposition and Inciting Incident (Act I)

Act I, scene i. The play opens ominously, at night, in the bitter cold, at a guard station overlooking the Danish coast. Two sentinels, Barnardo and Marcellus, have invited a young scholar named Horatio to stand watch with them to witness for himself an apparition that they claim to have seen twice previously. Horatio's skepticism about the ghost is soon dispelled when a figure in armor, looking like the dead Danish king Hamlet, appears before them. The ghost disappears without a word, and, in the ensuing discussion among the sentinels and Horatio, Horatio reveals that Denmark is preparing for war. The Norwegian prince Fortinbras has raised an army and threatens to attack Denmark to reclaim the lands that his father, also named Fortinbras, lost to the dead king Hamlet. Thinking the ghost of Hamlet is a sign of some terrible event to come, Horatio suggests that news of the ghost should be given to the young prince Hamlet, the elder Hamlet's son, so that the prince might speak with the ghost.

Act I, scene ii. In court the following day, the new Danish king, Claudius, brother to the late Hamlet, thanks the assembled council and courtiers for having freely accepted his marriage to Gertrude, the widowed queen. He then dispatches emissaries to the elderly and sickly king of Norway, Fortinbras's uncle, requesting that Fortinbras's warlike preparations, of which the Norwegian king knows little, be suppressed. Claudius then grants an audience to Laertes, son to Polonius, Claudius's Lord Chamberlain, and grants the young man permission to return to France, from whence he has come to attend Claudius's coronation. Claudius then turns his attention to the young prince Hamlet, addressing the young man as his son. Hamlet's response, his first line in the play, reveals that he is not pleased by the marriage of Claudius to his mother. Gertrude and Claudius urge Hamlet, who is still dressed in mourning black, to end what they regard as his excessive grief over the death of his father, something that Hamlet refuses to do. Claudius reveals that he considers Hamlet to be the rightful successor to his throne, and both Claudius and Gertrude ask Hamlet not to return to Wittenberg, in Germany, where Hamlet has been a student. Hamlet's lukewarm acceptance of this is greeted joyfully by Claudius, who resolves to hold a drinking party in celebration. Left alone, Hamlet reveals, in his first soliloquy, the extent of his unhappiness. He wishes that his flesh would melt away, that there were no divine command against suicide, and describes the world as an "unweeded garden," that is to him "weary, stale, flat, and unprofitable." The chief cause of Hamlet's distress is his mother's recent marriage, which Hamlet describes as "incestuous." His heart is broken by the "wicked speed" with which his mother has married Claudius, whom Hamlet considers a filthy satyr (a drunken, lecherous creature, half man and half beast). Horatio, who has been a student with Hamlet at Wittenberg, enters with Marcellus and Barnardo and tells Hamlet of the ghost. They agree to hold watch together that night, and Hamlet expresses his suspicion that there have been "foul deeds."

Act I, scene iii. Before leaving for France, Laertes speaks with his sister, Ophelia, warning her against Hamlet, who has made romantic overtures toward her. Laertes has two primary concerns: that his sister remain chaste and so not ruin her reputation, and that she recognize that Hamlet, being heir apparent to the throne, cannot choose for himself a person of lower station to be his bride. Ophelia accepts Laertes's "lesson," but reminds him to practice what he preaches while in France. Polonius enters and bids his son make haste to board the ship, which is waiting for him, and then, in a manner typical for Polonius, goes into a long, moralizing speech in which he gives his son precepts for proper behavior. After Laertes leaves, Polonius questions Ophelia about the subject of her discussion with her brother. Ophelia reveals to her father Hamlet's recent "tenders of affection," which have, she says, been accompanied by "all the holy vows of heaven." Outraged, Polonius forbids his daughter to have any interaction with Hamlet in the future, and Ophelia agrees to obey.

Act I, scene iv. Hamlet, Horatio, and Marcellus meet at the guard station. In the distance there are sounds of trumpets and cannon. Hamlet explains that these are accompaniments to Claudius's drunken feast and says that such behavior leads people in other nations to call the Danes drunkards and pigs. Hamlet then observes that a person born with a single defect of personality (such as an inclination to drink) can, despite many other virtues and graces, be completely undone by that defect. The ghost then appears, and Hamlet's immediate response is to wonder whether this is "a spirit of health" or a "goblin damn'd." The ghost raises, for Hamlet, "thoughts beyond the reaches of our souls." When the ghost beckons Hamlet to come away with it, Horatio protests that the ghost might tempt Hamlet to a cliff, take on some terrible shape, and cause Hamlet to lose his reason and fall into the sea. Horatio says that such a cliff overlooking the sea "puts toys of desperation, / Without any more motive" into every brain, tempting people to suicide. Refusing to be held back, Hamlet follows the ghost. Horatio asks, "To what issue will this come?" and then answers his own question, saying that "Heaven will direct it," thus introducing what is perhaps the major theme of the play—the relationship between human action and divine providence.

Act I, scene v. In the inciting incident of the play, the ghost reveals to Hamlet that he has been murdered by Claudius, who now wears the crown, and asks that Hamlet revenge his death. The ghost explains that he has been condemned to spend time walking the earth at night and suffering the fires of purgatory by day because Claudius killed him before he could be absolved of his sins. The ghost also tells Hamlet that Claudius has seduced Gertrude into adultery. The ghost then recounts his death. While King Hamlet was resting in the afternoon in his orchard, Claudius poured a poison into his ear. Critics have noted many parallels in this description to the account of the fall of Adam in Genesis. The murder takes place in an orchard, which recalls the trees of the garden of Eden. The instrument of the murder is poison, recalling the poisonous snake from the Genesis story. The poison is poured into an ear, as the snake in the Garden of Eden poured poisoned words into the ear of Eve. As a result of the murder, Claudius dies in a sinful, unconfessed state, a fact that recalls the original sin that was the legacy of Adam to his descendants. The ghost asks Hamlet to take revenge on Claudius but to leave his mother's punishment to heaven. Hamlet vows to wipe all other matters from his memory except the revenge that he will now undertake. When Marcellus and Horatio find him, Hamlet makes them swear not to reveal what they have seen. He then tells them that in the future he may see fit to "put an antic disposition on"— that is, to pretend madness (in order, one assumes, to hide his true intent from Claudius).

Rising Action (Act II)

Act II, scene i. Polonius instructs his servant, Reynaldo, to travel to France and spy upon Laertes. In particular, Polonius wants Reynaldo to seek out Laertes's acquaintances, to pretend some distant knowledge of Laertes, and to suggest that Laertes indulges in vices such as gambling and sexual license. Reynaldo is to do this, Polonius explains, so that he may "by indirections find directions out." In other words, by this indirect method, Reynaldo will learn, and then report back to Polonius, whether Laertes has been engaging in these vices while in France. After Reynaldo exits, Ophelia enters and tells her father that Hamlet has charged into her bedroom, with his clothes disheveled and a piteous look on his face. Polonius immediately assumes, and Ophelia echoes his opinion, that the cause of Hamlet's behavior is madness brought on by the prince's love for her. Ophelia recounts how Hamlet held her at arm's length and, with one hand on his brow, looked long at her face, then "rais'd a sigh so piteous and profound / As it did seem to shatter all his bulk / And end his being." He then silently left the room, keeping his eye on her as he went. Polonius tells his daughter that Hamlet's love madness must be reported to the king.

Act II, scene ii. Gertrude and Claudius meet with Rosencrantz and Guildenstern, two schoolmates and youthful companions of Hamlet's, whom the king and queen have brought to Denmark so that they might learn the cause of the prince's mental disturbance. Polonius enters and tells the king that he has discovered the cause and will explain all after the king has met with the ambassadors to Norway, who have just returned. Alone with Claudius, Gertrude ventures that her son's lunacy is probably due to "His father's death and our o'erhasty marriage." The ambassadors inform Claudius that their mission has been successful. The king of Norway, Fortinbras's uncle, has stopped Fortinbras from attacking Denmark and has set him, instead, on a campaign to recover some land from Poland, to which end the Norwegian king requests that Claudius allow Fortinbras safe passage through Denmark on his way to fight the Poles. Polonius tells the king and queen of Hamlet's distracted love for Ophelia and offers as proof a love letter Hamlet has written to Ophelia. Polonius suggests that they test the hypothesis that love for Ophelia has driven Hamlet to madness. Polonius will arrange for his daughter and Hamlet to meet, and Polonius will hide with Claudius within earshot to observe their interaction.

The king and queen exit, and Hamlet enters "reading on a book." There ensues the first of several "mad scenes" in the play in which Hamlet speaks in a way calculated to seem like madness. Indeed, to people like Polonius, Rosencrantz, and Guildenstern, who lack Hamlet's intellect, the prince's comments in these scenes do sound like madness, but they have an underlying sense. Hamlet refers to Polonius as a seller of fish, or fishmonger, which sounds like madness to Polonius. The term, however, was common slang for a panderer, or person who procures prostitutes. Hamlet then compares the possibility of Ophelia's conceiving a child to the sun breeding maggots in a dead dog and tells Polonius that he should therefore keep his daughter out of the sun. This is Hamlet's riddling way of referring to Polonius's keeping Ophelia from him (the sun = the son = Hamlet). That Hamlet should call Polonius a fishmonger is, perhaps, a suggestion that Polonius has acted as a panderer, disallowing the relationship between Hamlet and Ophelia in the favor of another suitor. That Hamlet believes, in fact, that Ophelia has taken another lover becomes clear later, in act III.

When Rosencrantz and Guildenstern encounter Hamlet, he tells them that he considers the world a prison and Denmark one of its worst confines. Immediately, Hamlet guesses that the two have been brought to Elsinore to spy on him. Hamlet then enlarges upon his general melancholy, saying that the earth seems to him "a sterile promontory" covered by "a foul and pestilent congregation of vapors" and that man is but the "quintessence of dust." "Man delights me not," he says, and "women neither." The suggestion is quite strong that any romantic or sexual involvement is repugnant to Hamlet. Rosencrantz and Guildenstern tell Hamlet that a company of actors has arrived at the castle, and this immediately changes Hamlet's disposition. Hamlet tells his old schoolmates that he is only sometimes crazy but does so in a way calculated to sound as though he were, indeed, mad. Polonius announced the arrival of the actors, and Hamlet calls Polonius by the name of a Hebrew warrior, Jephthah, who sacrificed his daughter and thus kept her from having a normal married life.

Hamlet greets the actors and requests that one of them perform for him a speech that deals with the revenge taken by the Greek warrior Pyrrhus for the killing of his father, Achilles. The actor delivers the speech, passionately telling of Pyrrhus's murder of the king of Troy, Priam, and of the grief of Priam's wife, Hecuba. Alone after the speech, Hamlet delivers his second great soliloquy, calling himself a "rogue and peasant slave" because this actor, with no real cause, has shown great feeling for Hecuba whereas he, with real motive, "prompted to revenge by heaven and hell," has done nothing. Hamlet calls himself a coward who unpacks his heart with words. He then devises a plan. The ghost, he says, may be a devil prompting him to do evil, and so he will test this by having the actors perform a play that will lead Claudius to reveal his guilt.

Climax (Act III)

Act III, scene i. Rosencrantz and Guildenstern report back to the king and queen. Gertrude tells Ophelia that she hopes that it is, indeed, Ophelia's beauties that are the cause of Hamlet's madness. In an aside, Claudius reveals that his deeds are weighing heavily on him. Polonius places Ophelia, with a prayer book in hand, where she might encounter Hamlet. Polonius and Claudius hide to listen to their conversation. Hamlet enters, alone, and delivers the "To be, or not to be" soliloquy, a lengthy meditation whose basic argument is that life is so full of troubles and misery that a person might well commit suicide if it were not for fear of what might happen after death. At the end of this speech, Hamlet goes further, saying that conscience makes people into cowards. Because of conscience, a person's resolutions, or determinations, are "sicklied o'er . . . with thought," rendering the person incapable of action.

On first seeing Ophelia, Hamlet asks that she remember him in her prayers. Ophelia asks Hamlet how he has been and says that she has "remembrances" of his to return. Hamlet denies having given them to her. Ophelia chides him, saying that he knows that he did and is being unkind, or unnatural. Hamlet then accuses Ophelia of being unchaste and tells her that she should go to live in a nunnery where she will not become "a breeder of sinners." He says that he himself is reasonably chaste but is nonetheless filled with sin, being proud, revengeful, and ambitious. He rails against women in general, saying that they make their husbands into cuckolds and behave wantonly while pretending to be innocent. He then expresses the opinion that there should be no more marriages and implies that one marriage (that of Claudius and Gertrude) and one currently married person (Claudius) will die. Ophelia is horrified that Hamlet has fallen into such madness and that she believed his previous declarations of love.

Speaking with Polonius after Hamlet and Ophelia exit, the king makes clear that he has heard Hamlet's threat and resolves to send Hamlet away on the pretext of collecting the tribute that England owes to Denmark. Polonius, still believing that Hamlet's madness is due to unrequited love, suggests that Gertrude should speak with her son and resolve this matter.

Act III, scene ii. Hamlet, himself an excellent actor, instructs the players before their performance, telling them not to overact but to "Suit the action to the word, / the word to the action." According to Hamlet, the purpose of playing has always been and will always be "to hold as 'twere the mirror up to nature." After praising Horatio as a man who is not passion's slave and who takes good and bad fortune with equal grace, Hamlet asks his friend to keep an eye on Claudius during the play. Again Hamlet suggests that the ghost might be from hell and explains that he is using the play to test the truth of what the ghost has said.

Before the play begins, Hamlet sits near Ophelia. Throughout the opening pantomime, Hamlet makes lewd, suggestive comments to her. At one point he suggests, again, that Ophelia has taken a lover. At another he says that the prologue to the play is brief "As woman's love." In the play within the play, which Hamlet refers to as "The Mouse-trap" because he is using it to capture Claudius, the wife of Gonzago, a duke, claims that she will not remarry after her husband's death because to kiss another man in bed would be to kill her husband a second time. Her husband, the duke, responds by saying that such strong emotions as his wife expresses spend themselves and disappear. When in the play the character Lucianus sneaks into Gonzago's garden and pours poison into the duke's ear, Claudius rises in anger and storms off. Hamlet is delighted to have proved Claudius's guilt. Polonius comes to tell Hamlet that his mother wishes to speak with him in her chamber. As the scene ends, Hamlet delivers another soliloquy in which he says that it is the witching hour and that he could, like a witch, drink hot blood. He resolves to speak daggers at his mother but to use none on her, despite his own unnatural inclination to do so.

Act III, scene iii. Claudius meets with Rosencrantz regarding his intention to send Hamlet to England, with Rosencrantz and Guildenstern as escorts. Rosencrantz and the king discuss the danger that Hamlet poses to Claudius, a fact that strongly suggests, but does not prove, Rosencrantz's knowledge of Claudius's intention (revealed later) of having the English king put Hamlet to death. Claudius, having just arranged his foul purpose in sending Hamlet to England, then tries to pray. Claudius is overwhelmed by guilt over the killing of his brother and says that prayer has a "twofold force." Prayer can both give a person the strength to keep from sinning and can bring about pardon after one has sinned. Claudius, however, cannot ask for forgiveness in prayer because to do so while he is still enjoying the fruits of his sins would be hypocritical. Hamlet, coming on Claudius alone at prayer, decides not to kill the king at this time because he assumes Claudius is in a state of grace and that killing him now would send the king to heaven. Hamlet wants, instead, to kill the king while he is sinning and so to doom him to hell.

Act III, scene iv. Hamlet enters his mother's room and confronts her about her relationship with Claudius. Gertrude, frightened, calls for help, and Polonius, hidden behind an arras, or hanging tapestry, calls out in response. Hamlet, hearing this, runs a sword through the arras, killing Polonius, whom he mistook for the king. Hamlet tells his mother that her late husband was killed, a suggestion to which Gertrude responds with surprise. Oddly, however, they do not discuss this point further. Hamlet then forces his mother to sit down, in the presence of Polonius's dead body, to listen while he castigates her for her lust and lack of judgment in choosing Claudius over her late husband. Gertrude expresses shame about these actions. The ghost then makes its second appearance, telling Hamlet that it has come to "whet" his "almost blunted purpose." Gertrude, who has just witnessed her son talking to what seemed to be the air, says that Hamlet is imagining things. Hamlet assures her that he is not insane and tells Gertrude to assume a virtue if she has none and not to go in the future to Claudius's bed. He asks for and receives from the queen the assurance that she will not reveal that he is "mad in craft" rather than truly mad. Hamlet's closing lines suggest that he knows what Claudius intends in sending him to England. Hamlet vows to turn the plan on its inventors and lugs the body of Polonius away.

Falling Action (Act IV)

Act IV, scene i. The king enters the queen's chamber and learns of the killing of Polonius, which the queen ascribes to Hamlet's madness. Claudius recognizes, however, that Hamlet had meant to kill *him*. He worries that Polonius's death may be blamed on him and cause trouble in the kingdom.

Act IV, scene ii. Rosencrantz and Guildenstern, acting on Claudius's orders, confront Hamlet, asking him where he has stowed the body of Polonius. Hamlet responds in riddles and runs off.

Act IV, scene iii. The king confronts Hamlet. Hamlet tells Claudius that Polonius is at dinner, "Not where he eats, but where 'a is eaten" and then explains how even a great king may die, be eaten by worms, which then are eaten by a fish, which is then eaten by a beggar. In this way, Hamlet says, a king may "go a progress through the guts of a beggar." Hamlet reveals where he has placed the body, and Claudius tells him that for Hamlet's own safety he shall be sent to England. Alone, Claudius reveals in a soliloquy that Rosencrantz and Guildenstern bear letters asking the king of England to execute Hamlet.

Act IV, scene iv. Hamlet encounters Fortinbras's army and asks a captain in that army where they are heading. The captain explains that they are going to recover a worthless piece of land previously lost to Poland. Alone, Hamlet delivers another soliloquy in which he castigates himself, again, for his delay in carrying out his revenge against Claudius. These men, he says, are willing to risk their lives to regain an insignificant piece of land because it is a matter of honor. In contrast, Hamlet, having much greater cause, has done nothing but indulge "some craven scruple / Of thinking too precisely on the event." Again, Hamlet vows to take action, but even this vow reveals his ineffectiveness: "O, from this time forth, / My thoughts be bloody, or be nothing worth!" In other words, even at the point when he is expressing his commitment to action, in his actual statement Hamlet is only committing himself to thoughts.

Act IV, scene v. As the scene opens, Gertrude refuses to see Ophelia, who has asked for admittance. The gentleman who has brought this news explains that Ophelia has been behaving madly, speaking of her father and of tricks in the world, beating at her heart, and making senseless statements that others interpret as having hidden meaning. Horatio suggests that it is best that Gertrude see Ophelia because what others conjecture from her speech might prove dangerous. On being allowed in, Ophelia asks, in the presence of the king and queen, "Where is the beauteous majesty of Denmark?", a question that can be taken to refer both to Gertrude and to the country as a whole. Ophelia, in her madness, sings lines from different ballads. These stanzas, as fragmented as they are, all deal with loss, with someone who has died, and with a maid who lost her virginity to a man who promised falsely to marry her. Ophelia seems to bewail the death of her father and her own betrayal in love. In her madness, she says, "My brother shall know of it, / and so I thank you for your good counsel." Actually, Ophelia has not received any counsel from the king and queen, but the question that she seems to have been considering is whether her brother should be told of the murder of Polonius. She makes this statement immediately after having said, "I cannot choose but weep to think they would lay him i' th' cold ground," suggesting not only grief over the coming burial of her father but also grief over the coming burial of Hamlet, a likely consequence when Laertes learns about his father's murder.

Alone with Gertrude, Claudius reveals that Laertes has returned from France and that people are stirring Laertes against him. When Claudius and Gertrude hear a noise outside, they reveal how frightened they have become. A messenger comes to tell them that Laertes has arrived at the head of a mob that is demanding that Laertes be made king. Claudius asks that Laertes be let in, saying, ironically, that God will protect him because he is a king. In sharp contrast to Hamlet, Laertes is ready, immediately, to draw blood to revenge his father and doesn't care that he risks damnation in doing so. Claudius protests his innocence in Polonius's death. Ophelia enters, still singing songs in her madness, and so Laertes learns the effects of the recent events on his sister. When Ophelia sings, "It is / the false steward, that stole his master's daughter," Laertes responds by saying "This nothing's more than matter," meaning that his sister's crazed words are more revealing that rational speech would be. Ophelia exits, and the king assures Laertes that on consulting with wise friends he will learn that Claudius is guiltless and his friend. Claudius ends by saying "where th' offense is" (that is, with Hamlet), "let the great axe fall."

Act IV, scene vi. A sailor arrives with a letter for Horatio from Hamlet. In the letter, Hamlet asks Horatio to deliver letters from himself to the king, tells Horatio that he was captured by pirates and has negotiated his release, and says that the sailors will bring Horatio to meet with Hamlet.

Act IV, scene vii. Laertes meets with Claudius and tells him that it does appear that Claudius is guiltless in Polonius's death. When he asks why Claudius did not proceed against Hamlet, Claudius responds that both Gertrude and the common people are too fond of Hamlet for that. Claudius assures Laertes that he has taken appropriate action. At that time, a messenger arrives bringing a letter from Hamlet that says that he is back from England and wishes to see the king on the following day. Laertes and Claudius then plot a way to kill Hamlet. Laertes is well known for his ability as a swordsman, and Hamlet has previously expressed jealousy in this regard. Claudius says that he will lay a wager on a friendly duel between Hamlet and Laertes but that they will arrange for Laertes's sword to be "unbated," or uncapped. Laertes suggests that, in addition, he will place poison on the tip of the sword. To make sure that Hamlet dies, Claudius says that he will put poison in a cup of wine and, if Hamlet is not killed by Laertes's sword, he will give the cup to Hamlet.

The queen enters with the news that Ophelia has died by drowning. Laertes tries to hold back his tears but cannot. The king tells Gertrude that he has had a difficult time calming Laertes down and fears that the death of Ophelia may enrage him again.

Resolution and Dénouement (Act V)

Act V, scene i. The scene opens with two "Clowns," gravediggers who are preparing a grave for Ophelia. The first gravedigger questions the idea that Ophelia is to be given a Christian burial given that she killed herself. (In fact, Ophelia cannot be said to have committed suicide, if suicide is defined as a willful act of self-destruction. A close reading of act IV, scene v, lines 172–183 will reveal that Ophelia was trying to hang flowers on a willow bough near the brook when "an envious sliver broke" and she fell in. For a time, Ophelia's clothing held her up and she sang snatches of songs, but then her heavy garments dragged her down. After Ophelia fell in the brook by accident, she was too distracted by her madness to save herself. That Shakespeare was himself aware of this distinction between a willful act and an accident is made clear by the comments of the First Clown, who recalls, incorrectly, a relevant legal precedent. The Clown says that "an act hath three branches—it is to act, to do, to perform." The actual legal precedent is that a willful, or witting, act involves the imagination of the act, the resolution, and the performance. The description of Ophelia's death lacks both the prior imagining and the resolution, the two legal tests for actions that are done while one is in one's right mind and therefore responsible.) Hamlet and Horatio arrive on the scene. Seeing the gravedigger tossing up skulls leads Hamlet to expostulate on the brevity of human life and the ultimate worthlessness of human activity. The person who was in his life a great buyer of land, Hamlet says, inherits no more than the plot in which he is buried. Hamlet is particularly taken aback when the gravedigger informs him that one of the skulls is that of Yorick, the late king's jester. Looking at Yorick's skull, Hamlet thinks of the many times when Yorick carried him on his back and of the many times when Hamlet kissed the place on the skull where Yorick's lips once hung. The dust of Alexander the Great, Hamlet points out, might well be used, years after, to stop a hole in a barrel of liquor.

A group of people, including Laertes, Gertrude, Claudius, and a priest arrive, following the body of Ophelia, which is being borne to the grave. The priest refuses to give Ophelia the usual burial rites because her death was "doubtful." Laertes, in anger, tells the priest, "A minist'ring angel shall my sister be / When thou liest howling." Gertrude expresses her lost hope that Ophelia would be Hamlet's wife. Laertes, in his grief, leaps into Ophelia's grave and cries out for the earth to be heaped on both him and his sister, "the quick and the dead." Hamlet, realizing who has died and seeing Laertes's display of emotion, will not be outdone in grief but himself jumps into the grave with Laertes. Hamlet and Laertes grapple. The king orders that they be separated. Hamlet exclaims that his love for Ophelia was more than that of forty thousand brothers. Claudius tells Laertes to remember their plan and to wait to take his revenge.

Act V, scene ii. At the beginning of the scene, Hamlet explains to Horatio what happened to him aboard the ship bound for England. Thinking one night about how his plans had been thwarted, Hamlet realized that "There's a divinity that shapes our ends." Thinking of this, he rose and found the commission given to Rosencrantz and Guildenstern by Claudius. There he read Claudius's request that the king of England put him to death. Hamlet then rewrote the commission, changing it to a request that the bearers of the commission be executed. Hamlet points out that here, too, heaven ruled, for, as God would have it, he had in his pocket his father's ring, bearing the royal seal of Denmark, with which he was able to reseal the commission, making it official. Hamlet expresses no regret about having sent Rosencrantz and Guildenstern to their deaths, saying that they "made love to" their "employment" by Claudius and received what they themselves had conspired in. Hamlet then reiterates his reasons for wanting revenge on Claudius, which include killing the king, compromising his mother, standing between Hamlet and his hopes for the crown, attempting to kill Hamlet, and doing all this with great deceit. Horatio points out that Claudius will soon know what happened in England, to which Hamlet responds, "the interim's mine."

Osric, a courtier, enters and tells Hamlet of the duel. Hamlet reiterates his disdain for things of this world, saying that Osric, a land owner, is "spacious in the ownership of dirt." Hamlet accepts the challenge to duel with Laertes and tells Horatio that, given the odds and his recent practice, he shall probably win the fencing contest. Nonetheless, Hamlet feels misgivings, and Horatio tells him that if there is anything about the matter that Hamlet dislikes, he should forget about the duel. Then, in what may well be the central passage in the play, the one in which the conflict in Hamlet's mind is finally resolved, Hamlet says that all things are ruled by providence, that what will be will be, and that "the readiness is all."

Hamlet tells Laertes that what he did, in killing Polonius, was done out of madness and requests that Laertes think of him as of a brother. Claudius arrives and drops into a cup of wine a valuable pearl which, he says, will be Hamlet's if Hamlet gets the first or second hit. In the ensuing sword-fight, Hamlet twice gets the better of Laertes. After the first time, Claudius offers the cup to Hamlet, but Hamlet waves it off and strikes Laertes again. The queen takes the cup and, despite the king's attempts to stop her, drinks to Hamlet's health. Laertes wounds Hamlet. Then, in the ensuing fight, Hamlet grabs the untipped sword and wounds Laertes. Laertes reveals that he has been killed by his own treachery. The queen cries out that she has been poisoned. Hamlet, realizing that he will soon die, stabs the king and then makes him drink from the poisoned cup. Hamlet and Laertes exchange forgiveness. Horatio, seeing this, threatens to take his own life, but Hamlet begs him to remain alive to tell his story. Just before Hamlet dies, Fortinbras arrives, and Hamlet, with his dying voice, expresses his will that Fortinbras become king of Denmark. Horatio asks that Hamlet's body be brought to the stage and expresses his intention to tell "th' yet unknowing world / How these things came about." Fortinbras orders that this be done and expresses the opinion that had Hamlet lived to become king, he would have "prov'd most royal."

Creative Writing Activities

Creative Writing Activity A: Another Scene for the Play

Write another scene for the play based on one of the following ideas or on one of your own:

1. Write a scene to appear after act I, scene iii, in which Ophelia speaks with her friend Rosalind about her father's injunction not to see Hamlet anymore. In the scene, clarify Ophelia's feelings toward Hamlet.

2. Write a scene to appear after the so-called "closet scene," act III, scene iv, in which Gertrude visits a priest and confesses her sins.

3. Write a scene showing Hamlet aboard the pirate ship, negotiating for his release.

4. Write the speech that Horatio might have delivered after the closing scene of the play. Draw upon what Horatio says in act V, scene ii, lines 372–379.

Creative Writing Activity B: Ballad

Hamlet contains a number of verses from ballads, but none of these ballads is given in its entirety. Choose one of these ballads and write the rest of it.

As an alternative, write a ballad, pop song, or rap song retelling the story of *Hamlet*. If you wish to do so, you can make your song a humorous parody or satire.

Creative Writing Activity C: New Ending

Imagine that the story of Hamlet ends with act IV. Using prose, write a new and different ending for the story.

Creative Writing Activity D: Ghost Story

Hamlet is one of many thousands of ghost stories that have been told over the years. Write your own story about a ghost that appears to make a request of someone living.

Creative Writing Activity E: Journal Entry

Write a journal entry from the point of view of Ophelia after act IV, scene i, or of Gertrude after act III, scene iv. In your journal entry, express your feelings about your recent interactions with Hamlet.

Creative Writing Activity F: Newspaper

Newspapers did not, of course, exist in Hamlet's day, or in Shakespeare's for that matter. Nonetheless, imagine that you are on the staff of a newspaper in Elsinore. Work with other students to prepare a series of newspaper articles telling about the events related in the play, from the threat of invasion by Fortinbras to the ill-fated sword match at the end.

Critical Writing Activities

The following topics are suitable for short critical essays on *Hamlet, Prince of Denmark*. An essay written on one of these topics should begin with an introductory paragraph that states the **thesis**, or main idea, of the essay. The introductory paragraph should be followed by several paragraphs that support the thesis using evidence from the play. This evidence may be presented in the form of quotations or summaries of events or dialogue. The essay should conclude with a paragraph that summarizes the points made in the body of the essay and that restates the thesis in different words.

Critical Writing Activity A: Alternate Readings of *Hamlet*

Over the years, critics have differed widely in their interpretations of *Hamlet*. Each of the following statements has been supported, in print, by one or more interpreters of the play, but each is quite controversial. Choose one of these statements and write an essay telling why you believe it to be true *or* false.

1. The ghost that appears at the beginning of the play really is a demon, or devil, who causes Hamlet to engage in terrible acts that endanger his soul.

2. The primary message of the play is that one should be a "man of action" like the late king Hamlet or like Fortinbras rather than a man of thought like Hamlet.

3. The primary message of the play is that all action is futile because no one can see very deeply into life and because, at any rate, divine providence, not human actions, determines what happens.

4. Hamlet is at no point in the play actually suicidal.

5. The real reason for Hamlet's delay in taking his revenge is that he realizes, at some level, that revenge is wrong.

6. The real reason for Hamlet's delay in taking his revenge is that Claudius has enacted Hamlet's own unconscious wish to kill his father and marry his mother.

7. The real reason for Hamlet's delay in taking his revenge is that after he learns that Claudius did, in fact, murder his father, he doesn't have the opportunity to act.

8. The real reason for Hamlet's delay in taking his revenge is that he scorns this world and all that it has to offer and doesn't want to have anything to do with it.

9. Hamlet doesn't just pretend to be insane; he actually is insane.

10. Hamlet's treatment of Ophelia is due to the fact that she actually has taken another lover.

11. Hamlet's treatment of Ophelia is due to the fact that because of his mother's unfaithfulness to his father, he scorns all things having to do with love, romance, women, sex, and having children.

12. Ophelia is driven insane by the guilt that she feels over having rejected Hamlet, having driven him to madness, and thus having indirectly caused her own father's death.

13. Ophelia is driven insane because after having compromised herself in taking Hamlet as a lover, she lost him.

14. Ophelia is driven insane because in spite of the fact that she has tried to remain pure and to obey her father—she nonetheless loses everything she cares about.

15. Gertrude was a de facto accomplice in the murder of her husband, someone who looked the other way because she was carrying on an adulterous affair.

16. Ophelia's death was not a suicide.

17. Hamlet is a violent, callous, self-centered, egotistical young man with no regard for the effects of his actions on others.

18. Hamlet is a deeply sensitive man, too good and too noble to cope with or remain in the wicked world in which he finds himself.

19. Hamlet says in act V that all things are governed by providence, but the actual events of the play show that events occur accidentally, bringing doom to both the innocent and the guilty.

20. The central struggle in the play is an internal one between the Christian, who knows that revenge is wrong, and the natural person, who is prompted to revenge by passion.

21. The something that is rotten in Denmark is Hamlet, for the Danish court is actually full of life, vitality, strength, and purpose, whereas Hamlet is full of melancholy, misanthropy, and nihilism.

22. The play is a dramatic failure because it does not provide sufficient reason for Hamlet's delay, for his treatment of Ophelia, or for his deep despair.

23. Hamlet's major concern is with the truth, and he is ruthless, both with himself and with others, in pursuit of the truth.

24. Hamlet is a hero.

25. Hamlet is not a tragic figure because, in the end, he gets what he wants.

Critical Writing Activity B: Comparison and Contrast

In *Hamlet,* many parallels and comparisons exist among the characters. Fortinbras and Hamlet are both sons of dead kings, both stand to become kings themselves, and both have uncles who are now on the throne. Laertes and Hamlet are both young students whose fathers are murdered and who thus have reason to take revenge. Hamlet and Ophelia both lose their fathers and display signs of madness. Both Gertrude and Ophelia are accused, by Hamlet, of improper behavior. Polonius, Claudius, Laertes, Rosencrantz, and Guildenstern all have their own wicked stratagems turned on themselves. Write a paper comparing and contrasting any of the following characters:

Hamlet and Fortinbras
Hamlet and Laertes
Hamlet and Ophelia
Gertrude and Ophelia

Make sure to point out both the similarities and the differences in the characters and to explain what these similarities and differences reveal.

Critical Writing Activity C: Reviewing a Dramatic Interpretation

The usual interpretation of Hamlet's famous "To be or not to be" soliloquy in act III, scene i, is that Hamlet believes himself to be alone and is speaking to himself about his own concerns. In the film version of *Hamlet* directed and performed by Kenneth Branagh, Hamlet speaks the "To be or not to be" soliloquy to Claudius, hiding behind a mirrored door. The staging makes clear that Hamlet is aware of Claudius's presence and is directing his words to Claudius. Analyze the soliloquy with Branagh's interpretation in mind. What does the soliloquy mean if it is about Claudius rather than about Hamlet? Does Branagh's unique (and debatable) interpretation of the soliloquy make sense? Write a paper explaining your view of this interpretation and why you hold that view. (If possible, view the scene from Branagh's film before writing your essay.)

Critical Writing Activity D: Analysis

Choose any of the following soliloquies and analyze it in detail. Begin by explaining where the soliloquy appears in the play and its connection to the plot. Then go through the soliloquy, line by line, explaining what it says. Finally, summarize the primary message of the soliloquy.

Act I, scene ii, lines 129–159: "O that this too too solid flesh would melt . . . "

Act II, scene ii, lines 542–597: "O, what a rogue and peasant slave am I! . . ."

Act III, scene i, lines 55–87: "To be, or not to be, that is the question . . ."

Act III, scene ii, lines 384–395: "'Tis now the very witching time of night . . ."

Act IV, scene iv, lines 32–66: "How all occasions do inform against me . . ."

Critical Writing Activity E: Theme

Choose one of the following themes and discuss, in an essay, the message the play teaches regarding this theme.

1. the relative value of thought and action
2. the consequences of duplicity or deceit
3. the relationship between normalcy and madness
4. the relationship between the natural and supernatural worlds
5. the relative power, in life, of fortune (or chance) and providence

Critical Writing Activity F: The Nature of Drama

Hamlet's advice to the players in act III, scene ii is often taken to be the definitive statement by the greatest dramatist of all time about the purpose and nature of the dramatic arts. Assuming that Hamlet's advice and Shakespeare's own beliefs are identical, write a paper explaining what you believe Shakespeare's opinions were about what makes a good play.

Critical Writing Activity G: The Elizabethan Conception of Kingship

A common belief in Elizabethan times was that kings were divinely appointed and protected and that they ruled by divine right. Another belief was that the king's person was symbolic of the body politic, that the king, metaphorically, was the head of a body that was made up of the people. With these two ideas in mind, study the following passages:

Act III, scene iii, lines 11–23
Act IV, scene v, lines 125–127

In a paper, explain the principles by which the Elizabethans defined kingship, how the murder of Hamlet's father violated these principles, and how Fortinbras's arrival at the end of the play restored these principles.

Critical Writing Activity H: Play Structure

Write a paper on the structure of the play. Explain the following:

1. what central conflict is introduced in act I and what inciting incident introduces this conflict
2. how the central conflict is complicated in act II
3. what turning point, or crisis, occurs in act III
4. what events occur in the falling action of act IV to bring about the final resolution of the central conflict
5. what event in act V resolves the central conflict

Projects

Project A: Preparing an Acting Edition of the Play

Hamlet is a long play, and Shakespeare's acting company probably presented a much shorter version in the theater. One of the three surviving versions of the play, the First Quarto, is, in fact, much shorter than the other two and is generally considered to be an actor's poor reconstruction of the play as he remembered it from performance. Imagine that you are going to present this play on the stage but that you need to delete several hundred lines so that the play might be presented in a couple of hours. Work with other students to decide on which passages or scenes you might delete while retaining the most important plot elements and themes. You may wish to make a photocopy of the play and to mark passages for deletion.

Project B: Set Design

Choose one scene from *Hamlet* and design a set for it. Begin by making sketches. Then create a finished illustration of the set or construct a model of the set out of balsa wood, foam rubber, or other materials. You might wish to design a set using a computer draw/paint or computer-aided drafting (CAD) program.

Project C: Modernizing the Play

Imagine that you are a theater director and that you want to produce a version of *Hamlet* in a radically different setting, such as sub-Saharan Africa in the 1800s, Chicago in the 1920s, or Washington D. C. in the present. Describe in detail what social positions the various characters in your version of the play would have. For example, instead of being king of Denmark, Claudius might be a gangland crime boss.

Project D: Costuming

Design a costume for one of the characters in the play, such as the ghost, Hamlet, Polonius, or one of the gravediggers. Create an illustration of the costume and explain, in writing, why you have designed the costume as you have.

Project E: Board Game

Create a board game in which the players are Rosencrantz and Guildenstern, attempting to advance themselves at court.

Project F: Twenty Questions

Have a classmate assume the role of some character from the play and ask yes or no questions of that character until you figure out which character it is.

Project G: Writing and Performing Music for the Play

Write tunes for one or more of the ballads in this play. Set the ballads to music and perform them.

Glossary

PRONUNCIATION KEY

VOWEL SOUNDS

a	hat	ō	go	ʉ	burn
ā	play	ô	paw, born	ə	extra
ä	star	oo	book, put		under
e	then	ōō	blue, stew		civil
ē	me	oi	boy		honor
i	sit	ou	wow		bogus
ī	my	u	up		

CONSONANT SOUNDS

b	but	l	lip	t	sit
ch	watch	m	money	th	with
d	do	n	on	v	valley
f	fudge	ŋ	song, sink	w	work
g	go	p	pop	y	yell
h	hot	r	rod	z	pleasure
j	jump	s	see		
k	brick	sh	she		

a • bate (ə bāt´) *vt.,* make less

a • bate • ment (ə bāt´mənt) *n.,* amount deducted

a • bridge • ment (ə brij´mənt) *n.,* reduction, or curtailment; interruption

ab • sti • nence (ab´stə nəns) *n.,* act of doing without pleasure

ac • cord (ə kôrd´) *n.,* agreement

ad • der (ad´ər) *n.,* poisonous snake

af • fec • tion (ə fek´shən) *n.,* fond or tender feeling

al • le • giance (ə lē´jəns) *n.,* loyalty to a person or cause

al • ti • tude (al´tə tōōd´) *n.,* height

ap • pa • ri • tion (äp ə rish´ən) *n.,* strange figure that appears unexpectedly, especially a ghost

ap • pre • hen • sion (ap´rē hen´shən) *n.,* understanding; anxious feeling of foreboding

ar • raign (ə rān´) *vt.,* call to account; accuse

as • sail (ə sāl´) *adj.,* attack with arguments

a • sun • der (ə sun´dər) *adv.,* into parts or pieces

au • dit (ô´dit) *n.,* account; record

aus • pi • cious (ôs pish´ əs) *adj.,* looking to a happy future

a • wry (ə rī´) *adv.,* away from the correct course

base (bās) *adj.,* inferior; valueless

bat • tal • ion (bə talʹyən) *n.*, large group joined together

bat • ter • y (batʹər ē) *n.*, act of beating; pounding

be • get (bē getʹ) *vt.*, bring into being

be • guile (bə gīlʹ) *vt.*, deceive

be • seech (bē sēchʹ) *vt.*, ask earnestly; implore, beg

be • smirch (bē smʉrchʹ) *vt.*, make dirty; bring dishonor to

bier (bir) *n.*, platform for a corpse

blank verse (blaŋkʹ vʉrsʹ) *n.*, unrhymed verse having five iambic feet typical of Elizabethan drama

bois • ter • ous (boisʹtər əs) *adj.*, noisy; unruly

bough (bou) *n.*, branch of a tree

bray (brā) *vt.*, make a loud, harsh cry like a donkey

bra • zen (brāʹzən) *adj.*, made of brass (and, like it, bold)

brev • i • ty (brevʹə tē) *n.*, quality of being concise

ca • lum • ni • ous (kə lumʹnē əs) *adj.*, slanderous

cap • i • tal (kapʹət l) *adj.*, extremely serious; calling for the death penalty

ca • rouse (kə rouzʹ) *vi.*, engage in boisterous drinking and merrymaking

ce • les • ti • al (sə lesʹchəl) *adj.*, heavenly

cen • sure (senʹshər) *n.*, disapproval

chal • ice (chalʹis) *n.*, cup for holy wine

chaste (chāst) *adj.*, pure

churl • ish (chʉrlʹish) *adj.*, stingy; mean

clam • or (klamʹər) *n.*, loud outcry; uproar

cleave (klēv) *vt.*, divide or split

clem • en • cy (klemʹən sē) *n.*, forbearance; leniency; mercy

com • men • da • ble (kä menʹdə bəl) *adj.*, praiseworthy

com • mis • sion (kə mishʹən) *n.*, authorization

com • post (kämʹpōst) *n.*, decomposing vegetables used for fertilizer

con • dole (kən dōlʹ) *vi.*, express sympathy

con • fine (känʹ fīn) *n.*, bordered region

con • sum • ma • tion (känʹsə māʹshən) *n.*, completion; fulfillment

con • ta • gion (kən tāʹjən) *n.*, agent causing disease or the spreading of disease

cor • o • na • tion (kôr ə nāʹ shən) *n.*, ceremony in which a sovereign is crowned

coun • te • nance (kounʹtə nəns) *n.*, facial expression

coun • te • nance (kounʹtə nəns) *vt.*, condone; give approval to

cour • ti • er (kôrtʹē ər) *n.*, attendant at a royal court

dal • li • ance (dalʹ yəns) *n.*, playing at love

dal • ly (dalʹē) *vi.*, waste time; loiter

de • vout • ly (di vout´lē) *adv.*, earnestly; sincerely

dire (dīr) *adj.*, having dreadful consequences

dirge (dɵrj) *n.*, funeral hymn

dis • cre • tion (di skresh´ən) *n.*, good judgment; care to behave properly

dis • po • si • tion (dis´pə zish´ən) *n.*, one's nature or temperament; inclination; desire

dis • tem • per (dis tem´pər) *n.*, disturbance

di • stilled (də stild´) *adj.*, reduced

dis • trac • tion (di strak´shən) *n.*, confusion; diversion

dow • ry (dou´rē) *n.*, property that a woman brings to her marriage

el • o • quent (el´ə kwənt) *adj.*, vividly expressive; persuasive

en • mi • ty (en´mə tē) *n.*, hostility

en • treat (en trēt´) *vt.*, ask earnestly; plead, beg

en • treat • y (en trē´tē) *n.*, begging favors

ep • i • taph (ep´ə taf´) *n.*, inscription on a gravestone

ex • hort (eg zôrt´) *vt.*, urge by strong argument; make urgent appeal

ex • pend (eks pend´) *vt.*, spend; use up

ex • pos • tu • late (eks päs´chə lāt´) *vt.*, reason with or about

ex • tort (eks tôrt´) *vt.*, to get something from someone by violence or threat

ex • trem • i • ty (eks strem´ə tē) *n.*, extreme danger

fe • lic • i • ty (fə lis´i tē) *n.*, happiness; bliss

fet • ter (fet´ər) *n.*, restraint; anything that serves to restrict

fla • gon (flag´ən) *n.*, container for liquids

flax • en (flak´sən) *adj.*, pale yellow; straw-colored

foil (foil) *n.*, long, thin fencing sword

fore • stall (fôr stôl´) *vt.*, prevent; hinder

for • ward (fôr´wərd) *adj.*, too bold; too soon

frail • ty (frāl´tē) *n.*, weakness, especially moral weakness

gam • bol (gam´bəl) *n.*, skipping or frolicking about

gam • bol (gam´bəl) *vi.*, frolic; skip about

gar • land (gar´lənd) *n.*, wreath or chain of flowers

gar • ri • soned (gar´ə sənd) *adj.*, fortified with military troops

gen • try (jen´trē) *adj.*, rank resulting from birth

ger • mane (jər mān´) *adj.*, truly relevant

gibe (jīb) *n.*, jeer; taunt

gild • ed (gild´əd) *adj.*, coated with gold; made more attractive

gore (gôr) *n.*, blood from a wound

grave • ness (grāv´nis) *n.*, seriousness

griz • zled (griz´əld) *adj.*, streaked gray and black

hal • lowed (hal´ ōd) *adj.,* holy

har • bin • ger (här´ bin jər) *n.,* something which comes before, announcing what is to come

her • ald (her´əld) *n.,* person who makes official announcements

hom • age (häm´ij) *n.,* anything given to show allegiance

im • mi • nent (im´ə nənt) *adj.,* close to happening; impending

im • part (im pärt´) *vt.,* make known; tell

im • pi • ous (im pī´əs) *adj.,* lacking reverence for God or for a parent

im • por • tu • nate (im pôr´choo nit) *adj.,* urgent; persistent

im • por • tu • ni • ty (im´pôr toon´ i tē) *n.,* persistent demand

in • dict (in dīt´) *vt.,* charge with committing a crime

in • di • rec • tion (in´də rek´shən) *n.,* roundabout means

in • dis • cre • tion (in´di skresh´ən) *n.,* lack of good judgment

in • fal • li • bly (in fal´ə blē) *adv.,* without error

in • so • lence (in´sə ləns) *n.,* boldly disrespectful, impudent manner

in • stru • men • tal (in strə men´təl) *adj.,* useful

in • ter • im (in´tər im) *n.,* period of time between

in • vul • ner • a • ble (in vul´nər ə bəl) *adj.,* not open to harm

jo • cund (jäk´ənd) *adj.,* cheerful

ju • di • cious (joo dish´əs) *adj.,* showing wise judgment

kin (kin) *adj.,* related

late (lāt) *adj.,* recently deceased

lev • y (le´ vē) *n.,* tax

li • ber • tine (lib´ ər tēn) *n.,* one who leads an immoral life

liv • er • y (liv´ər ē) *n.,* identifying dress of a particular group

loam (lōm) *n.,* rich, fertile soil

maimed (māmd) *adj.,* imperfect; defective

mal • e • fac • tion (mal´ə fak´shən) *n.,* wrongdoing; crime

ma • li • cious (mə lish´əs) *adj.,* ill-willed

man • date (man´dāt) *n.,* written order or command from authority

mar • tial (mar´ shəl) *adj.,* soldierlike

ma • son (mā´sən) *n.,* person who builds with stone

ma • tron (mā´trən) *n.,* married woman of mature appearance

mince (mins) *vt.,* cut or chop into little pieces

mirth (murth) *n.,* joy

mor • tise (môr´tis) *vt.,* join; fasten securely

mote (mōt) *n.,* speck

ob • sti • nate (äb´stə nət) *adj.,* stubborn, unyielding

pal • pa • ble (pal´pə bəl) *adj.,* that can be felt; solid

par • a • gon (par´ə gän) *n.,* highest model

parch • ing (pärch´iŋ) *adj.*, drying up with heat

parch • ment (pärch´mənt) *n.*, paper-thin animal skins used instead of paper from wood

par • ley (pär´lē) *vi.*, meet for conversation

pen • e • tra • ble (pen´i trə bəl) *adj.*, that can be penetrated or affected

per • ni • cious (pər nish´əs) *adj.*, causing great harm

per • turbed (pər tʉrbed´) *adj.*, troubled

pe • ru • sal (pə ro̅o̅´zəl) *n.*, study

pes • ti • lence (pes´tə ləns) *n.*, dangerous infectious disease

pes • ti • lent (pes´tə lənt) *adj.*, contagious; dangerous; likely to cause death through contagion

pi • te • ous (pit´ē əs) *adj.*, exciting pity or compassion

pith (pith) *n.*, essential or central part; essence

por • tal (pôrt´l) *n.*, doorway; entrance

por • ten • tous (pôr ten´təs) *adj.*, warning of coming evil

prate (prāt) *vi.*, talk idly; chatter

pre • cept (prē´sept) *n.*, principle

pre • script (prē´skript) *n.*, direction

prod • i • gal (präd´i gəl) *adj.*, carelessly wasteful

pro • fane (prō fān´) *vt.*, treat with irreverence or contempt

pro • fane • ly (prō fān´lē) *adv.*, showing disrespect for sacred things

prop • er • ty (präp´ər tē) *n.*, quality; characteristic

prov • i • dence (präv´ə dəns) *n.*, foresight; care or preparation in advance

purge (pʉrj) *vt.*, get rid of, here as tears

quin • tes • sence (kwin tes´əns) *n.*, pure, concentrated essence

ra • di • ant (rā´dē ənt) *adj.*, shining

re • cord • er (ri kôrd´ər) *n.*, wind instrument with eight finger holes

ren • dez • vous (rän´dā vo̅o̅´) *n.*, agreed meeting place

re • qui • em (rek´wē əm) *n.*, hymn for the dead

re • quite (rē kwīt´) *vt.*, reward; retaliate against

res • o • lu • tion (rez´ə lo̅o̅´shən) *n.*, firm determination

rite (rīt) *n.*, formal, ceremonial act

riv • et (riv´it) *vi.*, fix or hold the attention

rogue (rōg) *n.*, idle person of little worth or repute

sanc • ti • fied (saŋk´tə fīd) *adj.*, holy

sa • vo • ry (sā´vər ē) *adj.*, pleasing to taste; appetizing

scru • ple (skro̅o̅´pəl) *n.*, doubt; feeling of uncertainty as to whether an action is right

se • pul • cher (sep´əl kər) *n.*, burial vault

sheen (shēn) *n.*, brightness; luster

sig • net (sig´nit) *n.*, official seal; stamp

slan • der (slan´dər) *n.*, statement harmful to someone's reputation

sole (sōl) *adj.*, one and only

sound • ed (sound´əd) *adj.*, willing to speak honest feelings

stowed (stōd) *adj.*, safely packed away

sty (stī) *n.*, filthy enclosure, usually for pigs

sul • try (sul´trē) *adj.*, oppressively hot

sum • mons (sum´əns) *n.*, official order to appear as a defendant before a court

su • per • flu • ous (sə per´flo͞o əs) *adj.*, surplus; excess

sup • press (sə pres´) *vt.*, abolish by authority; keep back or down

sur • mise (sər mīz´) *vi.*, imagine

te • di • ous (tē´dē əs) *adj.*, tiresome; boring

tem • per • ance (tem´pər əns) *n.*, self-restraint; moderation

tem • per • ate • ly (tem´pər it lē) *adv.*, moderately; with self-restraint

ten • ant (ten´ənt) *n.*, person who pays rent on a house or land

ten • ant • less (ten´ənt ləs) *adj.*, empty of people (here, the dead)

te • ther (te´thər) *n.*, leash

to • ken (tō´kən) *n.*, gift as symbol of the giver's affection

trans • for • ma • tion (trans´fər mā´shən) *n.*, change of form or appearance

tread (tred) *vi.*, walk; step

tri • fling (trī´fliŋ) *n.*, frivolous play

tru • ant (troo´ənt) *adj.*, staying away from school

tur • bu • lent (tur´byo͞o lənt) *adj.*, wildly agitated or disturbed; stormy

ul • cer • ous (ul´sər əs) *adj.*, having an ulcer, an open sore

un • fledged (un flejd´) *adj.*, not yet feathered, like a bird; thus, immature

val • iant (val´yənt) *adj.*, brave

val • or (val´ər) *n.*, marked courage; bravery

var • i • a • ble (ver´ē ə bəl) *adj.*, changeable; varied

venge • ance (ven´jəns) *n.*, desire to punish another in payment for a wrong

ven • omed (ven´əmd) *adj.*, poisoned

vial (vīl) *n.*, small glass bottle

vis • age (vis´ij) *n.*, face; features

wan • ton (wän´tən) *adj.*, undisciplined

war • rant (wôr´ənt) *vt.*, deserve

whet (wet) *vt.*, make keen; stimulate

wretch (rech) *n.*, despised person

Handbook of Literary Terms

Antagonist. See *character.*

Aside. An **aside** is a statement made by a character in a play, intended to be heard by the audience but not by other characters on the stage.

Central Conflict. A **central conflict** is the primary struggle dealt with in the plot of a story or drama. See *conflict* and *plot.*

Character. A **character** is a person (or sometimes an animal) who figures in the action of a literary work. A *protagonist,* or *main character,* is the central figure in a literary work. An *antagonist* is a character who is pitted against a protagonist. *Major characters* are those who play significant roles in a work. *Minor characters* are those who play lesser roles. A *one-dimensional character, flat character,* or *caricature* is one who exhibits a single dominant quality, or *character trait.* A *three-dimensional, full,* or *rounded character* is one who exhibits the complexity of traits associated with actual human beings. A *static character* is one who does not change during the course of the action. A *dynamic character* is one who does change. A *stock character* is one found again and again in different literary works. An example of a stock character is the mad scientist of nineteenth- and twentieth-century science fiction.

Cliché. A **cliché** is a tired or hackneyed expression such as *quiet as a mouse* or *couch potato.* Most clichés originate as vivid, colorful expressions but soon lose their interest because of overuse. Careful writers and speakers avoid clichés, which are dull and signify lack of originality.

Conflict. A **conflict** is a struggle between two forces in a literary work. A *plot* involves the introduction, development, and eventual resolution of a conflict. One side of the *central conflict* in a story or drama is usually taken by the *main character.* That character may struggle against another character, against the forces of nature, against society or social norms, against fate, or against some element within himself or herself. A struggle that takes place between a character and some outside force is called an *external conflict.* A struggle that takes place within a character is called an *internal conflict.* See *central conflict* and *plot.*

Crisis. In the plot of a story or a drama, the **crisis** is that point in the development of the conflict at which a decisive event occurs that causes the main character's situation to become better or worse. See *plot.*

Drama. A **drama** is a story told through characters played by actors. The script of a drama typically consists of characters' names, dialogue spoken by the characters, and stage directions. Because it is meant to be performed before an audience, drama can be distinguished from other forms of non-performance-based literary works by the central role played in it by the spectacle—the sensory presentation to the audience, which includes such elements as lighting, costumes, make-up, properties, set pieces, music, sound effects, and the movements and expressions of actors. Another important distinguishing feature of drama is that it is collaborative. The interpretation of the work depends not only upon the author and his or her audience, but also upon the director, the actors, and others involved in mounting a production. Two major types of drama are comedy and tragedy. See *tragedy.*

Foil. A **foil** is a character whose attributes, or characteristics, contrast with, and therefore throw into relief, the attributes of another character.

Freudian Criticism. **Freudian Criticism** is analysis and interpretation of literature based on theories of the father of psychoanalysis, Sigmund Freud.

Inciting Incident. See *plot.*

Irony. **Irony** is a difference between appearance and reality. Types of irony include the following: *dramatic irony,* in which something is known by the reader or audience but unknown to the characters; *verbal irony,* in which a statement is made that implies its opposite; and *irony of situation,* in which an event occurs that violates the expectations of the characters, the reader, or the audience.

Irony of Situation. See *irony.*

Mimesis. **Mimesis,** as defined by the Greek philosopher Aristotle, is the imitation of life in art.

Mood. Mood, or **atmosphere,** is the emotion created in the reader by part or all of a literary work. A writer creates a mood through judicious use of concrete details.

Motivation. A **motivation** is a force that moves a character to think, feel, or behave in a certain way. Revenge is one of Hamlet's motives for taking action against Claudius.

Oedipus Complex. The **Oedipus Complex** is the name that Sigmund Freud gave to a conflict that he believed to be universal among male children, a repressed desire to kill their fathers and so supplant them and have their mothers to themselves. In a footnote in his book *The Interpretation of Dreams,* Freud argued that Hamlet suffered from an unresolved Oedipus Complex.

Plot. A **plot** is a series of events related to a central *conflict,* or struggle. A typical plot involves the introduction of a conflict, its development, and its eventual resolution. Terms used to describe elements of plot include the following:

- The **exposition,** or **introduction,** sets the tone or mood, introduces the characters and the setting, and provides necessary background information.
- The **inciting incident** is the event that introduces the central conflict.
- The **rising action,** or **complication,** develops the conflict to a high point of intensity.
- The **climax** is the high point of interest or suspense in the plot.
- The **crisis,** or **turning point,** often the same event as the climax, is the point in the plot where something decisive happens to determine the future course of events and the eventual working out of the conflict.
- The **falling action** is all of the events that follow the climax.
- The **resolution** is the point at which the central conflict is ended, or resolved.
- The **dénouement** is any material that follows the resolution and that ties up loose ends.
- The **catastrophe,** in tragedy, is the event that marks the ultimate tragic fall of the central character. Often this event is the character's death.

Plots rarely contain all these elements in precisely this order. Elements of exposition may be introduced at any time in the course of a work. A work may begin with a catastrophe and then use flashback to explain it. The exposition or dénouement or even the resolution may be missing. The inciting incident may occur before the beginning of the action actually described in the work. These are but a few of the many possible variations that plots can exhibit. See *conflict*.

Protagonist. See *character*.

Psychodrama. A **psychodrama** is a play that deals with the state of mind of its central character. The term is generally used to describe twentieth-century plays and films that deal with madness or other extreme psychological states. Nonetheless, one can legitimately call *Hamlet* a psychodrama.

Resolution. See *plot*.

Soliloquy. A **soliloquy** is a speech delivered by a lone character that reveals the speaker's thoughts and feelings.

Symbol. A **symbol** is a thing that stands for or represents both itself and something else. Writers use two types of symbols—conventional, and personal or idiosyncratic. A *conventional symbol* is one with traditional, widely recognized associations. Such symbols include doves for peace; laurel wreaths for heroism or poetic excellence; the color green for jealousy; the color purple for royalty; the color red for anger; morning or spring for youth; winter, evening, or night for old age; wind for change or inspiration; rainbows for hope; roses for beauty; the moon for fickleness or inconstancy; roads or paths for the journey through life; woods or darkness for moral or spiritual confusion; thorns for troubles or pain; stars for unchangeableness or constancy; mirrors for vanity or introspection; snakes for evil or duplicity; and owls for wisdom. A *personal* or *idiosyncratic symbol* is one that assumes its secondary meaning because of the special use to which it is put by a writer.

Theme. A **theme** is a central idea in a literary work.

Tragedy. A **tragedy** is a drama (or by extension any work of literature) that tells the story of the fall of a person of high status. It celebrates the courage and dignity of a tragic hero in the face of inevitable doom. Sometimes that doom is made inevitable by a tragic flaw in the hero, such as the hubris that brings about the fall of Sophocles's Oedipus. In the twentieth century, writers have extended the definition of *tragedy* to cover works that deal with the fall of any sympathetic character, despite his or her status.

Turning Point. See *plot*.